DATE DUE

BRODART   Cat. No. 23-221

The Annual of Bernard Shaw Studies
Volume Nine

---

continuing

The Shaw Review

Stanley Weintraub, *General Editor*

John R. Pfeiffer	Shirley Rader	Judith Rayback
Bibliographer	Editorial Assistant	Editorial Assistant

SHAW 9

SHAW OFFSTAGE

THE NONDRAMATIC WRITINGS

Edited by

Fred D. Crawford

The Pennsylvania State University Press
University Park and London

All quotations from the published plays and prefaces, unless otherwise identified, are from the *Bodley Head Bernard Shaw (Collected Plays with their Prefaces)*. Quotations from published Bernard Shaw writings are utilized in this volume with the permission of the Estate of Bernard Shaw. Shaw's hitherto unpublished writings © 1989 The Trustees of the British Museum, The Governors and Guardians of the National Library of Ireland, and the Royal Academy of Dramatic Art.

Library of Congress Cataloging-in-Publication Data

Shaw Offstage / edited by Fred D. Crawford.
     p. cm.—(Shaw ; v. 9)
  ISBN 0-271-00652-8
  1. Shaw, Bernard, 1856–1950—Criticism and interpretation.
I. Crawford, Fred D. II. Series.
PR5366.A15 vol. 9
[PR5367]
822'.912 s—dc19   88-19770
[822'.912]   CIP

Note to contributors and subscribers. *SHAW*'s perspective is Bernard Shaw and his milieu—its personalities, works, relevance to his age and ours. As "his life, work, and friends"—the subtitle to a biography of G.B.S.—indicates, it is impossible to study the life, thought, and work of a major literary figure in a vacuum. Issues and men, economics, politics, religion, theatre and literature and journalism—the entirety of the two half-centuries the life of G.B.S. spanned was his assumed province. *SHAW*, published annually, welcomes articles that either explicitly or implicitly add to or alter our understanding of Shaw and his milieu. Address all communications concerning manuscript contributions (in 2 copies) to Ihlseng Cottage, University Park, Pa. 16802. Unsolicited manuscripts are welcomed but will be returned only if return postage is provided. In matters of style *SHAW* recommends the *MLA Style Sheet*.

CONTENTS

Fred D. Crawford

INTRODUCTION: OFFSTAGE?

One contributor's amused response to the title SHAW OFFSTAGE was to ask, "was he ever not 'on-stage'?" Indeed he was, and well he knew it.

In the early years in London, Shaw was offstage in the sense that no one knew who he was, or cared. During the years of his emergence as a playwright, he was offstage in the sense that his plays seldom went into production, and then only for short runs. He was also offstage in his devotion to his socialist and political writings, which not only distracted him from his plays but also interfered frequently with his popular success as a playwright. Today we recognize Shaw as second only to Shakespeare in the British theatrical tradition, the chief modern dramatist, the innovator of serious farce, the infuser of moral purpose into the drama, the proponent of the theater of ideas, the striker of the deathblow to nineteenth-century melodrama, and a precursor of the avant-garde theater, but he was never exclusively a playwright to himself or to his contemporaries. During his literary apprenticeship and long after he had proven himself as a dramatist, he devoted much of his energy to well-crafted prose. In short, Shaw's nondramatic writing was more than a series of early false starts in his search for his literary medium, and it continued to occupy him throughout his life as he devoted himself to a variety of purposes outside the theater.

When Shaw arrived in London in 1876, he had virtually no prospects for achievement or recognition. However, he had determined to win a place in the limelight of public esteem, and he worked indefatigably to do so, beginning by educating himself in the British Museum Reading Room and at public lectures. During two decades of frustrating poverty and obscurity, he forged a public image that became almost impossible to ignore. His efforts at self-advertisement took many forms, including making his presence felt at public debates, dressing idiosyncratically, uttering iconoclastic opinions on a wide variety of subjects, and sprinkling his controversial views with liberal doses of paradox, irony, and the

incomparable Shavian wit. In 1898 he claimed that, "with an unprece-
dented pertinacity and obstination, I have been dinning into the public
head that I am an extraordinarily witty, brilliant, and clever man. My
reputation is built up fast and solid, like Shakespeare's, on an impregnable basis of dogmatic reiteration." Even as he wrote, his reputation was
not "fast and solid," nor had he won quite the recognition he sought. He
had managed to achieve widespread notice as something of a crank, with
strong views on vegetarianism, antivaccination, antivivisection, and his
own worth, and he had attracted some favorable attention from a few
who had responded intelligently to his published works, but he was still
not onstage.

Shaw's nineteenth-century London years were, then, chiefly offstage
in the nature of his literary endeavors, yet shortly after the turn of the
century, he was in an ironical position. By the end of 1901 he had
published ten plays that would justify naming him among the chief
dramatists of the nineteenth century. However, with the exceptions of
the unfinished *Passion Play* (which he abandoned in 1878) and an ill-
fated 1884 collaboration with drama critic William Archer that later
evolved into *Widowers' Houses*, the rest of Shaw's writing was nondramatic. His first serious literary effort, *My Dear Dorothea*, written in 1878,
was a prose piece subtitled "A Practical System of Moral Education for
Females Embodied in a Letter to a Young Person of That Sex." Between
1879 and 1883 he completed five novels (he also began a sixth, which he
did not finish). After joining the Fabian Society in 1884, he produced
many socialist tracts as well as preparing and delivering scores of public
lectures. He wrote book reviews for the *Pall Mall Gazette* from 1885 to
1888, art criticism for the *World* from 1886 to 1890, music criticism (as
Corno di Bassetto) for the *Star* from 1888 to 1890, music criticism (as
G.B.S.) for the *World* from 1890 to 1894, and theater criticism for the
Saturday Review from 1895 to 1898. He published *The Quintessence of
Ibsenism* in 1891 and *The Perfect Wagnerite* in 1898. During this period of
overlapping genres he also tried verse in the form of anonymous political ballads for the *Star*, he collaborated on a multi-author novel for the
1890 Christmas Number of the *World*, he wrote scads of letters, and he
kept a diary. Had there been an exhaustive edition of *The Complete Bernard Shaw* in 1901, his ten plays would have formed only a small fraction
of his collected works.

Ironically, Shaw's method of gaining public recognition as a playwright also was offstage. He reached his audiences through the publication of his plays rather than through performances. He had little choice,
in some part due to censorship when the Lord Chamberlain refused to
license *Mrs Warren's Profession* (at that time one-third of Shaw's dramatic

canon), but chiefly because few would produce his plays, which had only limited runs in suburban and matinee performances. He won a wider audience through the pioneering publication of his scripts, complete with Shavian prefaces raising the significant issues of the plays and Shavian stage directions designed to accommodate readers rather than directors or actors. Critics, reacting more to his public persona and to his role as the *Saturday Review*'s drama critic than to what happened on the stage, had difficulty responding objectively to his plays as plays, and the prefaces made some critics even more reluctant to recognize his worth as a dramatist. In *Iconoclasts* (1905), J. G. Huneker, annoyed by the didacticism he perceived in the plays, used the prefaces to demean Shaw's dramaturgy, writing that the prefaces "are literature, and will be remembered with joy when the plays are forgotten." Frequent charges that the plays were "decidedly not drama," that the plays had not proven themselves on the stage, and that the plays were really political pamphlets in costume continued to limit Shavian productions.

Shaw eventually attained recognition as a dramatist after the 1904–1907 Vedrenne-Barker [Royal] Court Theatre productions had demonstrated that the plays could attract large audiences for long runs, but this by no means assured his success on the London stage. After the 1905 command performance of *John Bull's Other Island*, as T. F. Evans commented in *Shaw: The Critical Heritage*, "The age of Bernard Shaw may be said to have begun. From then on, his plays commanded the greatest attention accorded to any living dramatist." Even so, the attention was not always favorable. The critics continued to pan Shaw, and the responses of the *Morning Post* and other papers may have contributed to *Major Barbara*'s relative failure (unlike *John Bull's Other Island, Man and Superman*, and others, *Major Barbara* was not revived at the [Royal] Court after its initial run). *Getting Married* and *Misalliance* both failed on the commercial stage, and in his disgust with the London critics, Shaw gave his plays increasingly to Germany for their premieres. This might well have been the fate of *Fanny's First Play* had not Shaw written it for Lillah McCarthy and withheld his name as the author. In 1911, however, *Fanny's First Play* had a 622-play run in London, and in 1914 *Pygmalion*, after premiering in Vienna, ran 118 times in London, so Shaw finally had substantial successes on the commercial stage. In the sense of avoiding London, however, he was offstage during the Edwardian years, and his onstage successes occurred only after considerable neglect and abuse.

Shaw's hard-won and enviable popularity was short-lived, for he soon found himself offstage again as a result of his nondramatic writing. Following the outbreak of World War I, he retreated to write *Common*

Sense About the War, which appeared in November 1914 and sold more than 75,000 copies. *Common Sense* alienated practically everyone by pointing out that England had to bear a share of responsibility for the war and that the war would be ruinous for all parties. In response to his widely misquoted suggestion that soldiers of both sides should shoot their officers and go home, his emphasis that England was as responsible for the war as Germany, and his mocking tactical suggestion that the English could best crush Germany by killing 75 percent of its women, the war-frenzied British public regarded him as a traitor. He was even expelled from the Dramatists' Club, although he was its most eminent member. *Common Sense* destroyed overnight the onstage popularity and success that had taken more than two decades to establish. When John Leslie Palmer, somewhat prematurely, entitled his 1 March 1915 *Fortnightly Review* article "Bernard Shaw: An Epitaph," many found the title apt. During the war Shaw began work on two of his greatest plays—*Heartbreak House* and *Back to Methuselah*—and wrote a few light pieces for the stage, but he was offstage again as far as the British public was concerned.

After the appearance of *Saint Joan* in 1923, public reaction to Shaw completed a shift from abhorrence to adulation, but again he did not remain onstage for long. When he received the Nobel Prize for Literature for 1925, he joked that he had probably won the honor in return for not having written a play that year. Actually there was a six-year hiatus in Shavian stagecraft, for from 1923 to 1928 he worked almost exclusively on his political magnum opus, *The Intelligent Woman's Guide to Socialism and Capitalism.* When he returned to the stage, he began with a play that dramatized many of the concerns raised in the *Guide,* and he followed *The Apple Cart* with other political plays that alienated many who objected to his between-the-wars flirtations with dictatorships. He also aroused considerable controversy in 1932 with *The Adventures of the Black Girl in Her Search for God* (which he called his "large pamphlet"), and he continued to involve himself in pursuits that took him from the stage, including traveling around the world, working with the BBC Advisory Committee on Spoken English, and writing for the cinema (in 1938 he won an Academy Award for his screenplay of *Pygmalion*). These and other activities, coupled with the waning of his dramatic effectiveness during his last years, somewhat undermined his onstage influence.

Shaw's early offstage writing, including *My Dear Dorothea,* political ballads, criticism, novels, and short stories, introduced many concerns that would remain important to him throughout his long literary career. In addition, these works frequently suggest the genesis of techniques that served him well in his plays. His later nondramatic works, including *The*

Intelligent Woman's Guide to Socialism and Capitalism and *The Adventures of the Black Girl in Her Search for God,* not only reveal his mastery of prose forms but also show that, for Shaw, drama remained only one of the many vehicles available for conveying the Shavian viewpoint to an audience. In short, Shaw's offstage works lead to a greater appreciation of the full range of his genius.

Laura Tahir

MY DEAR DOROTHEA: SHAW'S EARLIEST SKETCH

Bernard Shaw wrote *My Dear Dorothea, A Practical System of Moral Education for Females* in January and February 1878, two years after he arrived in London. It is his first prose work, a short piece (approximately 4,200 words) written as a letter of advice to a five-year-old girl from one who feels for her "the romantic affection of a parent, tempered by the rational interest of an experimental philosopher."[1] In this early effort we see the emergence of Shavian form and content: humor, paradox, moralizing, the use of the letter as a means of expression, a female as the main character, and many inchoate ideas that would later become major themes of Shaw's work. GBS gave the manuscript of *My Dear Dorothea* to his good friend and biographer, Stephen Winsten, who published the work in 1956 as a book—not quite in its entirety—with illustrations by Clare Winsten. In a brief afterword to *My Dear Dorothea*, Stephen Winsten comments that "this piece is the very quintessence of all [Shaw's] work and may well be regarded as the germinating ground of his genius." *My Dear Dorothea* also offers suggestions about what the author's recent past in Dublin must have been like. This early Shaw work both reflects the author's youth and provided for him a sketch that would guide his thinking as he developed his later work.

In the first line of *My Dear Dorothea*, Shaw writes, "As you have just completed your fifth year, a few words of wholesome counsel as to your conduct and feelings may not be unreasonable." The year 1878 was a fifth year for Shaw, too. In 1873 the Shaw-Lee household had broken up when George John Vandeleur Lee's musical career became so successful that he ambitiously left Dublin for London. In that same year Mrs. Shaw followed her voice teacher, taking her two daughters, Lucinda and Agnes, with her and leaving behind her husband, George Carr, and son, George Bernard. Although Shaw described his early childhood as "domestic anarchy," and wrote that his mother "accepted me as a natural and customary phenomenon, and took it for granted that I should go on occurring in that way,"[2] there had been a family structure that must have provided some stability for young Shaw. Lee had offered the Shaw household his "impetuous enterprise and his magnetism," which, according to GBS, were more than welcome to the "thoroughly disgusted and disillusioned woman [who was] suffering from a hopelessly disappointing husband and three uninteresting children grown too old to be petted like the animals and the birds she was so fond of, to say nothing of the humiliating inadequacy of my father's income."[3]

By 1873 Shaw was already quite capable of taking care of himself, but with this move of part of his family to London, he lost what had become an important family activity—music—and had to rely even more on his own resources. He wrote that during his boyhood in Dublin, "music had been my daily food,"[4] and lamented that in 1873, "I suddenly found myself in a house where there was no music, and could be none unless I made it myself."[5] Fortunately for Shaw, his mother had left her piano in Dublin, and Shaw taught himself to play the instrument. Later he recalled that during 1875–76 he had had "a few pianoforte lessons from T. Moore without result."[6] It seems that his self-sufficiency had been well established. He continued his self-education in other areas as well, visiting museums, concerts, and plays, and filling his diaries with fragments of verse.

Shaw encourages Dorothea to develop self-sufficiency. "Everybody in this world is expected to take care of themselves, and live without asking help from their fellow-creatures." Self-sufficiency, the author tells Dorothea, is what will eventually establish her as an adult. Adults are people who "have grown up completely in mind and body and are therefore expected to take care of themselves. . . . Always strive to find out what to do by thinking, without asking anybody. If you continually do this, you will soon act like a grown-up woman." Shaw points out how grown-up people are different from Dorothea: they are taller and stronger, have money to spend, are allowed to walk about by themselves, and deceive one another. Unfortunately, however, "a very great number of grown-up people act like children" because they do not think for themselves.

Self-sufficiency is also a source of improvement. "By learning to decide for yourself, you will improve greatly, and will not have to be running continually to your mother when she is reading or sewing, and disturbing her with questions." Dorothea must never think of herself as "clever enough or neat enough," and this way she will always be learning more and improving herself. Shaw acknowledges that Dorothea probably feels no need for improvement. She has "excellent persons" such as her Aunt Tabitha and Godpapa Whenzentoul to watch over her. But, Shaw warns, these people are adults and can never be expected to understand a little girl. That is, adults are not perfect, and Dorothea must understand their shortcomings. This attitude is reminiscent of an opinion Shaw expressed in a letter from Dublin to his sister Lucinda in London in 1875. Lucy was performing in one of Lee's amateur operas, and Shaw wrote, "As to Lee, I would decline to listen to him. We all know what his tirades are worth, and I think his coming to Victoria Grove and launching out at you as he did, simply outrageous."[7] Other adults in Lee's production were not spared either: "They have not been acting squarely with you at all, they are afraid of you, don't understand you in the least, and consequently have fallen into a wretched policy of half coaxing and half coercing, by indirect influences and threats."[8]

Another important part of growing up for Dorothea is learning how to maintain self-control. "Never cry," Shaw writes, "and never lose your temper." But he knows that Dorothea will become angry, and he points out that this is not the same as losing one's temper. "[P]eople cannot help being angry when they are offended. It is when your anger makes you forget what you are doing, that your temper is lost. Then you say or do things which you are sorry for or ashamed of afterwards." One could infer from this that Shaw was not the emotionally cool person he often posed as, but that in fact he had very strong feelings over which he wanted to achieve control. He tells Dorothea that she will gain nothing by freely releasing tears or anger and that by keeping these feelings in check she "will have a great advantage in any dispute over others who may not equal you in self-control." Similarly, Shaw advised Lucy, "The sum of my advice to you is, to cultivate of all things, serene philosophy. Never under any circumstances lose temper, and never let yourself be put out. If you are, don't shew it."[9]

Shaw wishes to teach Dorothea to teach herself, and reading books is one good way to learn. Dorothea should disregard Aunt Tabitha's tracts since they are "somewhat dull." She should also disregard any tiresome books that adults tell her to read. But *Pilgrim's Progress*, Shaw's own childhood favorite, is highly recommended. "You must read this before you are ten years old. Be sure and do not let your opportunity slip." In the manuscript to *My Dear Dorothea*,[10] Shaw had also advised Dorothea to read *The Arabian Nights Entertainments* and Lamb's *Tales From Shakespear*, but for some reason this was deleted in the published version.

While adamantly opposing Dorothea's taking advice, Shaw has endless advice for her. This is not a Shavian paradox. Shaw suggests that, if Dorothea cannot find the right course for herself, she ask somebody, as long as she does not make a habit of this, and as long as she makes sure that the person who advises her is right. Apparently the young author felt certain of the correctness of his own thought, or at least attempted to convince himself that he was.

Shaw includes in his counsel on education a warning about the miseries of attending school. At school, Dorothea will find herself "suddenly in the midst of a barbarous community. They will not care about you." The schoolmistress is described as "the natural enemy of all." Shaw described one of his schoolmasters as "the common enemy of me and my schoolfellows. In his presence I was forbidden to move, or to speak except in answer to his questions. Only by stealth could I relieve the torture of immobility by stealthily exchanging punches (called 'the coward's blow') with the boy next me."[11] Dorothea should not expect to be understood by her classmates. "Knowing nobody, and feeling uncertain whom to trust, you will feel lonely, and wish heartily that you might go home again. Console yourself by remembering that this will only last a week, and let nothing tempt you to let any girl know what you feel." Here Shaw is advocating emotional isolation, a more extreme form of self-sufficiency, as a means of dealing with discomfort. One is reminded of his own boyhood preference to be alone, "mostly a solitary wanderer in enchanting scenery to the magic of which I was very susceptible."[12] And mischief is advised for Dorothea: "Attend to your lessons as much as you can without fatiguing yourself; and get into mischief as often as you can. This will give you the habit of working and enjoying yourself at the same time." Shaw wrote that his own childhood did not include any sort of control from his "amiable and most uncoercive parents," and that he and his boyhood friends "made mischief for its own sake in mere bravado."[13]

It is curious that Shaw does not recommend aesthetics to Dorothea. Aside from his counsel that "story books are much better than lesson books," Shaw does not seem to think that music, art, or literature might save Dorothea. Of his own education, he wrote, "It is evident that my schooling was a complete failure, and that the aesthetic education I received out of school was my salvation."[14] In *My Dear Dorothea* Shaw seeks to scrutinize and clarify issues that confused him. His interest in the arts was something that he took for granted.

There is a vague reference to religion at the beginning of *My Dear Dorothea*, and throughout the letter Shaw preaches about proper moral conduct. His attitude here is as iconoclastic as it is about education. Dorothea must think for herself and not be guilty of idolatry. But she will have to admit that she is in fact an idolater when she answers Shaw's question: "Would you not hate me if I told you that Aunt Tabitha was a foolish old maid, your mother a frivolous and selfish woman, your father a perverter of truth for gold, and the clergyman the worst man in church?" If Dorothea grows up to be thoughtful, she will inevitably become disillusioned and disappointed. This was certainly Shaw's experience with religion. In the Preface to *Immaturity*, he described a scene from his boyhood in Ireland during which he questioned his compulsion to pray every night, even though he did not believe his prayers could be answered. Prayer, Shaw began to feel, was an act that encouraged people to live dishonest lives. Therefore, he gave up prayer, and he later claimed that "this sacrifice of the grace of God . . . to intellectual integrity synchronized with [the] dawning of moral passion in me. . . . Up to that time, I had not experienced the slightest remorse in telling lies whenever they seemed likely to help me out of a difficulty: rather did I revel in the exercise of dramatic invention involved."[15] Religion was an important concern for young Shaw. He had once confided to his boyhood chum, Edward McNulty, that he would be the founder of a new religion. But in 1878 that religion had not yet been established.

Much of Shaw's religious counsel to Dorothea takes the form of biblical aphorisms, but not without a Shavian twist. He quotes the golden rule and then inverts it, saying Dorothea need, for the present, only take care not to do unto others anything that she would not wish others to do to her. For example, "Never on any account conceal anything from [your mother] or tell her what is not true. If you will think how much perplexed you would be if you could not be sure that whatever she said was the truth, you will understand what she would feel if she could not be certain that every word of yours was true, and see how foolish it would be to tell her a lie."

Shaw provokes Dorothea to thought and implies the importance of empathy when he says, "If your mother is always kind to you, love her more than you love anything except your doll; but never forget that she was once a little girl like yourself grown up; and that she is kind because she remembers how she liked people to be kind to her. If she is cross for a moment, recollect that you are sometimes cross yourself, and forgive her." Dorothea will learn to empathize if she uses reason to understand her mother. For instance, she may feel neglected, but she should remember that "your mother, having long since exhausted the novelty of having a child of her own, thinks of you only as a troublesome and inquisitive little creature, whose dresses are continually dirty, and whose face is too sticky to be kissed with pleasure."

Some of Shaw's biblical references in *My Dear Dorothea* are more amusing than insightful. For example,

> Some of the holiest men have been terribly unhappy. King Solomon, who first spoke of a merry heart as having a continual feast, wrote a book so

> full of grief that you would almost cry if you read it. Elijah the prophet, a good man who never died, but went straight to heaven in a horse-and-car, asked God to kill him because he could not bear to live. Jesus Christ was so melancholy that he never smiled, or took any amusement, except boating occasionally.

No doubt Shaw was influenced by his mother's brother, Dr. Walter Gurly. Of him Shaw wrote, "To the half dozen childish rhymes taught me by my mother he added a stock of unprintable limericks that constituted almost an education in geography. . . . Being full of the Bible, he quoted the sayings of Jesus as models of facetious repartee."[16]

Shaw supports part of his moralizing with footnoted quotations from the Bible, indicating a substantial knowledge of that work. For instance, he notes that Dorothea's Aunt Tabitha and Godpapa Whenzentoul may not agree with him, but they will "admit that the system of which they approve is neither so consistent in its application, nor so uniformly successful in its results, as to warrant a universal adoption of it." From the Bible he quotes Proverbs 14:12: "There is a way that seemeth right unto a man, but the ends thereof lead to death."

Along with Shaw's exhortation that Dorothea question the conventional thoughts and actions of her elders, he emphasizes the importance of politeness and tact. To be pleasing is to be "properly hypocritical." The world is full of hypocrites, people who say what they do not mean, or pretend to be greatly concerned about affairs that do not affect them. In order to be liked, Shaw writes, one has to be a proper hypocrite. Dorothea should strive to be adept at the kind and proper type of hypocrisy if she wants to get along with people. Shaw himself felt awkward among people when he first arrived in London and thus knew the value of skills that would enable him to achieve ease in social situations. He "suffered agonies of shyness." At the same time, he was well aware of his interpersonal needs. To shy away from people was his first reaction, but he realized "that I must never let myself off in this manner if I meant ever to do anything in the world."[17] Thus, his fear of social encounters led to courage and a need to fit in with the crowd. He went out of his way to learn the skills that would enable him to attend social gatherings where his curious mind would be stimulated. Dorothea also should struggle to achieve these skills. "If you are careful about these things, [your mother's friends] will most likely ask you to their houses and give you cake." As an example of how to cultivate social grace, Shaw asks Dorothea to suppose that she had a kind friend who died.

> You would be very sorry for your loss, and you would feel (knowing how kind the friend was) that everyone else ought to be sorry too. And if your

> companions laughed at your grief, you would feel hurt. By this you may
> perceive that when those whom you meet tell you that they have lost their
> friends, you must, in order to avoid paining them, look as sorrowful as
> possible. This will be an act of hypocrisy on your part, but a very proper
> and kind one. You must also pretend to think that all your acquaintances'
> dead friends are in heaven, although you may privately feel quite certain
> that they are in hell. Indeed, you may lay it down as a rule for practising
> Hypocrisy, that unpleasant things which you may know about people
> should never be mentioned.

Shaw writes that "though your behaviour may be as proper as that of
any other girl, your manner can never be the same any more than your
nose can." This results from individuality. A hundred little girls at a
party may observe the same rules of behavior, Shaw writes. "They will all
curtsey to the lady of the house, and eat as much cake as their parents
will allow them to, they will not eat with their knives, drink tea out of
their saucers, or take bones in their hands to gnaw the flesh from; and
still each will have quite a different manner." Dorothea must be careful
never to imitate others lest she lose her individuality.

Shaw's advice is not to be understood without some thought. He does
not give Dorothea easy directions or proscriptions. He seeks to show her
that concepts such as hypocrisy, pride, selfishness, and contentment are
not necessarily one-sided. Just as a little hypocrisy enables one to be
proper, pride is also a useful sentiment. Pride at its best will make Dorothea wish to know as much as other people, but if pride is not kept in
check, it becomes vanity. Vanity is the "desire for things or affectation of
qualities which you can never possess." He points to the difference between selfishness and greed: "Let your rule of conduct always be to do
whatever is best for yourself. Be as selfish as you can." Greedy people, on
the other hand, are "only silly people trying to be selfish without knowing how," people who want to have what they cannot have. Greedy
people are not content. No one, however, is content.

> You have been told so often that contentment is a good thing, that you
> will probably feel sorry and disappointed to hear that it has no existence.
> But if you think about it for a minute, you will perceive that in reality it
> would destroy all your pleasure if you possessed it. The reason why
> people praise it so much is, that it is natural to them to esteem the things
> they have not and to despise the things they have.

Shaw became discontented with Dublin. He was aware of the "enor-
mity of [his] unconscious ambition" but was "not enamored of failure, of
poverty, of obscurity, and of the ostracism and contempt which these
imply; and these were all that Dublin offered."[18] Shaw arrived in Lon-

don on 31 March 1876, only four days after his sister Agnes had died of consumption at Ventnor, on the Isle of Wight. He immediately went to Ventnor, and after a brief stay there returned to London to live with his mother and sister Lucy. Only nineteen years old, he needed to deal with a mixture of feelings about being an immature boy from Dublin who had vague but certain hopes of being a successful man in London. He needed a way to organize his thoughts and feelings into a meaningful purpose. Many years later he looked back on that time and described his view:

> I had the intellectual habit; and my natural combination of critical faculty and literary resource needed only a clear comprehension of life in the light of an intelligible theory: in short, a religion, to set it in triumphant operation. It was the lack of this last qualification that lamed me in those early days in Victoria Grove.[19]

The intelligible theory, or religion, would be developed in Victorian London. While the economic condition of most Victorians during this time was not good, ideas flourished, in print and on the platform. The ideas of such thinkers as Darwin, Marx, Spencer, and the Mills created an intense intellectual climate in which people could discuss and argue scientific, social, philosophical, and political issues. There were hundreds of Victorian periodicals, and the literacy rate of the English population had been rising steadily since mid-century. According to one historian, it was also a time in which more thought than action took place, "a period of gestation in which little legislation was produced while new philosophies of reform were being developed and changes made in the assumptions on which social reformers based their plans."[20]

My Dear Dorothea was written during this very active time in Shaw's mental development. His need for a religion or creed led him to write to the imaginary five-year-old girl who perhaps symbolizes his own struggle during the five years immediately prior to the letter. Shaw wants to show Dorothea life's complexities and contradictions, to provoke her with the concerns he struggled with himself. Many of these concerns would become preoccupations, even obsessions, which he elaborated on for the next seventy years. Stephen Winsten claims of *My Dear Dorothea* that "[m]ost of the conclusions arrived at stayed with [Shaw] for the remainder of a long and active life, and if we were not aware of the fact that it was written in 1878, we might have been deceived into thinking that he was quoting his own plays and prefaces." Margot Peters similarly writes, "*My Dear Dorothea* offers evidence of a mind born wise."[21]

It might be more accurate to say that *My Dear Dorothea* offers evidence of a mind born *to become* wise. There are numerous features of this first work of Shaw's that reflect his recent past and serve as models for later work. For example, Shaw refuses to give Dorothea a silly nickname. He, in fact, was dissatisfied with his given name, and in 1879 would publish an article, "Christian Names," denouncing names given to children. And Shaw's advice to Dorothea that she cause mischief whenever possible is reminiscent of his own attempts to amuse himself in school and prefigures Agatha Wylie and her friends in *An Unsocial Socialist*. Shaw spent many years (1878–93) writing prose, including five unsuccessful novels, before he became known as a playwright. But during this period he was doing more than perfecting a form, in spite of his own claim that "I have a great respect for the priggish conscientiousness of my first efforts. They prove too that, like Goethe, I knew all along, and have added more to my power of handling, illustrating, and addressing my material than to the material itself."[22]

One way to study the development of thought is the evolving systems approach, a method constructed by Howard Gruber and his associates.[23] A creative individual is an evolving system that regulates creative activity, which in turn regenerates the system. Creative thought is a product of such a system and occurs as a constructive process involving a series of changing and growing structures. This process evolves over time; it is a protracted epigenesis. For instance, GBS did not simply discover the idea of creative evolution by reading Samuel Butler, nor did he somehow pick up ideas about class injustice by reading Marx. These ideas were constructed through repetition and variation of structures, and the foundation for that construction can be seen in *My Dear Dorothea*. Since structures change, we cannot look at one point in the life of a creative individual and expect to capture the essence of that person's thought. By looking at the *development* of thought, we can often account for inconsistencies and contradictions. In *My Dear Dorothea*, for instance, the rudiments of Shaw's life philosophy are many and stimulating, but a close look shows this work to be a first draft, an experiment of the Life Force, with tenuous arguments to be developed and perfected by the author for the rest of his life.

Shaw intended *My Dear Dorothea* to be part of a longer work portraying his philosophy of life. The original manuscript indicates that the work is Shaw's "1st sketch," "Letter 1," a letter embodied in a *series* of letters. It is most likely the only letter Shaw ever wrote of this proposed series. Perhaps the proposed letters to Dorothea were abandoned for *Passion Play,* which Shaw began in February 1878, almost in tandem with *My Dear Dorothea. Passion Play* is an iconoclastic versified drama about New Testament events in which Shaw continued to develop themes about growth and youthful rebellion from *My Dear Dorothea.* Both works were aborted in February 1878. Another work, the outline for a novel Shaw called *The Legg Papers,* was also left incomplete in 1878. Shaw was involved in a dense network of social activities and self-educative enterprises during his early years in London, and perhaps this was more conducive to preparation and incubation of thought than to the kind of discipline necessary to bring a work to full realization.

The inside cover of the manuscript title page of *My Dear Dorothea* offers a fascinating insight into how the young Shaw was organizing his thoughts at this time. He did not write a preface to the letter, but instead created an index (appended to this essay) made up of thirty items from the letter, indicating on which of the twenty-nine pages each item is discussed. Given such evidence, it would be tempting to say that all Shaw's ideas were there from the beginning, that in January and February of 1878 twenty-one-year-old Shaw came up with a list of thirty terms that would describe his work for the next seventy-three years. The list is certainly comprehensive, but the concepts serve as a sketch for further development, a commitment to understand and grow with the knowledge that grappling with these concepts would bring.

Shaw makes several attempts to broach the topic of religion with Dorothea, but his advice stops short. He clearly states that idolatry is "wicked," but what is this individuality that should replace it? In the next-to-last paragraph of the letter he writes, "Never listen to religious instruction. I have already promised to write to you on that subject when you are old enough to care about it," and one might infer that he is less than certain about what to say to Dorothea about religion. But over time, with repetition and variation in the structures of thought, Dorothea will learn to understand the world. She should keep this letter: "Keep it and read it occasionally. The older you grow, and the better you know the world, the more easily you will understand it."

Instead of instructing Dorothea on religion at this point, Shaw emphasizes growth. He uses words relating to growth (such as "little," "child," and "grown-up") more than fifty times in this piece. There is a constant juxtaposition between Dorothea and adults. He urges Dorothea to have a commitment to growth and improvement. To grow is to search, especially amid the confusion that Shaw was certain lay ahead for Dorothea. His letter would prepare her "for the grim confusion into which you will descend, after you have successfully passed through the whooping cough, the scarlatina, the measles, and any other perilous experience which the infinite benevolence of the Omnipotent may impose upon you." The Omnipotent would eventually become a more abstract force

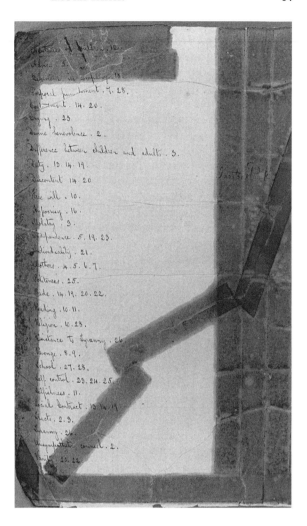

Fig. 1. Shaw's unpublished index to *My Dear Dorothea*. Courtesy Harry Ransom Humanities Research Center, University of Texas at Austin.

of creative evolution, and many years later Koheleth will be able to describe it to the Black Girl. Dorothea's god is not yet a power that she can find in herself, but the Black Girl will be able to claim that "to know God is to be God."[24]

The glimmerings of creative evolution in *My Dear Dorothea* are implied in Shaw's discussion of idolatry, contentment, discontent, and free will. The idolaters feel that authorities "can neither commit sin nor make a mistake." But years later Shaw would write that growth can only be achieved by trial-and-error experiments of the Life Force. Dorothea should not be content as an idolater, but should strive to understand and to improve herself. Shaw's index reference for free will is to page 10 of his manuscript, which identifies the kinds of books Dorothea must read. Free will later will become the force propelling creative evolution, but at this point free will refers to Dorothea's choice of reading material.

Growth is presented as the outcome of a dialectical relationship between an unknowing child and a superior adult. But Shaw is unclear about whether the child or the adult is wiser. In many ways the child is inferior to the adult and must learn to become like the adult, and yet if the adult forgets what childhood is like, he or she is not wise. Ultimately the synthesis shows that the wise adult and the wise child are similar. "I know how clever you are, and I advise you just as I would an older person," Shaw writes to Dorothea.

The entry "social contract" in Shaw's index refers to a discussion that prefigures his socialism. The world in which we live is a "very badly arranged one," Shaw writes.

> Some people are born with a great deal more money and clothes than others; some are even born without any at all. Everybody likes money and clothes, and the consequence is, that the people who have none want to take some from the people who have plenty; and the people who have plenty are angry because they have not as much as the Queen. But if they were to steal whatever they wanted, and hurt those with whom they were angry, the world would be so full of thieves and murderers that nobody could live happily in it.

This unhappy world is "only made bearable by each person agreeing to bear some share of the trouble. No matter how heavy a load is, its weight is scarcely felt when it is divided between many persons." Again we hear the golden rule and are reminded that much of Shaw's early thinking was shaped by his knowledge of the Bible. It would not be until 1882, when he heard Henry George's lecture on land nationalization, that Shaw's ideas about a "social contract" would be organized around a socialistic economic theory.

My Dear Dorothea is clearly autobiographical. In addition to giving the reader an idea of the author's recent youth and foreshadowing later Shavian themes, the work was also a means by which Shaw came to deal with his anger toward authority figures. The letter is iconoclastic, and even violent at times. Having been a neglected child, Shaw learned early on to take care of himself by making up stories. In *My Dear Dorothea*, Shaw creates several stories of hypothetical mothers that Dorothea may have to encounter. The wicked mother is portrayed with the horror of a child's fairy tale (unfortunately some of the description was edited out of the 1956 published edition). The published text advises Dorothea about this mother: "First of all, you must learn not to hate her and so you will be delighted at occurrences which other girls cry over." The manuscript has,

> First of all, you must learn to hate her with all your heart. Then, every-thing that annoys her will be a pleasure to you, and so you will have the advantage of being delighted at occurrences which other girls cry over. Whilst she is ill in bed, she cannot beat you, and you can enjoy yourself by thinking that she may die at any time. Always tell her lies, except you are [sic] absolutely sure of being found out. Even if you have not the pleasure of deceiving her, you will be none the worse; for whether you confess or deny, you will be punished equally.

Shaw was working out his anger toward authority figures in a healthy, imaginative, and creative way.

Graham Wallas, one of Bernard Shaw's close friends, described a four-stage process of creative problem solving in his book, *The Art of Thinking*. During the first stage, preparation, the thinker actively investigates a problem. Then there is a period of incubation, during which no active thought on the problem takes place. Incubation leads to insight, or a solution to the problem. Finally, the thinker must verify the insight. This four-stage linear process is not a totally accurate account of how creative problem solving takes place. For instance, an incubation period may not occur at all, or insight and verification may occur simultaneously. Or an error might provide insight, which needs no verification but instead may lead to other hypotheses which can then start a new preparation. In the case of Bernard Shaw, it seems that there was a long period of preparation in which he was involved in an elaborate network of related enterprises such as music, prose writing, and public speaking. Incubation then can be reinterpreted as a temporary period of inaction in one enterprise while work is being done in a similar enterprise. Insights occur, but rather than sudden inspirations, they are best seen as a result of a complex history of development in which the thinker commits himself or herself to a purpose. In *My Dear Dorothea*, Shaw laid the foundation of his life's purpose. It was a preliminary sketch to be developed over a long productive life. Some of the ideas would be abandoned for a period of time, incubating perhaps, later to become insights, reworked, verified, and then part of a new configuration of ideas. In *My Dear Dorothea* we can see the author had set for himself an intelligent and ambitious task.

Appendix: Shaw's Index to *My Dear Dorothea*

Acuteness of children, 12
Advice, 5
Behaviour in company, 18
Corporal punishment, 7, 28
Contentment, 14, 20
Crying, 23
Divine benevolence, 2
Difference between children and adults, 3
Duty, 13, 14, 19
Discontent, 14, 20
Free will, 10
Hypocrisy, 16
Idolatry, 3
Independence, 5, 19, 23
Individuality, 21

Mothers, 4, 5, 6, 7
Politeness, 25
Pride, 14, 19, 20, 22
Reading, 10, 11
Religion, 10, 28
Resistance to tyranny, 26
Revenge, 8, 9
School, 27, 28
Self-Control, 23, 24, 25
Selfishness, 11
Social contract, 13, 14, 19
Tracts, 2, 3
Tyranny, 26
Unsympathetic counsel, 2
Vanity, 20, 22

Notes

1. Bernard Shaw, *My Dear Dorothea* (London: Phoenix House, 1956), p. 52. All further quotations from *My Dear Dorothea* are from the Phoenix House edition unless noted otherwise.

2. Shaw, Preface to *London Music in 1888–89*, in *Bernard Shaw, Selected Prose*, ed. Diarmuid Russell (New York: Dodd, Mead, 1952), p. 69.

3. Ibid., p. 78.

4. Shaw, *Sixteen Self Sketches* (New York: Dodd, Mead, 1949), p. 59.

5. Shaw, Preface to *London Music*, p. 90.

6. *Bernard Shaw: The Diaries, 1885–1897*, ed. Stanley Weintraub (University Park: The Pennsylvania State University Press, 1986), p. 29.

7. Shaw to Lucinda Frances Shaw, 24 February 1875, in *Collected Letters, 1874–1897*, ed. Dan H. Laurence (New York: Dodd, Mead, 1965), p. 9.

8. Ibid.

9. Ibid.

10. Shaw, *My Dear Dorothea*, original manuscript, 1878, p. 10. I wish to thank the Harry Ransom Humanities Research Center, The University of Texas at Austin, and The Society of Authors on behalf of the Bernard Shaw Estate for permission to quote from this manuscript.

11. Shaw, Preface to *Farfetched Fables* (London: The Bodley Head, 1974), pp. 422–23.

12. Shaw, *Everybody's Political What's What?* (New York: Dodd, Mead, 1944), p. 160.

13. Ibid.

14. Ibid., p. 182.

15. Shaw, Preface to *Immaturity* (London: Constable, 1930), p. xx.

16. Shaw, *Sketches,* p. 32

17. Shaw, Preface to *Immaturity,* p. xlii

18. Ibid., p. xxxiii.

19. Ibid, p. xliv.

20. Janet Roebuck, *The Making of Modern English Society from 1850* (London: Routledge & Kegan Paul, 1982), p. 65.

21. Margot Peters, *Bernard Shaw and the Actresses* (New York: Doubleday, 1980), p. 5.

22. Shaw, Preface to *Immaturity,* p. xxxix.

23. See Howard E. Gruber and Sara Davis, "Inching Our Way Up Mount Olympus: The Evolving Systems Approach to Creative Thinking," in *The Nature of Creativity,* ed. Robert J. Sternberg (New York: Cambridge University Press, 1988), and Doris B. Wallace and Howard E. Gruber, eds., *Creative People at Work* (New York: Oxford University Press, 1989). I also wish to thank Howard E. Gruber and Colin G. Beer for their comments about the evolving systems approach.

24. Shaw, *The Adventures of the Black Girl in Her Search for God* (London: Constable, 1932), p. 30.

Ray Bradbury

ON SHAW'S "THE BEST BOOKS FOR CHILDREN"

After half a lifetime of reading Shaw, quite often out loud because I can't help myself, I still have the feeling that if you had run up to him early or late in his life and asked, "Do you know everything?" he might well have cried, "But most certainly, yes!"

He would have joined your shocked laughter and then added, "What do you want to know?"

Well, in this instance, children and children's books.

Shaw's "The Best Books for Children" reminds me, if you will pardon the intrusion, of a character in one of my own stories who, after listening to a dead, dull, and horribly realistic dinner lecture, turned on the dullard and cried, "Sir, have you *proof* of childhood! ? "

For indeed, as Shaw points out, the reason why so-called adults are no fun is that they have set about eradicating such proofs. The child in them, shot dead, is their idea of being full-grown. They are first cousin to the vampire, but worse; they do not even walk and live at night.

Reading his essay reminds us, as if we needed reminding, that all Shaw ever does is treat us to his uncommon common sense. What he says about children and reading and libraries is, it seems to me, undeniable. But still, long before Shaw's time and well into ours, we have the teacher or the librarian who would cram funnels down our throats and shove books in as if this force-feeding could make literary *foie-gras*.

Shaw's comment on quality for kids, and the second-rate for adults, hits the nail. I can remember librarians who herded this boy time and again out of the grown-up sectors of the stacks, fearing that the quality I might find there would melt my brain or destroy my innocence. When the librarians charged off on their terrible mission to prevent education, I snuck back into the forbidden corridors and had me a good self-righteous read.

So it was, we see, with Shaw, and should be with every adventurous child reader.

If Shaw were alive today, he would find a similar example in the librarians and teachers who stare at the floor while théir children look to the stars. While these laggards are busy declaring that fantasy and science fiction will turn boys into layabouts, those boy-readers become astronauts, and fly to leave their shoe-treads in the lunar dusts.

The trend is changing, of course. The librarians and the teachers have begun to run to the planetariums. It is hard to get in, however. The places are crammed with children who know what to read in order to know what to see.

And Shaw's ghost is in there with them, asking their advice on books that he should scan in order to catch up. Catch up, hell, he's been ahead of us all of our lives. It is we who must do the running.

Bernard Shaw

THE BEST BOOKS FOR CHILDREN

Shaw wrote "The Best Books for Children" for the Pall Mall Gazette *on 7 November 1887 in response to a series of five articles on children's books. The editors cut the piece to one paragraph, published (unsigned) on 29 November 1887 as "A Batch of Books for Boys." The complete essay has remained unpublished until now.*

My opinion on this subject derives all its value from the fact that I am one of the people who have not forgotten their own childhood—one indeed by whom the sense of being grown up has been but imperfectly acquired. Somehow the tone of one or two of the ladies who have already opinionated so judiciously in this column reminds me of the books I sometimes got as birthday presents from aunts and others who had views about little children, but whom to this day I cannot conceive as having ever been children themselves. I despised their books, which were usually about rainbows, faithful dogs, or detestable people like the Swiss family Robinson, who made life one long Puritan Sunday. In revenge, as it seemed to me, these ladies wanted my mother to take away, as unfit for a boy's reading, the books I did like; but fortunately my mother had been very strictly brought up, with the reactionary result of convincing her that the opposite system was the proper one. She refused even to take away the Arabian Nights; and though my aunt was so much in earnest that she actually stole the book from me, I traced it to its hiding place, and stole it back again, placing it beneath my mattress in case she should renew the attempt. Except for this interference, I was allowed to read whatever I could lay my hands on. As a result of it all, I have only two obstinate opinions: one, that there are some books which are half closed for ever to those who have not opened them in childhood; and, two, that what are called immoral episodes in books have no more effect on a child than the birth of its younger sisters and brothers.

I have no recollection of a time when I could not read; and the first book

I remember is the Pilgrim's Progress, the chief among those great books of which you defraud your child for ever if you withhold it even for ten years. The next was the Arabian Nights, as aforesaid, in an old calfcovered edition which may have been as plain spoken as Captain Burton's for all I know, but which contained no harm for me. Then came a translation of About's Roi des Montagnes, which greatly pleased me. Robinson Crusoe I jibbed at, because I did not discover it for myself. It was given to me to read; and at first I could not stomach it. But by some chance I waded through the first few pages; and then I need hardly say that the whole joyless but interesting narrative held me until Crusoe left the island, after which I did not care so much about him, though I intensely admired Bill Atkins. Meanwhile, the Arabian Nights had set me reading all the fairy tales I could get; and when a new volume of them arrived, I generally came to blows with my sisters for possession of it. I remember that they never disputed possession of the Ancient Mariner and John Gilpin, which were my pet poems. Robinson Crusoe had introduced me to the romance of adventure; and my second great sensation in that line was Captain Mayne Reid's Scalp Hunters. At this time (the child being now a boy) the love affairs in the books began to interest me, not perhaps in the way the authors intended; but at any rate so far that I began to accept constancy in love and chivalry towards women as heroic qualities, though I regret to say that heroes who made a great point of telling the truth struck me as being Sunday School sneaks, contemptibly inferior to highwaymen and pirates. Indomitable courage in personal combat thrilled me the more because I soon discovered, to my intense humiliation, that it was a quality I did not myself possess. No doubt I was over credulous in assuming that my deficiency was an exceptional one; but it may be that constitutionally brave boys do not care for deeds of daring in fiction as I did.

By this time I had a knowledge of [a] great many scraps from Shakespear, acquired in a way worth considering. I was fond of turning over the numerous illustrations by H. C. Selous in Cassell's Shakespear. Each illustration had a few lines of the text attached. The metre stuck these well into my memory long before I had any notion that Shakespear was a man instead of a book. Lamb's tales from the plays first strung these scraps together for me. But instead of reading Shakespear, I followed up the vein opened by Captain Mayne Reid, and read all the novels I could get. In some volumes of All the Year Round I read A Tale of Two Cities and Great Expectations; and they affected me strongly, though I was so very young that the discovery that Pip's fortune came from the convict—obvious as it is—quite took me aback. Then, as I got on for ten, I devoured everything except my school books, which I shirked incorrigibly.

Scott's novels were hard to get into, but good when you got there. Ivanhoe was of course a great find; but I was conscious that it was a showy novel, and considered that The Heart of Midlothian was better. The Ingoldsby legends struck my fancy; I did not catch their vulgarity (if, as I am told, they really are vulgar); and I did catch the fantastic imaginative side of them. Lord Derby's translation of The Iliad was inexhaustible; and I believe that if William Morris's Sigurd the Volsung had existed then, it would have been the very thing for me. I tried Trollope; but he was a fearful failure—dry as sawdust. I was so convinced beforehand that I should not like Thackeray, that I did not attempt him. Withal I read a lot of trash in penny numbers and the like, quite well knowing that it was trash; for I was, it seems to me, just as competent a critic as I am at present: indeed, that part of my critical work which I most enjoy now consists in giving reasons—probably wrong ones—for opinions formed in my nonage. The better the books were, the earlier I could like them. For instance, Great Expectations succeeded with me when Martin Chuzzlewit or Dickens's inferior and so far more popular books would have failed; and the Pilgrim's Progress and the Vicar of Wakefield came long before Alice in Wonderland, which, however, is hardly a fair example of a child's book.

This practically covers what I can recollect of my reading until, at twelve or thereabout, I began to disapprove of highwaymen on moral grounds, and to read Macaulay, George Eliot, Shakespear, Dickens, and so on in the ordinary sophisticated attitude. I read some books because I thought I ought to, not because I liked them. A boy whom I knew, moved to envy by my having read Robertson's Charles V, outdid me by reading Locke's Essay on the Human Understanding, whereupon, out of bravado, I read the Bible straight through, and settled him. Perhaps if I had been allowed to discover the Bible as I had the Pilgrim's Progress, I should never have thought of it when I wanted to select a particularly long and disagreeable feat in reading.

My general conclusion is that second rate fiction is good enough for grown-up people, but that first rate fiction is needed for children. Every child should have read some of the greatest books in its language before it is seven years old; and also know by ear (if it has one) some of the greatest melodies in the world. Here is my list.

For a Child	For a Boy
The Pilgrim's Progress	The King of the Mountains (About)
The Arabian Nights	Robinson Crusoe
Immoral Fairy Tales	The Scalp Hunters

The Ancient Mariner	The Ingoldsby Legends
John Gilpin	Don Quixote
A Tale of Two Cities	Homer (not Pope's)
Great Expectations	Sigurd the Volsung
The Vicar of Wakefield	The Waverley Novels
Lamb's Tales from Shakespear	The Novels of Dumas (*père*)

These will teach the future man how to dream. When he has learned that, it will be time to give him Macaulay and Tyndall on Sound, which will start him very well through his teens. But above all, only put the books in his way. Dont shove them down his throat if you want him to relish them.

Stanley Weintraub

BALLADS BY SHAW: THE ANONYMOUS *STAR* VERSIFIER OF 1888–1889

Shaw's identified published verse to date demonstrates that Bernard Shaw was an execrable poet. His 1888–89 attempts were no better, and clearly justify his anonymity.[1] Shaw loved to exercise his pen with indifferent poetry, although he knew that its quality was inferior. His diaries of 1885–97 are full of references to his attempts at verse, most of them fortunately never published. Some show a playful side of Shaw, such as his pseudonymous epistolary spoofs as "Amelia Mackintosh" or "Horatia Ribbonson," but his *Star* ballads of 1889–89 reveal a politically aroused Shaw.

The government's punitive Irish policy inspired Shaw early in 1888 to focus his ire on Arthur Balfour (1848–1930). Eight years Shaw's elder, the well-born Balfour was considered by many to be a young political dilettante when his Cecil uncle, the Marquess of Salisbury, then Conservative prime minister, appointed him Chief Secretary for Ireland early in 1887. The Irish Crimes Bill had just come into effect to punish intimidation of rapacious Irish landlords, and Balfour began making use of his new powers in September 1887. Local violence was met with force; two rioters were killed and others imprisoned, earning the Secretary the name "Bloody Balfour."

Eventually public outrage at the disproportionate penalties meted out (forcible strippings were apparently part of the police tactics) caused suspension of the bill, but not before the new policy had achieved its purpose of reducing the incidence of violence, at least temporarily. Shaw's mock-Gilbertian ballad in the persona of Balfour makes very clear what side he took. It was first published in *The Star* on 23 January 1888 (C392), and reappeared in *Platform and Pulpit* (A282). It appears here with the others to complete the cycle of Shaw's 1888 ballads, and to correct misprints in the earlier reprinting:

A Balfour Ballad

I am a statesman bold,
And I've frequently been told
There are other ways of killing dogs than hanging 'em;
And my plan to make it hot
For the Irish patriot
Is subtler far than bludgeoning and banging him.

When the hero of the West
Isnt strong about the chest
I cultivate his tendency to phthisis
By giving him a cell
In my Tullamore hotel[2]
Where the balmy air in winter time like ice is.

And the manager and waiters
In the morning grab his gaiters,
His ulster, and his trousers, and his cardigan;
And he cuddles in his quilt,
And reflects upon his guilt,
Vowing never to put in for three months' hard again.

The nature of his bed
Makes his shoulder blades all red,
Till he longs to have some padding for his skeleton;
And the story of his woes
So long and poignant grows,
That he finds the prison slate too small to tell it on.

And the hacking of his cough
As his coil he shuffles off,
Never strikes me through with shudders of repentance,
Nor spoils my wine and wassail
At the Four Courts and the Castle;[3]
No! consumption wasnt mentioned in my sentence.

Though the dogs may make a fuss
They cant find fault with us
If a higher Power relieves the land they lumbered;
And we reverently say,

"He gave. He took away."
Every hair we left upon their heads was numbered.

Repression of civil liberties was again Shaw's theme in April, although to that he added corruption. Two paid Tory agitators (the fact was never in doubt), Samuel Peters and an otherwise unidentified Kelly, had been involved in a "Fair Trade" demonstration in Trafalgar Square in February 1886. Afterwards Radical freethinker hero Charles Bradlaugh (1833–91) charged that they had been paid by Lord Salisbury and other leading Conservatives to stage the rally, which, in effect, was intended to support sugar protection interests. Salisbury indeed had sent a check for £25, which was not illegal on his part, and it appeared no libel to claim that it had been sent to promote the Trafalgar Square demonstration. But Kelly and Peters asserted that only £4 had been spent that way, "to obtain bands and banners," despite the fact that someone had paid for all the posters and placards and, very likely, for the people who carried them.

As Shaw notes in the opening of the ballad, the cover story told to the court when the case went to trial early in 1888 was that the money was to go for Christmas cuts of beef for deserving (and hungry) longshoremen in Kelly's "Riverside Labourers Association." Where the "shiners" (gold or silver coins, originally guineas or sovereigns) actually went was never determined.

An action for libel was taken against Bradlaugh for his imputation of wrongdoing (however legal), and a jury ordered payment of £300 in damages. Bradlaugh's indignant fellow M.P.s took up a subscription to pay it.

Peters, as Shaw observes, was among other things a lobbyist for English sugar refiners, who wanted cheap imported sugar: secretary of the puppet "Workmen's National Association for the Abolition of Foreign Sugar Bounties." Both Peters and Kelley had histories of accepting money for unedifying causes, but the judge, Baron Huddleston, thoughtfully suggested to the jury about Bradlaugh—a Member of Parliament—that little credence could be given to the testimony of a man who objected to taking the oath on the traditional courtroom Bible.

Cecil, as noted earlier, is the family name of the prime minister, Salisbury, whose party had been symbolized (since the days of Disraeli) by the primrose. Since he was not a party to the suit, no one questioned whether he had been libeled.

Shaw's outrage took the form of a near-libelous ballad in *The Star* on 20 April 1888 (C427). When Bradlaugh's daughter (and Shaw's friend) Hypatia published a biography of her father in 1895, she reprinted

Shaw's verses in the second volume without identifying the balladeer.
Shaw may not have confided in her.

Halves (An Historical Poem)
December, 1885

Take this cheque, my gentle Kelly,
Fill our starving London's belly;
Hie thee down with dearest Peters
To the lowly primrose eaters;
Tell the unemployed refiners
Cecil sends them of his shiners;
Let each toilworn Tory Striver
Batten on this twenty-fiver.
    Spread my bounty
    Through the country;
But my right hand must not know
What my left hand doth; and so
If thou value my attention
Full details must thou not mention.

February, 1886

Riots! Whew! Too bad of Kelly,
I must ask him what the—. Well, he
Can't at least pretend that I
Had any finger in the pie.

April, 1888

Halves, Peter, Halves! Honor 'mongst *us*, my sonny!
    Had I but tipt the wink a year ago,
You might have gone and whistled for your money,
    And *my* straightforwardness been spared a blow.

I was ashamed of giving you the cash:
    You were ashamed of getting it from me.
Three hundred is the value of that splash
    On our fair fame, unspotted previouslee.

Remember, sonny, when your freethought flesher
    Showed Charles your name and mine upon that cheque:
Had I owned up, I think you must confess your
    Foot would not now have been on Charles's neck.

So halves, my Peters:—nay, I crave not coin:
    To touch the brass would not befit my station:
I only ask that Kelly you'll rejoin,
    And pay your debt in Tory agitation.

In June Shaw was at it again, this time attacking W. T. Stead (1849–1912), former editor of the *Pall Mall Gazette,* which had its offices in Northumberland Street. A crusading, publicity-seeking journalist, Stead had seized causes ranging from raising the age of consent from thirteen to sixteen, and concomitant juvenile prostitution (he served a jail sentence for proving one could purchase a thirteen-year-old virgin), to intrusions into foreign affairs in Africa and Asia. In April 1888, Stead had left the editorial chair to become a special traveling correspondent for his paper. Long pro-Russian (because he was anti-Turkish), he was able to arrange to interview the tyrannical Czar Alexander III, producing material for the *Gazette* as well as for a widely publicized 1888 book, *The Truth about Russia.* His first dispatch to the *Gazette* made the front page of the 18 June 1888 issue, and promoted a fanciful freedom-loving and peaceful Russia as the center of European power, since France was weak and Germany was under a new and untried monarch. Stead's subsequent articles were given poorer placement, which riled the self-styled "Special Commission" when he returned to London late on the following Sunday night, and used his old powers at the paper to write an unsigned and lengthy leader for the issue of Monday, 25 June. He loaded it with self-praise for "the unique nature and signal success of his Commission," and promised to print the articles yet again and at greater length to help the public "to follow the drift of his argument."

Shaw quickly (these were one-sitting efforts) produced another ballad, this one excoriating Stead's naïveté and egomania. Calling Stead "The Pope of the *Pall Mall*" was not Shaw's joking inflation of Stead's importance, but (as Shaw knew) the editor's own, for Stead's registered telegraph and cable office address was "Vatican, London." (Shaw's would later be "Socialist, London.") Michael Katkov (1818–87), mentioned unflatteringly in the verses, had been a Moscow professor of philosophy who had undergone a conversion from liberalism to become editor of the monthly *Russian Herald* and the daily *Moscow Record,* both organs of conservative opinion. George Kennan (1845–1924), clearly his opposite, was an American journalist and historian who regularly exposed Russian inhumanity. He would publish *Siberia and the Exile System* in 1891 and *Tent Life in Siberia* in 1902, and he was a supporter of the exile-led Friends of Russian Freedom. His article in "this month's *Century*"—*The Century Magazine* for June 1888—was the lengthy, artist-illustrated "Plains and Prisons of Western Siberia," in which Kennan detailed his visits to the "indescribably and unimaginably foul" jails in which the Czar kept his political prisoners. Friendship with Russia, Shaw put it bluntly, was a matter of commerce, where political idealism was swept aside.

Reading Kennan apparently just before Stead's self-congratulatory return was all Shaw needed. He dipped his pen in acid, and his verses appeared in *The Star* on 26 June 1888 (C456) as antidotes to Stead's litany of Czarist praise.

A Northumberland-street Ballad

There was a certain Mr. Stead,
      Went off to see the Tzar,
Who said, "Explain, Sir, whence you come,
      And who the blank you are."

Quoth Stead, "Most noble potentate,
      Let nothing you dismay,
My tes-ti-mo-ni-als you'll find
      Are perfectly O.K."

"Oh, if you come from *her,* all right,"
      The haughty sovereign cried;
"All O.K.'s pals are Alick's, and
      The Church's pals beside.[4]

"Come in and have a cup of tea;
      And to me quickly tell
If I, indeed, before me see
      The Pope of the *Pall Mall?*"

"Oh, mighty Tzar, no Pope am I
      (Though I have often thought
The berth would just have suited me;
      So if I aint, I ought)."

"I quite believe it," says the Tzar;
      "And what's more, dash my eyes
If I another Katkoff don't
      In you, Sir, recognize."

Then seeing Stead blush up quite red
      Over his collar's rim
The Tzar thought (winking to himself)
      "That's how to tickle him."

And then into his crimson ear
      A story he did tell,
How Russia's mission came from Heaven,
      And Austria from—another place;

And how the Russian gaols were all
      A prisoner could desire;
And how in this month's *Century*
      Kennan is just a—person not to be depended on;

And how the trade that England does
  In coal, would shortly come
To Baku, where the Russians have
  Lots of Pe-tro-le-um.

In short, the Tzar he gammoned Stead
  So neatly, that he fell
To taking notes enough to swamp
  For years the whole *Pall Mall.*

In August Shaw was at it again. On the 29th he noted in his diary that he had sent to *The Star* "a few doggerel verses in the foulest street language on the balloon incident which suddenly occurred to me. Curious, this impulse to utter rhythmically what one hears! "[5] Two days earlier a fatal balloon accident had occurred in Bishop's Wickham, Essex, in which a well-known aereonaut named Simmonds was killed and his two passengers injured. The balloon, *Cosmos,* had risen from the grounds of the Irish Exhibition at the Olympia in Kensington and was headed toward the coast, to cross the Channel, when Simmonds attempted an emergency landing. His grappling iron failed to take hold; then an explosion ripped through the bag, and the passenger basket crashed to earth, fracturing Simmonds's skull.

What Shaw had overheard in "street language" on the crash to inspire his jolly and tasteless verses remains unknown, for *The Star* found them inappropriate for print. Shaw's self-criticism seems to have anticipated that outcome, and his sudden concern about what had prompted such doggerel outbursts from him had the virtue of temporarily ending them, but only temporarily, for he was not yet done with W. T. Stead, whom he looked upon as hypocritical opportunist in the guise of social reformer. Reading the *Pall Mall Gazette* early in October 1889 inspired what he called in his diary "a few verses"[6] (NIL) for *The Star,* which this time were published on the 9th, the very next day, again anonymously:

From the Housetops

Said William S-T-E-A-D,
I will be even with T.P.[7]
For damning social puritee.

I've cherished as a poison'd dart
What he did privately impart.
He said it from his very heart.

All unsugared and unjamm'd,
Down his throat his words he ramm'd—
"Social Purity be [MS. illegible]."[8]

> Blush blood red, immoral *Star,*
> Now all men know what you are,
> From the mouth of your Papar.

After all, the self-discredited game of jogging political rhyme, at least
on the evidence of the diaries, was over, but Shaw continued to enjoy
his own earlier handiwork. "I horrified them [at Hubert Bland's
house]," Shaw claimed in a diary entry of 26 October 1890, "by reading
my old dogg[e]rel about the *Birkenhead.*" On the level of taste of his
Cosmos ballad, the verses celebrated the sinking of the *H.M.S. Birkenhead*
in 1852, which foundered on the rocks off Simonstown, South Africa,
at a cost of 445 lives. What intrigued Shaw was that the stirring injunction "Women and children first!" dated from the incident, and the
old doggerel amused him enough that he had kept it since at least
1882. A letter from Pakenham Beatty to Shaw dated 15 February 1882
refers to it, and the manuscript of the verses survives (in shorthand)
still.[9]

More usefully, Shaw was now putting his humor, mordant and otherwise, into his music reviews, first as *Corno di Bassetto* in *The Star,* then as
G.B.S. in *The World.* It was a more useful outlet for that vein of his
psyche. When he would write further verse, it largely represented a very
different emotion: love. But whether political versifier or love lyricist, he
remained no Byron.

Notes

    1. Code numbers of identified Shaw verses are from the Laurence *Bibliography.* A
parenthetical NIL identifies a Shavian work not in Laurence.
    2. "Tullamore hotel" refers to a gaol for Irish political prisoners.
    3. The "Four Courts and Castle" would refer to the British seat of government in
Dublin.
    4. The recondite "O.K." was Mme. *O*lga Novi*k*off, a sycophantic and charming admirer
of the Czar ("Alick" in the poem). She was annoyed at Stead's interview with Alexander because it was not sufficiently fulsome. "O.K." was an informal Russian ambas-
sadress in London at whose salon Stead was often present. He was "deeply attached to
her," he confessed in his journal (in 1880), with a "sinful passion" that threatened to
break up his "Christian home." Shaw's "O.K." pun was as close as he could come without
risking libel.
    5. Entry for 29 August 1888, in *Bernard Shaw: The Diaries 1885–1897,* ed. Stanley
Weintraub (University Park: The Pennsylvania State University Press, 1986), p. 406.

6. Entry for October 1889, indicating that he began the verses on the same day that he completed them, "copied them out," and sent them off, in *The Diaries,* p. 547.

7. Thomas Power O'Connor, popularly known as "T.P.," a liberal M.P. from Liverpool, had founded *The Star* in January 1888 and was its editor. He had first hired Shaw as a political writer, a job at which Shaw lasted three weeks.

8. The bracketed material—including Shaw's brackets—was a Shavian attempt at humor.

9. Beatty's MS. letter is in the BL; Shaw's shorthand draft of the verses is at the HRC (Texas).

Fred D. Crawford

SHAW'S COLLABORATION IN *THE SALT OF THE EARTH*

The "Christmas Number" of the *World* (19 November 1890) included *The Salt of the Earth,* a twenty-two-chapter collaborative novel by Archibald Forbes, Major Arthur Griffiths, Mrs. F. H. Williamson, C. J. Wills, and Bernard Shaw. Edmund Yates, founding editor of the *World,* began planning this issue some months before its release date. Under the editing and coordination of Griffiths, the novel was to exploit rising public interest in the socialist movement while catering to subscribers' tastes in fiction. The combination of Forbes, Griffiths, Williamson, and Wills seemed adequate to satisfy readers' aesthetic requirements (these four churned out popular fiction by the yard), but *Salt* also needed someone familiar with socialism to provide authentic background detail.

In his diary entry for 7 July 1890, Shaw recorded that he visited the office of Edmund Yates, who "wanted to enlist me for the 'Socialism' in the *World* Christmas number."[1] It was reasonable for Yates to think of Shaw since, as a Fabian socialist, he was the most suitable *World* contributor to provide realistic depiction of socialist activities. Shaw also had valid reasons for accepting the assignment. As the *World*'s art critic from 1886 through 1889 and the *World*'s music critic since early 1890, he had reason to be willing to help his employers, particularly for payment. He also appreciated Yates's editorial restraint. In a letter to the *Star*'s editor concerning his resignation as the *World*'s art critic, published 18 December 1889, Shaw had written that "I never trimmed a line in my articles to suit Mr. Yates, and he never asked me to."[2] Shaw agreed to provide the "Socialism" for the novel, and Yates agreed to pay Shaw £10. By 10 July Shaw recorded that he "Wrote to Major Griffiths about the Xmas number of *The World.*"[3] He worked cheerfully enough on his share, finishing a first draft in October.

However, when the Christmas issue appeared on 19 November, Shaw wrote to Yates to refuse any payment for his work. When Yates paid him anyway, Shaw returned the money. He found his public association with *Salt* both irritating and embarrassing. On 24 November 1890, he wrote to John Burns that,

> As my name has been mentioned by the press as one of the authors, and as I did actually write about three pages of it (the only three readable ones in it) you may as well know that when the rough plan of the thing was submitted to me I told the author (Major Arthur Griffiths) that it was ignorant rubbish; that I would not have helped at all had it not been better to rescue at least a couple of pages from Archibald Forbes & Co. than to let them have it entirely to themselves; and that I have refused to be paid for the work or to touch the unclean profits of the thing in any way.[4]

Shaw's rancor may "have had its source in a contretemps concerning the amount of remuneration, coupled with a refusal by Griffiths to accept any of Shaw's suggestions for the development of the novel," as Dan H. Laurence has suggested.[5] However, the development of the novel was more important to Shaw than the question of money.

In 1894, when Edmund Yates's death left the *World* without an editor, Shaw's correspondence indicates that the Christmas number and Griffiths's role in it continued to rankle. When Shaw wrote to C. D. Yates, the late editor's son, on 30 May 1894 that he "thought it possible that [editorship of the *World*] might be taken by Major Griffiths, of whose editorship I have had experience to the extent of a World Xmas number," he announced his desire to "drop out of the post of musical critic."[6] Shaw had already been considering his resignation, willing to rely on income from plays and from free-lance journalism, but Griffiths had no way of knowing this. When he learned of Shaw's desire to quit, he understandably wondered whether Shaw was personally reluctant to serve under his editorship.

Shaw wrote to Griffiths on 2 June 1894, stating that Griffiths's editing was not the reason for his resignation but also revealing that the Christmas number was still on his mind. Shaw referred directly to their former collaboration:

> As to that Xmas number, you certainly landed me most refreshingly over it; but I did not take it at all in bad part. Even if you propose to deal in future on the understanding that you will hold yourself free to land me again whenever it suits you, I am quite ready to take you on at those terms and to look after myself without being personally unpleasant. Why

then should we fail to hit it off in a relation which involves no conflict of our interests?[7]

Shaw ultimately agreed to remain until the end of the season, writing his last *World* music column in August.

Shaw's unhappiness with the novel might easily have resulted from its aesthetic shortcomings—it is a fourth-rate piece of Victorian magazine fiction abundant in contradictions, stereotypes, and the worst excesses of melodrama. However, his major objection was to the novel's sneering depiction of socialism. In his accounting of his income for 1890 (which totaled a mere £250/13/2), Shaw noted that he returned £10 which Yates had sent "for my part of the Xmas number. I refused to accept it because of the bearing of the rest of the number on my relations with the Socialists caricatured in it."[8]

One such socialist was Shaw's friend John Burns, who appears in *Salt*'s Chapter XVII as Fyres. Burns, with Cunninghame Graham, had been arrested for his role in "Bloody Sunday" (13 November 1887), a mass meeting supporting free speech at Trafalgar Square. The police dispersed the meeting with clubs. Burns spent six weeks in jail. Shaw, also involved in the demonstration, avoided arrest because, as he put it, his group "*skedaddled.*" Shaw wrote to Burns on 24 November 1890, "The Christmas number of the World is out. Dont buy it, as it contains nothing to enliven its doglike trash except a description of you, the value of which you may judge from such touches as 'the harsh Scotch intonation' of your voice."[9]

Fyres, as a caricature of Burns, is demeaning. On the one hand, Fyres delivers a speech which does indeed enliven the chapter and should have been much more effective with its audience than it was. Much of his speech echoes Shaw's comments on unearned sources of some socialists' incomes, reported in *The Practical Socialist*, January 1887.[10] However, Fyres is the unwitting dupe of the villain of the piece, does not care who his "real master and owner" might be so long as he receives "financial consideration," and is unaware that he is being manipulated for purposes that run counter to his own beliefs. In general, socialists in this novel tend to be naïve, venal, or simply stupid rabblerousers, a distortion that Shaw would naturally repudiate. How much Fyres's character owes to Shaw and how much to Griffiths's editorial liberties and scheme for the novel's development is difficult to determine, however.

According to Laurence, whose *Shaw Bibliography* includes *The Salt of the Earth* as item C762, "Chapter XVII (pp. 36–39, 41) was unquestionably his work. He may also have written Chapter XXI and a portion at least of

XXII."[11] Identifying exactly what Shaw wrote remains a problem, however. The nature of his participation required him to conform stylistically to the rest of the novel, and certainly Shaw's contributions suffered from editorial emendations. When Shaw wrote to Burns that he "did actually write about three pages" of the novel, he may have meant that only these pages escaped mutilation by the editor's blue pencil. If his estimate of three pages of the published version is accurate, he can have written only portions of the three chapters ascribed to him.

Despite the stylistic constraints imposed by Griffiths's plot, collaborators' compromises, and editorial discords, several Shavian elements of Chapters XVII, XXI, and XXII suggest his hand. First, there is a pervasive irony, even about the utopian claims of socialism, as well as hostility toward revolutionary radicalism, which accords with Shaw's professed Fabian commitment to gradual constitutional change. Second, there are elements of the Shaw known to readers of the *World,* where Shaw was music critic G.B.S. and had also written art criticism from 1886 to 1890. These include a reference to Colnaghi's print shop, a gallery often mentioned in Shaw's reviews. Third, despite the need to remain stylistically consistent with foregoing chapters, Chapter XVII differs markedly in the nature of topical, literary, and contemporary allusions and references, suddenly introducing more in that chapter than had appeared in the previous sixteen chapters combined. Fourth, Chapters XVII, XXI, and XXII draw directly from Shaw's socialist experiences, including "Bloody Sunday" in 1887 (which, like the demonstration in the novel, resulted in one death).

At the same time, these three chapters include material decidedly not Shavian. One striking example is the flashback passage in Chapter XVII, in which Rupert Wannless remembers his earlier relationship with Agneta Selby. This passage seems to be hastily added as an afterthought and demonstrates the worst of shoddy fictional conventions. Unintentionally, it anticipates Shaw's 1916 parody of Arnold Bennett's novelistic techniques in "Mr. Arnold Bennett Thinks Play-Writing Easier than Novel Writing,"[12] in which Shaw rewrote the ending of *Macbeth* in Bennett's style. Another is the editorial confusion between "Rupert" and "Reuben" Wannless in Chapter XXI, "James" and "Tom" Fyres in Chapter XVII, and the nature of Agneta's prior relationship with Wannless (in Chapter I, "her personal knowledge of Rupert Wannless had been slight," but in Chapter XVII she was a youthful and innocent Lady Chatterley to Wannless's inept Mellors).

One can ascribe most of Chapter XVII to Shaw, excepting the Wannless-Agneta flashback, which is markedly different in style from the rest of the chapter. Chapter XXI seems more like Shaw in its later sections, after the typographical separation two-thirds of the way through—the chapter begins with a distinctly antisocialist commentary that Shaw would not have written. Chapter XXII's description of the demonstration seems to draw extensively from Shaw's observations and experiences on "Bloody Sunday."

At some points Shaw rises above his collaborators, and one can only hope that the lifeless and stylized dialogue owes little or nothing to Shaw's pen. Shaw was hardly responsible for the sentimentality or the superficiality of the plot, or the weaknesses of the prose style as a whole. He apparently involved himself because he fancied himself an expert on socialism, warmed to the collaborative challenge, was willing to assist his *World* employers, and could use the extra money, which he ultimately rejected in disgust at the novel's treatment of socialism and at the way that Griffiths had "landed" him.

Notes

1. *Bernard Shaw: The Diaries, 1885–1897,* ed. Stanley Weintraub (University Park: Penn State University Press, 1986), p. 633.

2. Ibid., p. 569.

3. Ibid., p. 633.

4. Bernard Shaw, *Collected Letters: 1874–1897,* ed. Dan H. Laurence (New York: Dodd, Mead, 1965), p. 271.

5. Ibid., p. 438.

6. Ibid., p. 436.

7. Ibid., p. 439.

8. *Shaw Diaries,* p. 682.

9. *Collected Letters,* p. 271.

10. *Shaw Diaries,* p. 221.

11. Dan H. Laurence, *Bernard Shaw: A Bibliography* (New York: Oxford University Press, 1983), p. 571.

12. *Bernard Shaw's Nondramatic Literary Criticism,* ed. Stanley Weintraub (Lincoln: University of Nebraska Press, 1972), pp. 85–93.

Bernard Shaw

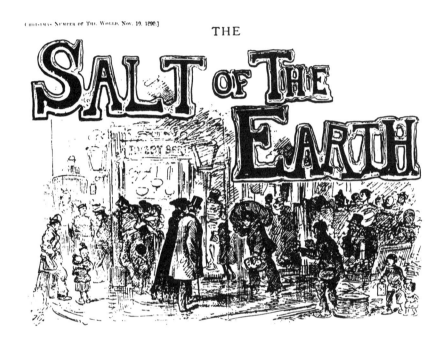

Fig. 2. Christmas Number of *The World*, 19 November 1890.

The ironical title of **The Salt of the Earth** *refers to the poor of London whom radical opportunists exploit. Chapters of the novel include illustrations which are generally caricatures of contemporary figures but which also bear frequently on the content of the novel (for example, the introduction of the noble Lord Ebor appears next to an illustration of the Duke of Clarence, Prince Albert Victor, and a caricature of Auberon Herbert is on the same sheet which describes Lord Ebor as "a strange compound of Auberon Herbert and Charlie Fraser").*

The widowed Lady Cramer lives in a London mansion with her son, Sir Anthony, a dilettante officer in the Scarlet Hussars. Lady Cramer has exploited a rather tenuous blood relationship with the wealthy heiress Agneta Selby and has made Agneta part of her household, ostensibly to avoid the impropriety of allowing the young Agneta to establish independent, and therefore unchaperoned, living arrangements. Lady Cramer hopes that her spendthrift son will marry Agneta, thus gaining control of Agneta's fortune. Neither Agneta nor Sir Anthony finds such a match appealing.

Riding one day in Hyde Park, the idealistic Agneta becomes interested in a demonstration of the poor, led by an impassioned socialist who invites those ignorant of the lives of the needy to visit an East End political meeting. The young socialist turns out to be Rupert Wannless, who knew Agneta in the country and who has since become an eloquent champion of the oppressed. Inspired partly by Rupert's newfound charisma and partly by a sudden social awareness, Agneta resolves to visit the East End. She rejects Sir Anthony's transparently halfhearted offer to escort her and enlists one of her suitors, Lord Ebor, to accompany her.

Ebor, like Sir Anthony, is an officer in the Scarlet Hussars, but he is also "a sentimental philanthropist, a theoretic leveller," and a member of Parliament. At the meeting, Agneta is sufficiently disturbed by one man's recital of woes to offer him money. However, Wannless appears and declares that alms are inappropriate at a political meeting, shaming the man and embarrassing Agneta. This incident attracts the attention of the deputy of a mysterious and wealthy Persian émigré, Mr. Oronzha, who lives stylishly at a Mayfair address in Bruton Street.

As the villain of the piece, Oronzha has an appropriately sinister past. In Persia he had been Iskender Khan, a potentate, who had attained his power by the expedient of murdering his uncle and his uncle's entire line. After a crop failure had reduced the income he derived from bribery and from bullying his Bakhtari subjects, he decamped rather than pay tribal taxes to the Shah. By prudently transferring his wealth beyond the Shah's reach and sending his wife and child to Bombay, he had provided the means for, and limited the hindrances to, his nefarious activities.

In England, Oronzha has become an expatriate gentleman, seeking opportunities to enrich himself. One scheme has been to found a sham socialist movement, the Regenerators, in order to abscond eventually with the funds. Another has been to court the wealthy Agneta, regardless of his wife in Bombay.

Meanwhile, Agneta has become increasingly disturbed by the plight of the poor and half-determined to dedicate her wealth to resolving the problems of the needy. She has turned to Lord Ebor, who pledges to support her. Salt's Chapter XVII, mostly by Shaw, begins here.—F.D.C.

CHAPTER XVII

Oronzha had not ceased since his return to plot against Agneta's property and peace of mind. The measures he took to secure a portion of the former have been already indicated, and will be more fully detailed in a later page. As to the young lady herself, he was more than ever resolved to win her, at all hazards and at all costs. But he felt that he was perpetually met and must eventually be foiled by the girl's undoubted preference for Lord Ebor. There was no misunderstanding or mistaking it; and the wily unscrupulous Persian's hatred of the young peer increased proportionately. He saw more and more clearly that every effort must be made to win Ebor morally, socially, physically if necessary. Anyhow, this detested but more favoured rival must be removed. It was in furtherance of these sinister designs that the Black Prince had contrived the meeting between Agneta and Lord Ebor which has been just described. The result of this meeting had not been altogether what Oronzha wished, in that it enabled the lovers to renew their old relations and to become mutually satisfied as to the real state of their hearts. But there was this much gained, that Lord Ebor was likely to join the ranks of the "Regenerators," and to show himself as a recruit newly enlisted under the banner which Oronzha's myrmidons had raised. To give full effect to this he secretly arranged—through the wire-pullers he directed without avowing himself—that a monster meeting should be held in the most public place and under the most ostentatious auspices. At this the quixotic Wannless was to speak. He had been secured some time previously to the "Regenerators," the great society which Oronzha had called into existence for his own purposes and for his own ends. The programme of this new society had appealed strongly to the fiery young enthusiast, and he had thrown himself into its operations heart and soul. Now, when a great meeting was contemplated, Wannless advised that it should be held in the enemy's camp, in the very heart of the West End. St. James's Hall was accordingly engaged for the occasion, invitations to be issued on a large scale to people of all classes and shades of opinion, but especially to those who, directly or indirectly, were supposed to sympathise with Socialistic tenets.

The Socialism which has its lair in this best of all possible countries of ours is a beast of many and varied stripes, ranging from a delicate paleness to an intense and gleaming luridness. There are the theoretical Socialists, who prefer Government securities to any other form of investment, and who keep their accounts with the Old Lady of Threadneedle

Fig. 3. Illustration in Chapter II's first
paragraph, which describes Lord Ebor's
character and background.

THE DUKE OF CLARENCE.

Street.[1] There are the sham Socialists, whose financial *penchant* is for
ground-rents, and who make the pretence of going into Socialism with a
view to the depreciation of other securities, so that investors may be
attracted by the superior stability of the kind of property of which they
are the holders for a rise. There are the pen-and-ink Socialists, who write
on the subject in the *Nineteenth Century* and the *Contemporary,* promptly
stirring up Mr. Knowles or Mr. Bunting if the "honorarium" is a trifle
slow in arriving, or if its amount is regarded as unsatisfactory.[2] Another
variety of the pen-and-ink species indite eleemosynary papers of portentous dulness and obscurity for the recondite review on which Mr. Samuelson wastes abilities worthy of a better cause.[3] The dilettante Socialists—
numerically a huge body—ramify in quite a bewildering manner. All
sorts of women are in this category, especially those who drive victorias,
and are at once strong-minded and partial to a little dinner at the Bristol

with a good-looking dilettante Socialist of the other sex. Grim maiden occupants of lofty flats, sundry erratic female persons with titles, and the tribe of obtrusive matrons whose husbands are understood to be prospecting for concessions in Athabasca or Namaqualand, are varieties of this type of Socialism. The utilitarian Socialists may be so denominated, not because they are of any service to the Socialistic cause, but inasmuch as they utilise Socialism for their own purposes. Of this phase are the commercially religious people, who would make a success of their affairs but for constitutional wrongheadedness which drives them from the conduct even of *Gutter Gazettes*,[4] and the smart men who lure a Yankee capitalist into the enterprise of buying up British newspapers for the purpose of propagating Socialistic doctrines, with the result that the misguided Yank drops his hard-earned dollars and the journals revert to their old accustomed Laodiceanism. The professional Socialists are for the most part *ci-devant* working men, to whom with a trifling alteration applies Lord Beaconsfield's well-known definition of critics.[5] The engineer who has been driven out of the "shop" for incompetence; the stevedore who has been notoriously clumsy in stowing a hold; the tailor who lost his seat on the "bench" because of loose stitching and gin; the collier who abandoned the pick he mishandled for the secretaryship wherein he embezzles the hard earnings of the fellows who intrust him with the conduct of their fund and their affairs—these, and such as these, are representatives of the pestilential class of professional Socialists. Of this class are the men who organise and trade upon strikes; who deal with strike-funds whose balance-sheets will not balance; who charge for cab-hire which they have not expended, and claim for "relief" which they have not disbursed. They are fluent in the vernacular of the poor devils they hoodwink, spice their oratory with oaths and blasphemy, are at once bullies and cowards, and enjoy the prefix of "Honest" awarded them, tongue in cheek, by their toadies and standers-in. The great mass of manual labourers may be reckoned as Socialists according to their lights, and in so far as they understand the meaning of Socialism, which they construe in an extremely direct and practical sense. Finally, there are the anarchical Socialists, the "dark devils," as the less unscrupulous of the great loosely-jointed confraternity call them, who in a large proportion are foreigners, and who "love darkness rather than light, because their deeds are evil."[6] [Drawing captioned "Mr. Livesey."[7]] They it is who are the fell, dangerous, and bloodthirsty demons of anarchy; who plot for revolution, slaughter, and chaos; who own no God, no nationality, neither ruth nor throb of tender emotion; whose lives are a sordid and loathsome hell, and who are reckless of them, because they believe, and rejoice in the belief, that they die as the beast perisheth.[8]

In spite of the police, carriages had blocked Piccadilly a good hour in advance of that named for the commencement of the proceedings. Long before Wannless took the chair the balconies were parterres of ladies, an occasional black coat interspersed serving simply as a foil for the brightness. On the floor there were many ladies in the front seats; the main area was, however, occupied chiefly by well-dressed persons of the male sex; but the gloomier spaces under the balconies and the rearward seats were closely packed by people whose aspect to the keen observer was not reassuring. Mr. Beerbohm Tree might have copied his make-up for Macari[9] from some of the dangerous-looking, evil-eyed fellows who hugged the shadow thrown down by the balconies, and whispered venomously to each other in every tongue of Continental Europe. Inspector Tomlin, of the C Division, so little liked the look of things, [in] spite of the seeming cheerfulness of the scene, that that experienced officer sent word to mass a body of reserve men in the adjacent police-station.

Conspicuous among the curiously mixed supporters of Wannless on the platform was a group of professional Socialists, among whom were James Fyres, Dick Oman, Jack Diggett, Harry Macmann, Milbay Sprowts, and other anarchists of the labour market. Contrasted with the coarse, vigorous, audacious faces of those men, the abstracted unworldly visage of Wannless, set in the long fair hair that fell on his shoulders, with the earnest blue eyes from which streamed a soft radiance, had something in it almost of divinity. In this man, at least, there was no taint of vulgar self-seeking. If he was not of the texture of which in these latter days practical and vigorous leaders of men are made, he was the kind of man to glory in martyrdom for a cause. The shadow of his fate even now lay across his countenance—a violent death in the passionate effort to avert violence and bloodshed.

Constitutionally nervous, Wannless was subject to every passing impression; and while at one moment full of enthusiasm for the cause to which he had devoted himself, at others he was inclined to despair of success; moreover, to doubt whether the principles he was one of the foremost to disseminate deserved it. He was no dreamer like Lord Ebor. It is not often that those who themselves have participated in *la lutte pour la vie*[10] cherish any lofty ideas as to the morality and disinterestedness of their fellows. That he sympathised with their grievances he had amply proved by his actions; but there were moments when he asked himself whether matters would be improved when the "white slave"—as the British workman, once famed for his independence and freedom of thought, is now termed in sensational "leaders" of Socialistic tendencies—became master of the situation. That the movement in which he was so deeply interested was for the ultimate benefit of mankind he dared not question, having gone too far to retrace his steps; but to give up everything for the sake of an unknown, even problematical, posterity is an unsatisfactory and impersonal sort of self-sacrifice which commends itself to few. Never did Wannless feel so utterly out of tune with his chosen surroundings as at the commencement of one of these huge gatherings, when the room was still half-empty, and no warmth of eloquence had as yet brought the different members of the community into complete sympathy with each other. Without an audience, not all cared to maintain even a semblance of the earnestness which was supposed to animate them; and the reckless jests and foolish laughter that filled an interval of waiting jarred upon one to whom the matter was almost a religion, and held as sacred as anything he had been taught to reverence in youth. At times he hated himself for his clear-sightedness; for reading the motives of his colleagues and crediting so few with sincerity and single-mindedness of aim. Yet how to deceive himself? how to remain blind to what was so apparent? A cynical fit was on him now. It seemed as though he were walking in a Palace of Truth[11] where all pretence was unavailing. One by one the masks slipped from the faces to which his cool dispassionate gaze was directed, and seemed to leave "not even Lancelot brave nor Galahad clean,"[12] until he came to one face, quite distinct from the rest, that forced back the blood to his heart, so that criticism was no longer possible.

It was Agneta, who had entered with one or two other ladies, and now approached the platform. Lord Ebor was close behind, not exactly one of her party, but he, too, took his seat upon the platform, at no great distance from Miss Selby.

To Wannless, Agneta had been a representation of the highest good, an ideal so far above the rest of the world that past and future had no meaning where she was concerned. Once they had been familiar friends.[13] As he looked across the space between them yearningly he became uncomfortably aware that a love he had fought down and conquered to the best of his belief was nevertheless as strong as ever. It could never die so long as Agneta was alive—and free.

The noisy crowd no longer had existence; even Agneta faded away from his blurred vision, and was replaced by another Agneta some years younger, and so simple in her attire that she seemed to have nothing in common with this lovely woman in velvet and soft furs, whose presence here was an episode apart from the luxurious conditions of her real life.

Instead of the large bare hall with its hard benches and flickering lights, he saw a wooded copse and a girl in a tumbled cotton frock, her hat slung across her arm to form a basket for the blackberries she carried. Her pretty mouth was darkened by the luscious fruit, and her eyes, into which the setting sun shone straight, so that the hazel hue looked

Fig. 4. The initial letter of the
text of Chapter I.

golden, were smiling at the idea of having been discovered by anybody in
such a plight. [Drawing captioned "Sir George Harman."[14]]

For months Rupert Wannless, the yeoman's son, had worshipped the
Squire's daughter from afar, and never dared to whisper of his hopeless
adoration; but now the very unconventionality of the position set him at
his ease. Neither the governess, who usually accompanied her, nor her
father, whose elaborate courtesy even more decisively emphasised the
gulf that separated Wannless from themselves, was present; not even a
footman was in attendance. For the time being at least the young people
were on a level, and as absolutely alone as though Agneta were some
farmer's daughter.

Quite frankly she asked him to join her, and unhesitatingly he as-
sented. As children they had gone frequently together on similar expeditions. It was only lately the Squire had awakened to a sense of responsibility where his daughter was concerned, that had resulted in exaggerated
precautions against which she naturally rebelled. It was an act of mutiny
in which Rupert Wannless assisted then; but no thought of that disturbed his delight in the chance which had presented itself. If he once

considered the fact of her being a great heiress, it was as a drawback, not only to the fulfilment of his hopes of winning her, but as contrary to his strong ideas of right and wrong, which even then were arranged on anarchistic principles. Nor did Agneta look down upon him as inferior in rank. At sixteen, social demarcations are not always clearly defined, and she forgot everything but that he was not very much older than herself, and good-looking by comparison with the fogies who were her father's friends and the only visitors at the Hall. A young girl is inclined to regard every young man in the light of a possible lover, and Agneta would have been blind indeed if she had not seen how she was exalted in Wannless's imagination. At church his eyes scarcely ever left her face; when she drove past him in the roads she saw the colour mount to his pale cheeks, and had a shrewd suspicion of the reason why. But this was the first time since her discovery of his secret that they had been alone together, and now it was her turn to grow confused. It was quite natural he should draw comfort from her embarrassed silence, and that his hopes mounted in proportion to her blushes as he ventured to possess himself of her hand and humbly kiss it.

But to all his eager questions she only answered shyly, "She had never dreamed of such a thing; she did not know if she loved him or not; it was so unexpected;" and then, with a delicious assumption of uneasiness, had raised her lowered eyes to ask him if he were quite sure he had made no mistake himself, if he really "loved her as"—with an alarming solemnity of accent—"men only loved once in a lifetime?"

Rupert Wannless always regretted that he had resisted the temptation which assailed him then to clasp her in his arms and give her a convincing proof of his affection. It struck him it would have been much wiser to have succumbed, since it is the boldest knocking at a woman's heart which secures a satisfactory response. And he was her first lover; no other had been before him, he could see by her surprised attention as she listened to his warm impulsive words. But the opportunity had passed, and he had stood there in the shadow of a mighty oak watching the distance widen between them, until the flutter of her blue cotton gown against the green trees and gold horizon could no longer be distinguished.

"I will write," had been his last words, and in pursuance of his promise he had penned a few passionate lines in which he had impressed upon her the unchangeable quality of his love, and implored for some, even an inadequate, return; yet in his heart was very little hope. It had died away as she departed. With her lovely face flushing and paling at his every word, it had been impossible to despair; but the very *naïveté* of her interest in his feelings might have forewarned him—indeed did so in a measure—that her own heart was not really touched. Agneta carried the note about with her for several days, and tucked it under her pillow at nights, that she might be reminded the first thing in the morning that the "common lot" had really come to her as to the rest of womankind. It seemed to assure her more satisfactorily than the length of her gown, or the fact of her hair being gathered into a knot instead of falling in a loose mass upon her shoulders, that she was really "grown up," and the stuff of which heroines are made. With unconscious cruelty she dissected every word that had been set down in uncontrollable emotion, and came to the conclusion that her own love, if actually in existence, fell far short of his in strength and fervour. After many communings with herself, she wrote a long and deeply-pondered letter, in which she told him she was not sure of her own heart, and gravely counselled him to seek for some one more worthy than herself. She would always be interested in his career, but did not think that she should ever marry, which communication drove her lover to distraction. In sheer desperation of spirit he addressed himself to the Squire, not hoping anything from his intervention, but feeling nothing could be worse than this uncertainty. Her father, not taking the matter quite seriously, had scolded his daughter, and in the same breath laughed at her for "a little rogue;" then wrote a note quite pleasant, even paternal, in tone, but in which Wannless was made quite aware that he had been guilty of an act of presumption in raising his eyes so high. What was intended to convince him at once of the hopelessness of his pretensions had, however, a contrary effect. "My daughter," wrote the Squire in a postscript, "is entirely dependent upon me. If she marries without my consent she will be penniless, and I could not, under any circumstances, sanction your addresses."

By this the last of Rupert Wannless's scruples was removed. Agneta, with no fortune, only her sweet self to recommend her, came infinitely closer to his heart than the heiress whose riches would have been a clog on his career.[15] Stimulated by the mere thought of this possible equality, he contrived to see her once more alone, and proposed they should elope together, painting in most glowing colours a future in which they should devote themselves to the service of their fellow-creatures, content with the barest necessaries, while the surplus of their income should help some of the poorer classes to the "comforts of life."

Perhaps Agneta, whose own pin-money exceeded the modest sum he had fixed as sufficient for their needs, was doubtful how this surplus was to be secured; in any case she could not conceal her reluctance to join the ranks of those who "get their coals by stratagem and pray to Heaven for their salad-oil." Moreover, the circumstances of this second meeting were unpropitious. It is possible to be very romantic in a sun-bathed wood, when Nature has put on a gorgeous garb of russet-brown and red and gold; but when the trees are bare and the first cold winds of winter seem to whistle through you, a more practical turn is given to your thoughts. Agneta felt certain now that she was not sufficiently devoted to the young Socialist to welcome an unknown quantity of discomforts for his sake, and managed to make her meaning painfully clear before they parted.

Whether or no[t] she was to blame in the matter, Rupert Wannless, violent in wrath as he had been hot in love, in the bitterness of his disappointment stigmatised her contemptuously as a coquette, and strove to drive out her memory from his mind in a crusade against the class to which she belonged. It had been a blow when he met her again, and on his own ground; but he had tried resolutely to persuade himself that she was no more to him now than any other dweller in Belgravia or Mayfair, and that she had only come among them out of idle curiosity, not from any true desire to do them service.

He felt irritated now by her presence; but something else was stirring in his heart—pity for her defenceless position, and a longing to protect her from dangers he foresaw, even if in so doing he hurt her and appeared ungracious.

If the old Squire had lived, this situation would have been impossible. She would never have been allowed to go alone with Lord Ebor to Shoreditch, nor to come here with no better escort than these advanced females.

Determined to do all he could to discover and circumvent whatever schemes might be in process of formation, Wannless was unwilling to come in personal contact with Agneta. They had parted once, as they thought for ever; and though chance had thrown her in his way again, he did not deceive himself with the notion that this would have any influence on his own future.

"Let sleeping dogs lie" is a good motto, and one he was quick to apply to the present case. Now his passions, if disturbed in their lethargic slumber, were still well under his control; but if he spoke to Agneta, touched the little hand he once had kissed, and gazed into the eyes which had been inclined to look with favour on himself, who could say what would be the consequences, or what harm might then be done? However, the business before him admitted of no delay. He was the chairman, and he was called upon to open the proceedings.[16]

"Let me, in the first instance," he began, when he rose, "put my audience in possession of the principles to which this association is devoted and pledged. This, in plain and direct words, is the programme of the 'Regulators:' Our unflagging efforts are aimed against every despotism, every established hierarchy; we war perpetually against kings, classes,

COLONEL NORTH.

Fig. 5. Illustration at the end
of Chapter XVII, shortly
after the caricature of
Colonel North as Colonel
South.

cash; our mission is to redeem mankind from slavery alike of monarch, aristocrat, or plutocrat; to secure universal freedom; to equalise and harmonise the lot of all."

This was the text on which for nearly two hours Wannless spoke with singular eloquence and earnestness. It was a strange scene. The orator shunned no item of his programme. He uttered sentence on sentence bristling with the sheerest treason. He revelled in sedition. He preached Communism in naked language. He proclaimed his readiness to pluck the flower of Socialism out of the nettle of Anarchy.[17] And withal he neither shocked nor scared nor angered his audience. The man was so unworldly, so unpractical, so amiable and tender, that people could not bring themselves to take him seriously. He was too mild a mannered man to be regarded as capable of scuttling a cockboat, far less a ship; and as for cutting a throat, the sight of naked steel would shatter his nervous system. In point of fact, poor Mr. Wannless was politely laughed at in undertones by the occupants of the balconies. He was almost jeered when he propounded the fine fundamental axiom, "No one has any right to superfluities when any one is in want of necessaries." In vain did he glow, and quiver, and entreat in advocacy of this theme. His peroration pleaded thus: "O ladies and gentlemen, be just to yourselves and just also to your fellow-creatures! I pray you from my heart to abjure the vile Philistine example of the spurious Socialist when starving Communists appealed to him: 'Monsieur, vous avez trop de luxe; donnez-nous qui sont en la misère de ces superfluités auxquelles vous n'avez aucun titre' ! "

Grim old Lord——muttered audibly, "See you d—d first!" and the only auditor who seemed really moved was Colonel South, who in his shy manner observed, "I suppose a collection will be taken up, and that last Latin quotation was so rattling good that I'm dashed if I don't put a tenner in the plate!"[18]

Well out of sight, Oronzha had been surveying the scene from above, where he sat unnoticed, cleverly disguised as a Lascar, side by side with his faithful lieutenant, Sheere Ali Beg. He was extremely dissatisfied with the situation. Nobody was compromised by the speech of Wannless—not even Wannless himself, apparently. His strong language had scared nobody away. There was Lord Ebor in his place beside Miss Selby, the more amused his order was abused, while Mrs. Lynx was trying to discover Wannless's address, in order that she might recruit him for her menagerie. The reporters, after the first ten minutes of Wannless's harangue, had given over taking him in shorthand, and were lazily dotting down an occasional sentence. The *Times* gentleman was actually asleep.

All this would never do. Oronzha was a man of resource. He pencilled a few lines on a page of his pocket-book, and sent a messenger on to the platform with instructions to hand the scrap quietly to Tom Fyres. This man was one of Oronzha's most useful underlings, although Fyres did not know who was his real master and owner. Nor indeed did that north-country philosopher care much, so long as the commissions intrusted to him—which, to do him justice, he executed with great thoroughness and success—were accompanied by the financial consideration which Mr. Fyres regarded as legitimate "perks." He read the scrap, tore it into small fragments, and with knitted brows sat watching for his chance.

The ripple of languid applause which followed the conclusion of Wannless's speech had not subsided when Fyres sprang to his feet, tossed back his shaggy forelock, and threw up his lean right arm above his head. Then at the pitch of his powerful voice he began to speak, the shrill strident accents, with their harsh Scotch intonation,[19] vibrating to the furthest corners of the great hall.

"Socialists! You Socialists!" with a sweep of his arm round the balcony. "Fine, whole-souled Socialists, truly! You are rank heathens; it is only the true Socialist who is the true Christian. It is he who obeys the injunction to sell all and give to the poor, and that other, to 'Forsake all and follow Me.' But you make-believe Socialists and sham sympathisers with Socialism, the clatter of your plated harness and the stamping of your high-bred carriage-horses are sounding in our ears! There you sit, you women, ladies of society, not of Socialism, dazzling the very sunshine with your costly raiment. 'I laff, I du,' like the Yankee in *Mugby Junction*,[20] when I think of you as honest, earnest Socialists. You, madam"— and the long forefinger shot out—"you, madam, are a Socialist, I suppose, in the sense that your husband was a Communist and a Republican before he ate the dirt of place and stipend, and kissed hands of the Sovereign he had insulted when the pariah became a Minister, and when he exchanged the blouse and Phrygian cap[21] for the cocked hat and Windsor uniform. And you, madam, in your college-cap and gown, emblems of a costly education; you, madam—for I assume that you are a married woman, although you think proper to ignore the name of the husband who led you to the altar, or mayhap the registry-office—you dare, forsooth, to pass for a Socialist while you inhabit that beautiful house whose rental value is some 800*l.* a year! But it is a waste of time to vituperate women-folk; and 'brutal' too, you call it, do you, my Lord Clerkenwell? So you are by way of being a Socialist, are you? Don't you think, my lord, that you might spend an afternoon better than in imitating good Wannless here, in visiting some of those loathsome rookeries up St. John's Road and Clerkenwell way, the pillage of which goes toward the maintenance in luxury of your fine old crusted family, including your high-toned and super-fine self? Ah, I know that melodious laugh and that soft mellifluous voice! Yes, my stout friend in the broadcloth there—once it was a red jacket, you may remember—you have risen from the ranks to Parliament; and you, too, would fain be reckoned a Socialist! You, who have forgotten now to denounce the use of the lash, and who raise your voice against the eight hours day for the labouring man! And you, worthy Mr. Scowl there, sitting next to our burly friend, whom you hate as much as he despises you, you are truly a noble specimen of an ardent Socialist! And, forsooth, you claim to be a labour representative too—you whom no honest working man would trust so far as he could throw a bull by the tail; you whose hands are soft and smooth as is your tongue, although I am bound to say that your fingers are nimble enough in cooking accounts and signing the minutes of shady companies. Odd mixture, isn't it, friends, that of banker and Socialist? Quite compatible callings in life, I'm sure you will admit. Behold them united in the person of our voluble friend here—Mr. Mahajun Jetty, M.P., no less. Pretty name that middle one of yours, Mr.

Jetty. Was it bestowed on you, may I ask, at the font, or did you pick it up in the Guikwar's[22] country? Anyhow, Jetty, whatever may be your proper middle name, Mahajun, Bunniah, Gomastah, or Shroff,[23] let me tell you that you are too rich a man—I say nothing as to how the riches were acquired—to be a Socialist of the right breed. A better fellow than you by a long chalk is that wild-eyed, scran-necked, bushy-headed ex-Gaucho down there in the area. It's not his fault that the smallest bobby in the force rolled him over and sat on his head in Trafalgar Square. But it is his fault that he continues to hold that old castle and estate up in Scotland; so long as he does he cannot, let me tell him, be a whole cloth Socialist, for which I think Nature intended him. And, truly, I think she did the same in regard to my winsome friend there from the New Forest, only that he had the misfortune to be born the son of a peer. Do you remember, sir, what the Wellsbourne labourer on strike said to you when you and one whom many a poor man mourns were entertaining him and his mates at tea in the great room of the Regent's Hotel in Leamington? 'I hope you're all at your ease, men; we're all friends and equals here.' 'Equals be blowed!' stolidly replied the labourer, slowly getting on his legs; 'how canst thou prate sic rot, when us chaps be wolfin' here at your expense, an' when oor wives an' young uns be clemmin' on nettle-broth an' byacon rind?' You're a good-hearted, free-handed fellow, but you are no more a Socialist than our taciturn friend here, Mr. Rabbitale, who raises Cain about an extra lick of wholesome whitewash and about a lively crop of personal insects, which, as like as not, he bred and nurtured himself. By the Lord, most men would have put up temporarily with half the plagues of Egypt to know that, while they were scratching, their Transvaal stock was advancing by leaps and bounds, and was enriching them beyond the dreams of avarice. But the cutaneous plutocrat is, like the rest of you, but a sham Socialist, for he clings to his superfluities while others lack for necessaries. As I scan these balconies, I see but one man whom I can hail from my heart as a genuine and self-sacrificing Socialist. Ay, my Lord Ebor, there you sit, an Israelite in whom there is no guile![24] You are rich, but your income is spent for the behoof of your poor fellow-men and women. You are no Sybarite, like Philip Waggonette there, or our candid friend of Palace Yard! [Drawing captioned "Colonel North."[25]] And more, her officer though you were, you are content to hear your Sovereign insulted, to endure denunciations of the dynasty and of the Monarchy, to listen to disparagement of the Constitution and objurgation of the Army in which you hold a commission; and all this, my lord and my brother, you do in the cause of Socialism!"

It was a clever device, and it was not badly executed, but it did not come off. The audience persisted in regarding Mr. Fyres simply as a

Fig. 6. From Chapter II, next to a description of Lord Ebor's political sympathies and shortly after Ebor's senior captain has called Ebor "a strange compound of Auberon Herbert and Charlie Fraser."

MR. AUBERON HERBERT.

phase of the entertainment. The people at whom he struck were only tickled by the rod with which he thwacked around, and grinned to see each other trounced. The reporters had left before Wannless had got off his peroration, and the sequel was only alluded to in casual paragraphs in the society papers. Oronzha's genial little *coup* had miscarried, and Lord Ebor for the time remained uncompromised.

Following Chapter XVII, the narrative shifts to Oronzha's growing influence over Agneta's affections through his suavity and his pretended interest in social regeneration. Part of Oronzha's plan is to use Agneta's involvement with the Regenerators to compromise her, thus forcing her to turn to him. The lawyer who had handled Agneta's father's estate visits Lord Ebor to warn him of Oronzha's growing influence over Agneta, and Ebor determines to join the Regenerators. He intends to penetrate the organization so that he can protect Agneta from her growing involvement with the movement.

Blindfolded, Ebor is taken to the society's headquarters. There he is interrogated by Wannless, who knows nothing of Oronzha's machinations and is pitifully trusting in his unqualified commitment to the Regenerators. Asked to swear unconditional allegiance to the Regenerators, Ebor hesitates, and when he is left in Wannless's custody pending the society's discussion of Ebor's situation, Ebor grills Wannless and concludes that Wannless is an idealistic dupe.

Ebor remains reluctant to commit himself too thoroughly, so the society, in its desire to gain Ebor's allegiance, alters the rules: Ebor can postpone the formality by agreeing to support the society in the meantime. Ebor, leaving with Wannless, confides that his primary object is to protect someone dear to him, and Wannless promises to warn Ebor should the need arise.

The final two chapters, in which Shaw seems to have had a hand despite his protestations to the contrary, follow.

CHAPTER XXI

The West End of London will not easily forget the last invasion by the East: those dark days when the dangerous and subversive elements which really preponderate in this great overgrown city effervesced to boiling point, and chaos seemed close at hand; at any moment the raging lava-like torrent might have burst through its barriers and spread ruin and desolation around. Now once again the same terrible disturbance threatened. If there was calm upon the surface it was the calm that precedes the storm, the fateful stillness that broods around before some awful cataclysm, some great seismic convulsion. Symptoms of the approaching upheaval were to be seen in the increased bitterness of the reckless agitators who constantly menace the public peace; in the constantly recurring collection of mobs in the parks and public places; in the blatant aggressiveness of demagogues, wherever they could find a platform for their pernicious oratory. The old methods were revived and developed; the outcry of labour wronged to benefit the bloated capitalists was renewed; a bad season, when trade, more than usually depressed, having multiplied the numbers of unemployed, repeated demonstrations were organised to give publicity to the indignant protests of the so-called champions of the working man. The wire-pullers were not satisfied with denouncing the rich, and pointing meaningly at the many outward signs of wealth in this opulent city, contrasting them with the abject poverty that rankled close at hand; but they plainly indicated that the balance could only be redressed by a general uprising of the down-

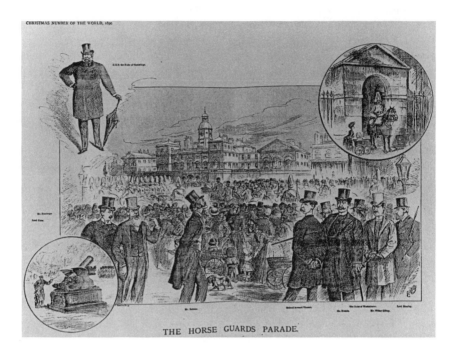

CHRISTMAS NUMBER OF THE WORLD, 1890

THE HORSE GUARDS PARADE.

Fig. 7. The general readership of *Salt* would undoubtedly have preferred the optimism
of this display to the view of the "quidnuncs at the clubs [who] remembered what had
happened at Wimbledon, shook their heads and said the troops were not to be
depended upon" (Chapter XXI).

trodden, suffering, and famished dregs. A current of deep ill-feeling was
daily gaining strength and volume, fed and fostered less by noisy decla-
mation than by the vague but portentous rumors, the more terrifying
that they were indefinite and unspoken, that some great revolutionary
change was imminent.

The coming troubles were intensified by anticipation. People went
about nervously asking each other what was going to be done; whether it
would be possible for the police to cope single-handed with disturbance on
so large a scale. There was a talk of increasing the garrison of London, but
quidnuncs at the clubs remembered what had happened at Wimbledon,[26]
shook their heads and said the troops were not to be depended upon. It
was a crisis in which, as on previous occasions, good citizens must arm for
their own protection. Once more special constables would be required to
support and strengthen the protective forces of the metropolis.

Yet, as usual, the unknown was magnified. Apprehension, although generally rife, was vague; it was impossible to give form and substance to the dangers that seemed imminent. No one seemed to know or realise what really impended, or where or when the blow might fall.

Lord Ebor was no better informed than the rest of the town. He, too, heard the rumours, and as he listened to them wondered whether the source of disquietude could be centered in that dingy club-room near St. Pancras. Still, he had received no message, no summons to reappear, nothing which could enlighten him as to the intention of the Regenerators, whose name was now so freely band[i]ed about as the backbone of the threatened agitation. While he still waited, hearing nothing, not even from Wannless, who had promised to give him the earliest intelligence, Mr. Jeffreys, the private detective, paid him a visit.

"Well, my lord," he began, "of course you know what's up, perhaps better than I do; but I have thought it my duty to come and talk matters over, for fear you might be tempted to go too far."

"It's very good of you," replied the young peer, "but I am more in the dark than you think. What is up, may I ask?"

"I suppose the society don't trust you much. You are too great a swell to know all their secrets. But they seem to trust others who sell them right away."

"But please enlighten me, Mr. Jeffreys. I have not exactly joined the society, although I have made a beginning."

And in a few brief words Lord Ebor told the story of his visit to St. Pancras.

"I see what it is: they'd like to have you with them, but consider you a little shy. All their plans are laid, and when the movement is quite ripe they hope to drag you into it. You will be carried forward with the stream, and may find it impossible to escape. That is why I have come to beg your lordship to be on your guard."

"Well, but tell me a little more about it all. What have you heard?"

"Simply this: that there is to be another monster demonstration in Trafalgar Square[27] at which the usual nonsense will be talked, and while it is in progress a series of smaller meetings, which mean serious mischief, will be held in other places, and followed by a combined movement against the banks and principal shops."

"Regeneration, in fact, means loot, rapine, and disorder. But are you sure this is true? And even if it is, do you think such a truculent and atrocious scheme has the smallest chance of success?"

"Not much, my lord. They are all alive and ready at the Yard; they know every move, and could put their fingers at once upon the ringleaders; but they wish to take them red-handed, to make a clean sweep of them all—all, you understand?"

"Including me, I suppose you mean?"

"Precisely. They know all about you—more, perhaps, than you do yourself."

"And what do you advise me to do now?"

"Take a trip abroad in a yacht, for choice on the high seas, where you cannot be heard of until the row is over."

"I cannot leave London. My presence here is imperatively needed in defence of others."

"It is not safe for you."

"I cannot think of my own safety. All I can promise you is to be on my guard."

"Well, my lord, you know your own business best, but if you are in any serious trouble you can count upon me. I will give you my private address: 'Northallerton Terrace, Shepherd's Bush.' It might be useful to you after office hours."

Mr. Jeffreys had hardly been gone half an hour before Reuben [*sic*] Wannless appeared.

"What's all this?" began Lord Ebor at once. "You promised to keep me fully informed."

"I came as soon as I could—as soon as I knew anything certain," replied Wannless in a low voice, seemingly very much dejected. There was little of the old fiery spirit about him now. "Even now I do not think I ought to tell you what is going to happen. Not only is it dangerous, but I am too much ashamed. To think that I should link myself with such scoundrels! I have been shamefully hoodwinked and deceived. I would throw them over; but if I did, I should be deserting her. We must save her, Lord Ebor, for she too is involved."

"It is the dearest wish of my heart. Miss Selby must be saved against herself; but how is it to be managed? I fear she will not listen to anything I may say. I have no influence, no right to interfere with her—"

Wannless interrupted him with a sad grave smile, as though he knew better than that.

"No one but you can do it; and it must be done. She has promised to appear in person in Trafalgar Square. Think of that, Lord Ebor! It was different at the St. James's Hall, where at least the meeting was under control, if not quite orderly. But among those roughs—the worse, I fear, in London—it is terrible to think of it."

"As you say, it must be prevented," Lord Ebor replied, with a very determined look. "But how? It is useless to reason with her. If she has made up her mind, neither argument nor compulsion will avail—she will certainly attend the meeting." [Drawing captioned "General Sir Lintorn Simmons."[28]]

"So must we, so as to be close at hand, and interpose between her and mischief the moment it threatens. I had not intended to join in the wretched business but for her sake."

"Tell me, Mr. Wannless, when did you know Miss Selby first?" asked Lord Ebor, touched at devotion he had never suspected, and which he saw was unrequited.

"Down at Wannsbeck, in Yorkshire. She will tell you the story some day, and then you can laugh together at the absurd pretensions I once entertained."

"Is it likely, Wannless?" said Lord Ebor gently, taking the other's hand. "What is there absurd in it? That you loved her? Who could help it? And why not you? You are as worthy of her as any man amongst us."

Wannless was more touched by Lord Ebor's kindly appreciative words than he cared to show. He spoke brusquely in reply, but it was to hide the emotion that might have unmanned him.

"Psha! Lord Ebor, that is coming it too strong. I am not going to believe such bosh as that. But I can give way, before *you*. It would be very galling to see her won by that—that—blackamoor."

"Oronzha? Can it be possible you have heard that story too?" cried Lord Ebor.

"It is common talk. I wish it was not. Still more do I pray that she may never fall to that. It would be worse for her, far worse, than death. He— that prince, as they call him—"

"I am persuaded that he is no more prince than you are."

"Prince!—of blackguards, I think. I firmly believe that—"

Wannless looked round rather nervously, then came close to Lord Ebor and whispered:

"That he is an arch-scoundrel playing some deep and desperate game of his own. From something let drop at the conclave—to which I am now admitted—I am confident that he is backing up this bogus society, if he did not originate it."

"But, why—why, in Heaven's name—should he call such an organisa- tion into existence? He is no philanthropist."

"He! Faugh! Anarchist and conspirator rather, with a strong leaven of the knave and imposter. The whole scheme has clearly been invented to delude and probably plunder Miss Selby."

"I see it all. He has curried favour with her by seeming to help in her great schemes, and has turned her childish desire to his own advantage. Of course he has robbed her."

"Of course—nominally for the society, actually for himself. Now he wishes to get her completely into his power. He will compromise her if [he] can at this meeting."

"Hoping thus to lay hands on her entire fortune as well as herself. This must be prevented."

Fig. 8. Illustration at the end of Chapter IV,
after Agneta had unknowingly encountered
Mr. Oronzha's "agent, emissary, factotum, . . .
but in all respects . . . devoted slave,"
disguised as a lascar seaman. Agneta "shrank
away instinctively from the evil Oriental
face." Later Oronzha "cleverly" employed the
lascar disguise to attend Wannless's meeting
in Chapter XVII.

RUSTEM PASHA.

"And we alone can do it. We must keep her away from the meeting or
follow her closely up, so as to be at hand if anything occurs."

The uncomfortable feeling that had long prevailed did not abate
before the day of the great demonstration arrived. It was clear that
serious mischief was brewing; some calamitous catastrophe might surprise London before the day was done. The worse feature of the agitation was the abstention of the noted leaders in what seemed kindred
movements—the well-meaning and generally straightforward men,
apostles of the higher and purer forms of Socialism; proud of their
principles, counting themselves the true aristocrats of society, and their
creed the real cream of politics. These were not heard of in connection
with the coming demonstration.

When the masses gathered independently at their various rendezvous,
it was at once apparent that London had been stirred to its bottomless
depths, and that the very lees and dregs of society had come to the
surface for the day. The dangerous classes—roughs, desperadoes, and

evildoers—mainly made up the contingents, and were easily recognisable among the crowd—wicked-looking, foul-mouthed, hungry-eyed, openly rejoicing at the chance they hoped had come at last of measuring their strength with their hated oppressors. When they had conquered the guardians of order, the town would be at their mercy, and they might feast their fill in license, plunder, and riot.

While the anarchical forces which he had secretly set moving were thus being marshalled in his diabolical cause, Oronzha, the arch-plotter, stood aloof, prudently leaving others to be his catspaws. Whether or not they succeeded in their fell designs he cared little; he hardly expected that they would. His experience in this country had been long enough to show him that the iron hand of authority, although generally concealed, is a very real and potent factor in every-day life. He had means of knowing—and, indeed, his own eyes had told him—that the measures taken to cope with the expected disturbance were more than ample to check and control it. As for this, he cared little; the demonstration would serve his purpose: the end he sought would be equally attained, even though it failed, provided only that those for whom the trap was set were caught and compromised beyond all hope of escape. He had secured Miss Selby's promise that she would show herself in an open carriage during the day. He hoped that Lord Ebor, although not actually an enrolled Regenerator, would also attend. Indeed, he had little doubt of this; for Wannless, after his last conversation with the young peer, had returned to the conclave with satisfactory assurances to this effect. To make this promise was the only certain way of being at hand to protect Miss Selby. [Drawing captioned "General Owen Williams."[29]]

It was of the utmost importance that Miss Selby should not fail, and very early in the day Oronzha called in Lowndes Square, and, being free of the house, was at once admitted to her presence.

"O Mr. Oronzha," she began at once, in a faltering voice, "I cannot do it. You must forgive me. I have tried hard to conquer my weakness, but it is impossible for me to take part in the demonstration to-day."

"Surely, lady, you would not go back from your plighted word?" said Oronzha sternly, but without anger. "Think, only think, what your support and encouragement mean. Think how bitter will be the disappointment, not to me only, but to others—to Lord Ebor."

"Will he be there? You are sure of that?" She seemed to waver for a moment. "But no, no; I cannot do it, not even for him."

"But you must," began Oronzha fiercely. "No, no, I did not mean that." He changed quickly, for the indignation already crimsoned her face. "Let me implore you. Stand by us to the last."

"I cannot. I cannot," Agneta repeated again and again, at last with an intonation that so plainly showed that "I cannot" meant "I will not," that Oronzha hurriedly left the room and sought Lady Cramer's aid.

Lady Cramer had long been as wax in the hands of the unscrupulous Persian; she had played his game with Agneta, and had continually instilled into the girl's ears, and with almost nauseous reiterance, the extraordinary merits of the man. He had bought up the right to her assistance. The help he had extended to her son had placed that son entirely in his power. He could ruin Sir Anthony, as he constantly threatened to do, whenever Lady Cramer proved restive. It was the same threat he used now, when, to his surprise, he found that she positively declined to use her influence with Agneta.

"You must and shall persuade her to do as she said," Oronzha insisted.

"No, Oronzha!" she replied defiantly, and for the first time her whole manner was changed. "Besides, it is sheer cruelty. And why? She can be of no use to you; she will only ruin herself."

"And then will all the more thankfully accept my hand," said the Persian, showing his gleaming teeth and the whites of his wicked eyes. "But this is no time to waste words. Will you, or will you not, do as I desire? If not, I will ruin your son utterly."

"My son is far beyond your reach. Set your people in motion, if you like. Before you can injure him perhaps you yourself will be in need of help."

"What do you mean? Explain yourself."

"I will let the police do that, Mr. Oronzha. I have heard, no matter where or from whom, some rather curious stories within the last few days. Possibly it would be well for you to keep out of the way for a time; at least, I should rather you did not call here again at present."

Oronzha, strange to say, made no reply for a time. Then he said gently, but with evil intonation:

"Whoever has been traducing me will have to answer for it, and those who disappoint me must take the consequences." And without another word he left the house.

CHAPTER XXII

A carriage was to have called for Miss Selby about noon—one of those which was to head the chief procession, which, following the Embankment, was to return by the Park, through Pall Mall to Trafalgar Square.

But no carriage came, and Lady Cramer, who, since her rupture with Oronzha, had displayed unusual affection to Agneta, congratulated herself that Lowndes Square was not to be involved in the coming demonstration.

Yet as the procession made its way, noisily and blatantly, with all the pomp of banners displayed, and brass bands making a hideous din, there was one carriage full of ladies at its head—ladies, that is to say, by courtesy, of the kind that do occasionally show themselves at such questionable gatherings. But there was one, closely veiled and fashionably dressed, sitting in the chief place, who might easily have been mistaken for Miss Selby. Her presence was further betokened by a flag which bore the name "Agneta," and which was carried on the box of the carriage.

The procession met with frequent interruptions: it was Saturday afternoon, and the traffic everywhere was great. Every time there was a check the temper of the great and multitudinous tail grew worse and worse. It surged onward, overflowing and threatening to overpower the mounted constables, who still controlled the thoroughfares. But although collisions seemed imminent at several points along the route, the procession moved forward, the carriages always leading, their way made clear for them by mounted assistants. Somewhere between Buckingham Palace and Marlborough House two fresh horsemen, bearing the distinguishing sash of the society, and coming from the direction of Constitution Hill, joined the little band around the leading carriage. These were Lord Ebor and Wannless. They silently took their places in the rear of the carriage, and followed on with the rest.

The plot thickened in Pall Mall.[30] There was a congestion of traffic, and the progress towards the Square was exceedingly slow. The route marked for the carriages was along Pall Mall East to the north side of the Square, and they had made the better part of the journey and were about abreast of Colnaghi's print-shop,[31] when they were brought to a sudden stop. The great multitude came rushing westward—a great mob, many-headed and mad, shouting, shrieking, wildly excited, and panic-stricken. Cries of "The Guards, the Guards!" "Soldiers!" "Tinbellies!" &c., were heard on every side, and just in the rear of the struggling mass, following them up closely, were the troopers—"big men on big horses"— using the flats of their swords, and driving all before them.

According to the accounts which afterwards appeared, there had been a free fight in the Square, drawn on by the impatience of the worse elements in the crowd, who, feeling themselves in strength, could not wait for the concentration of forces from other directions, but sought to try conclusions at once with their natural enemies the police. The blue-coated guardians of order had been momentarily overpowered, and it was necessary to bring up the reserve troops which were close at hand. The Life Guardsmen made short work of the mob, and while they promptly cleared the Square, bodies of fresh police formed in the rear, on whom their discomfited comrades rallied, and the whole moved forward with irresistible force.

The turmoil and the tumult around the carriages were indescribable. The crowd, as it came tearing along, parted in two streams on either side, followed up closely by the Cavalry, and behind came the police in a serried rank, with a broad front, occupying the width of the street. The superintendent in charge summarily ordered the drivers to turn. An angry altercation followed; a number of fugitives who had slipped through the horses of the Life Guards had returned to collect round these carriages; they were reinforced by others who had come round by Suffolk Street, and another serious affray began. The shrieks of the women in the foremost carriage were heard aloud above the din, when two horsemen fought their way gallantly to the side of the carriage, and while one cried "Miss Selby! Miss Selby! I am here to help you," the other lifted what seemed the fainting form of the closely veiled figure in his arm.

"Take her across your saddle, and force your way out," said the latter; "I will cover your retreat;" and then as the second horseman made his way with difficulty up Suffolk Street and into the Haymarket, the first turned to the *mélée* and began expostulating with the police.

"You are exceeding your powers. We claim the right of public meeting. Make way, I am Lord Ebor, a member of Parliament."

There was a hoarse roar of approval from the mob behind, answered by a few short undaunted words from the police.

"Beware, my lord," said the superintendent; "you are committing a breach of the peace. Give way; we are executing our orders."

"I will not give way," replied the other stoutly, as he turned in his saddle and asked the crowd whether they would allow themselves to be downtrodden and dragooned. It was evidently his intention to gain time for the escape of his companion by prolonging his harangue. But the police would brook no delay; their duty was plain and their temper was up. Once more the superintendent ordered the champion of the mob to make way, and, finding himself still resisted, he gave the signal to advance. A sharp scuffle ensued, in which, through some mischance, the horseman was thrown; his horse took fright, lunged out in furious kicks, one of which reached the unfortunate man as he lay prostrate upon the ground, and killed him then and there.

When, an hour or so later, the street being clear and comparative quiet restored, the police came with stretchers to the scene of the recent affray, the superintendent who had been in command recognised the prostrate form. The fair hair was all clotted with blood, the handsome face bruised and battered so as to be almost unrecognisable.

"It is Lord Ebor," said the superintendent in a pitying voice; "he said so himself. What madness led him to take the lead of such ruffians as these?"

It was all in the evening papers, the complete fiasco of the great demonstration, with the names, real or fictitious, of the principal persons engaged in it. A long paragraph was given to Lord Ebor; his biography followed a graphic account of his untimely death. His vagaries were lightly treated, full justice was done to his amiable qualities, and it was held that he had more than paid in his person for his foolishness. Little or no reference was made to Miss Selby—none directly or by name; but one or two specially knowing reporters spoke mysteriously of a young lady who had weakly lent the support of her presence to the meeting, and who had barely escaped with her life.

Agneta did not apply this to herself. She cared nothing for herself; she could think of nothing but the awful catastrophe. Lord Ebor dead! and she was responsible, as she had led him into this disastrous affair. The shock came upon her with a sense of acute physical pain; she was all but heartbroken. Everything seemed at an end for her. She could never forgive herself, never look up or smile again. Regret, remorse, deep, endless, unavailing, must be her portion for ever; and Lady Cramer, since her last interview with Oronzha, would have been glad to have quieted the pangs of conscience by showing kindness, by attempting consolation to the wronged and suffering girl. But Agneta had shut herself up in her own room, refusing to be comforted. She was there in that dumb agony of grief that finds no outlet in tears, when a note was brought up to her marked "Most urgent." She opened it listlessly, mechanically. Only a few words:

"Ebor is unhurt, but in imminent danger. You may save him. Can I see you here? I must not go to you.   O."

Agneta accepted the summons with all the alacrity born of hope. Despair had fled; her lover was alive, and she might save him.

Hastily throwing on a warm wrap, she left Lowndes Square, and, hailing a hansom, was driven to Bruton Street.

Oronzha at once entered the room into which she had been shown.

"Lady," he said, bowing low, "you do me too much honour. I hardly dared to hope that my poor house would be thus graced by your fair presence. May your footsteps be fortunate!"

"Oronzha," said Agneta with quiet dignity, "this is no time for compliment; I came because you sent for me—because of the great good news you convey—if, indeed, it is true? Tell me, I implore you, is Lord Ebor alive, and unhurt?" she added, with heightened colour, in which newly-risen anxiety was mixed with maiden shame at what was really a confession of her love.

"Alive and unhurt, but in peril and great pain. You alone can save him."

"How? Do not waste words; only tell me how."

"The police would be after him—if it were known he was alive they would certainly track him down. He must get abroad, or he will be arrested, arraigned, disgraced. But he cannot leave the country without means."

"Impossible! Surely Lord Ebor can command ample means?"

For the moment Agneta's suspicions were aroused.

"How can he?" answered Oronzha ingenuously. "You forget that he is supposed to be dead. He cannot show himself, still less draw a cheque. Yet to escape he must have a substantial sum. He does not ask it, mind—not at least from you."

"He has asked you, you mean?"

"Alas, yes! and I am unable to assist. I am utterly impoverished, all but ruined. To-day's abortive proceedings, and the preparations for them, have swallowed up all I have. I must begin again as I did before, in the far East, and build up a fresh fortune—no fear for me. But this poor young fellow—what shall I say to him? I thought at least that your generous hand would enable me to supply his needs. He must leave England at once, you understand?"

"Of course he must have all he wants; only—only I do not see how it is to be managed. The banks are closed; I have but little—a few sovereigns and a note or two in my desk at home."

"You have jewels, I presume?" Oronzha asked, in a careless casual way.

"O yes, plenty. But of what use would they be? Ah, I see! Perhaps you could raise money on them."

"I might," said Oronzha doubtfully, but with an inward chuckle of delight, "if I had them at once."

"I will bring them—all I have. Let me go for them—now, this instant," asked Agneta eagerly.

"Yes; go, lady—do not delay. Hasten back here—but at once, within half-an-hour—do you understand?—and all may yet be well."

When Agneta had hurried away, Oronzha, smiling with evil content-ment, returned to his study. He sat down at his writing-table, and, being evidently a methodical man, he took out his pass-book and studied it carefully. He added up the columns of either side of the little book; then he added them up once more. Next he did a little subtraction sum; and

JI. R. II.

Fig. 9. From the opening of Chapter XVIII, perhaps in ironical
juxtaposition to the description of Mr. Poundsted, the lawyer of
Agneta's late father, who has come to warn Lord Ebor of Oronzha's
insidious influence on Agneta: "Respectability, responsibility, a deep
sense of the importance of his functions were marked characteristics, and fully explained while they justified the cautious gravity of
his speech."

then he drew a cheque for the amount of the result to self or bearer. "One has to be very particular with trust-moneys," remarked Oronzha. So much for the Regenerators. Then the Persian went to what looked like a bookcase, but was really a Chubb's safe, and, opening it, he took out a cash-box, which he opened. There was no money in the cash-box, but there was something much more valuable—jewels. There were big strings of pearls, great uncut emeralds, rough rubies, and other stones. Oronzha looked at them affectionately, and toyed with them lazily. After which he began to pack them away in the pockets of a money-belt; when he had completed this operation he buckled on the belt beneath his vest.

"With these and what that idiot girl will bring I shall still be rich. I can turn them into money when and where I please. Ay, but where? Where shall I take refuge? In the East? Yes; I shall be safest in the East. Stamboul first, then Poti or Tiflis. We shall see. To Paris to-night—if she but brings the jewels—may her footsteps be speedy!—and to-morrow to Vienna by the Orient express. Hi!"

He summoned Sheere Ali, his faithful slave.

"The farce is played out. We are no longer safe here. All is known, my friend, or will be in a day or so. Make everything ready. We leave London in half-an-hour—Eastward."

"Thanks be to God!" devoutly answered his attendant. "And the lady? Have you lost her? Does she not go too?"

"That is my affair; your business is, make all ready."

As soon as Miss Selby crossed the threshold in Lowndes Square she was met by Lady Cramer.

"Agneta, where have you been? It is not right that you should leave the house after dark and alone—on such a day as this, too!"

"I was sent for. It was an urgent message affecting the safety of some one— some one—"

"I do not like it, Agneta, I tell you candidly. Now a second messenger has come."

"From—?" She could not trust her aunt with the news about Lord Ebor.

"From the police, I should say. He looks like a constable in plain clothes, and he insists upon seeing you. He must, he says; and he has waited half-an-hour."

Lady Cramer was satisfied in her own mind that Agneta was about to be arrested for high treason at least.

This second caller was Mr. Jeffreys, and he brought a *boná-fide* message from Lord Ebor.

"My lord sent me straight to you, miss, first to make sure you were safe and well. You see, when he found it was not you he rescued from the fight in the Square—"

"In Trafalgar Square? I never went to the Square. Don't you know that?"

"We didn't till the lady who was rescued came to again. Then my lord saw his mistake. It was a case of personation—the woman was made up to look like you, miss, just to drag you into the business, don't you see? to let all the world suppose you had been in the shindy."

"But who would dare do such a thing?" asked Agneta, horrified.

"Only one person. Can't you guess? That blackguard Oronzha."

"Oronzha!"

A light began to break in on Agneta all at once.

"Did he—is he—tell me, where is Lord Ebor now? You need not be afraid—I know he is safe and well."

"Yes; sound and hearty: he was at my house in Shepherd's Bush an hour ago. It was the other, poor Wannless, who was killed. But who told you?"

"Oronzha. He assured me that Lord Ebor wanted help to—to escape, and I have just come back to get the means."

"Which you were to hand over to Oronzha, eh? Money?"

"I had not enough. I was to give him all my jewels, which he was to convert into money."

"For his own use, I see. Miss Selby, you may be sure Lord Ebor never commissioned him to make such an appeal to you."

"But how could Oronzha have known that Lord Ebor was unhurt?" said Agneta, utterly bewildered.

"The woman who personated you must have told him. She ran off directly she could from Lord Ebor, and seemed to know him perfectly. Of course she went straight to Oronzha."

"What treachery, what wicked falsehood!" cried Agneta, almost in tears. "It is too hateful, too despicable! What *shall* I do?"

"Nothing, Miss Selby. Leave that to us—the police, I mean. Unless you would like to see the scoundrels run in, as they will certainly be in less than half-an-hour."

"No, no; I cannot go to that man's house again."

"You see, miss, if you were to hand him the jewels we might seize him with them, and then add a charge of false pretences, theft perhaps. They will take him, I believe, for inciting to tumult, fraud, half-a-dozen things. But the more the better. Will you come?"

"Indeed, it is impossible. I could not bear it. I never wish to set eyes on Oronzha again."

"Wisely determined, my dear," said Lady Cramer, who entered at that moment. "Won't you come into the drawing-room and have some tea? A friend of yours—Lord Ebor—is there."

This sudden change of feeling in her chaperon was not the least of the startling surprises that Agneta experienced on that eventful day. It was explained, as she afterwards discovered, by Lady Cramer's anxiety to shield Agneta, and indirectly herself, from the scandal that might possibly spring up when Oronzha's collapse became known. This could best be prevented by taking shelter under an avowed engagement to Lord Ebor.

The lovers looked at each other wistfully but silently, until Lord Ebor, with one passionate cry of "Agneta!" took her into his arms, and she nestled there joyfully, feeling that at last she was safe.

The police did not arrest Oronzha after all. When, after much difficulty, they effected an entrance into the house in Bruton Street, both the Orientals had disappeared. They were tracked as far as Dover, bound evidently for Paris, but it was no one's business to pursue them, and they both passed away into the vague obscurity of the far East, where we may thankfully leave them.

Lord and Lady Ebor have done with their quixotic efforts to remedy evils that are perennial, and they are now highly esteemed in society as models of common sense.

Notes

1. "The Old Lady of Threadneedle Street," the title of a 1797 cartoon by political caricaturist James Gilray (1757–1815), is the Bank of England.

2. Sir James Knowles (1831–1908) was editor of the *Contemporary Review* from 1870 to 1877 and the founding editor of the *Nineteenth Century*. Sir Percy William Bunting (1836–1911), an acquaintance of Shaw, was editor of the *Contemporary Review* from 1882 to 1911.

3. This probably refers to James Samuelson (1829–91?), who edited *The Journal of Science, and Annals of Astronomy, Biology, Geology, Industrial Arts, Manufactureres, and Technology* from 1864 to 1885. From May 1890 to February 1891 he edited *Subjects of the Day: A Quarterly Review of Current Topics*. Samuelson's prolific bibliography includes several books on the working class, drink, corrupt election practices, slum children, labor disputes, women workers, and other socialist concerns, as well as a book on the honeybee.

4. *Gutter Gazettes* may refer to the *Pall Mall Gazette*, often known to take a sleazy tone.

5. In Chapter 35 of *Lothair* (1870), Benjamin Disraeli, Earl of Beaconsfield, provided his definition of critics: "You know who the critics are? The men who have failed in liiterature and art."

6. John 3:19–"And this is the condemnation, that light is come into the world, and men loved darkness rather than light, because their deeds were evil."

7. Sir George Thomas Livesey (1834–1908) was an early promoter of labor co-partnership. In 1889 he initiated profit-sharing among his workmen, and by 1894 he replaced his profit-sharing scheme with workmen shareholding. Placing his caricature next to a catalogue of the strange bedfellows of socialism is singularly apt.

8. Psalms 49:12, 20—"Nevertheless man *being* in honour abideth not: he is like the beasts *that* perish" and "Man *that* is in honour, and understandeth not, is like the beasts *that* perish."

9. Robert Macaire is the rogue hero of Robert Louis Stevenson and W. E. Henley's *Macaire* (1885). Shaw recorded in his diary that he read *Macaire* on 3 June 1888 prior to seeing actor-manager Sir Henry Irving play Macaire on 4 June. Sir Herbert Beerbohm Tree had originated the role when the play first appeared.

10. The phrase *la lutte pour la vie* may derive from Herbert Spencer's *Principles of Biology* (1864–67): "This survival of the fittest which I have sought to express in mechanical terms, is that which Mr. Darwin has called 'natural selection,' or the preservation of favored races in the struggle for life" (Part III, Chapter 12). Earlier, Darwin called the third chapter of *The Origin of Species* "Struggle for Existence" and cited Spencer's use of the term "the survival of the fittest."

11. W. S. Gilbert wrote *The Palace of Truth* (1870), an adaptation of a novel by Madame de Genlis (1746–1830). Cf. *Pericles:*

> Prithee, speak:
> Falseness cannot come from thee; for thou look'st
> Modest as Justice, and thou seem'st a palace
> For the crown'd Truth to dwell in: I will believe thee.
>   (V, i, 120–23)

12. Cf. Tennyson's *Merlin and Vivien:*

> Defaming and defacing, till she left
> Not even Lancelot brave nor Galahad clean.
>   (ll. 801–2)

13. In Chapter I, "Her personal knowledge of Rupert Wannless had been slight." This cliché-ridden flashback, roughly one-fourth of the chapter, seems less likely to be Shaw's work than the rest of the chapter.

14. Sir George Byng Harman (1830–92) was a Lieutenant-General who had distinguished himself in the Crimea and in the Indian Mutiny.

15. Is it likely that Shaw could have written this sentence without alluding to Cordelia's dowerless state in *King Lear* (I, i)?

16. The opening of the meeting seems to signal Shaw's return to his share of the collaboration.

17. Cf. *Henry IV*, Part One: "Out of this nettle, danger, we pluck this flower, safety" (II, iii, 11).

18. Colonel South is a thinly disguised caricature of millionaire Colonel John T. North, who figures in an illustration later in the chapter. Shaw records in his diary that he went to North's Avery Hall to hear the eminent violinist Edward Reményi on 12 February 1891. Shaw wrote that North "wound up the concert by . . . remarking that this classical music was all very well, but that we wanted something that we knew something about, [and] he

called upon Reményi to give us Home, Sweet Home, which was accordingly done with imperturbable complaisance." Although this occurred after *Salt* appeared, it suggests why North might invite caricature as South, who confuses French with Latin and is moved by what he cannot understand.

19. Earlier in the chapter this was "James" instead of "Tom" Fyres. In a letter to John Burns (24 November 1890), Shaw identified Fyres as a caricature of Burns, one of the socialist heroes of "Bloody Sunday," when Shaw pointed to "the harsh Scotch intonation" of Burns's voice. Burns spent six weeks in jail for his role in the 1887 demonstration, was prominent in the Social Democratic Federation until 1889, and engineered the settlement of the great London Dock Strike in 1889.

20. *Mugby Junction* was in the 1866 Christmas number of *All the Year Round*, edited by Charles Dickens. In "The Best Books for Children," Shaw recalls first reading Dickens's *A Tale of Two Cities* and *Great Expectations* when they were serialized in *All the Year Round*.

21. The Cap of Liberty, or Phrygian Bonnet, was a conical cap placed in Roman times on the head of a slave on his emancipation. It became a symbol of liberation (the *bonnet rouge*) for the French Revolutionary Jacobins in April 1792, when the Swiss survivors of the mutiny at Nancy of 1791 were released from the galleys. The red "Phrygian bonnet" was the headdress of the galley slaves at Marseilles, where these men had been confined.

22. *Guikwar* is a corruption of *Gurkha*, a term often loosely applied to any Nepalese soldier in British service.

23. Shroff: a banker or moneychanger in South Asia; an Anglo-Indian corruption of *saraf* still in current use.

24. John 1:47—"Jesus saw Nathanael coming to him, and saith of him, Behold an Israelite indeed, in whom is no guile!"

25. This is the Colonel North caricatured as Colonel South (see note 18).

26. "The Wimbledon scandal of 1880. The National Rifle Association held its annual rifle-shooting championships on Wimbledon Common from 1860 until 1889. Then the event was moved to Bisley, where it is still held, Bisley becoming for rifle-shooting what Wimbledon remains for tennis. The scoring was conducted by Army non-commissioned officers, at least until 1880, when a ring of NCOs was court-martialled for taking bribes from the gentleman-volunteers who were doing the shooting, to rig their scores. Many of the weekend sharpshooters would have been London clubmen." Captain Alan Hanley-Browne and Eileen Hanley-Browne, Walton-on-Thames, Surrey, very kindly provided this information.

27. The implied earlier monster demonstration in Trafalgar Square was that of "Bloody Sunday," 13 November 1887. In reality, the next mass demonstration in Trafalgar Square would not occur until 13 November 1892. Shaw would be there. The later demonstration did not encounter police suppression.

28. Sir John Lintorn Arabin Simmons (1821–1903) was field marshal and colonel-commandant of the Royal Engineers.

29. Lieutenant-General Owen Douglas Cope Williams (1836–1904) was JP for Anglesey and Buckinghamshire. He was equerry to His Royal Highness, Prince of Wales (later Edward VII), during his 1875–76 Indian tour. A caricature of HRH appears in *Salt's* Chapter XVIII.

30. The plot thickens indeed. Could Shaw have inserted this in confidence that the editor would miss it?

31. In his capacity of art critic for the *World*, Shaw frequently visited Colnaghi's print-shop and gallery.

Stuart E. Baker

SHAVIAN REALISM

Shaw's claim to be a "dramatic realist," made so emphatically in response to the critical reaction provoked by *Arms and the Man,* has been treated gingerly by most critics. Some dismiss it out of hand; others endorse his claim but generally restrict it to the area of character psychology.[1] The implicit assumption is that Shaw was making an important point, but overstated his case in order to make it.

There are many reasons for disregarding Shaw's claim to be a realist playwright. For one thing, the title of "realist playwright" has become a rather dubious distinction; it has not been felt necessary to defend that claim while critical bias has been so overwhelmingly antirealistic. For another, few literary terms prove more slippery and elusive when we attempt to trap them in neat, objective definitions. Most important, at least for a great many readers and spectators, Shaw quite shamelessly sprinkled his plays generously with incidents and actions that defy our commonsense notions of realism. Still, we have learned that it can be dangerous to dismiss what Shaw said about himself and his work, especially when he said it with such particular and careful emphasis.

In fact, if we look beneath the surface and carefully clear away the considerable confusion that surrounds—indeed permeates—the question of dramatic realism, we discover that in this, as in so many other issues, Shaw knew better than his critics, and another of his paradoxes appears as the simple truth. The "truth" beneath this Shavian paradox is that while Shaw's realism is quite different from either "commonsense" realism or the "scientific" naturalism of Zola and his followers, it is also superior to them—it is actually more deserving of the name "realism."

Shaw's version of realism not only lies at the heart of his dramatic method (although it is by no means the whole of it), but was a lifelong way of seeing the world that pervaded his political, economic, religious, and philosophical ideas. "Realism," however it might be embellished with

fantasy, imagination, or merely the unfamiliar, is the very core of everything that can be called Shavian.

For Shaw, as for Zola, realism is not simply a dramatic technique or
theatrical style; it is first of all a way of looking at and understanding the
world. For Shaw, that means that a dramatic realist is first of all the kind
of realist first discussed in *The Quintessence of Ibsenism*. Unfortunately, this
means we must follow—at least for a ways—a very well-worn path. The
trip is necessary, both because the focus hitherto has always been Shaw's
attack on *idealists* rather than on the nature of realism itself and because,
despite the numerous discussions, many misunderstandings remain.
Confusion as to the meanings of "realist" and "idealist" still persists, in
spite of their universally acknowledged centrality to Shaw's work, because Shaw himself was notably evasive in providing definitions. It is as if
he recognized that the prominence he gave the terms demanded fuller
explanation, but he would not or could not clearly define them. His
clearest statement on the nature of idealism is in the notes for the lecture
on Ibsen from which the *Quintessence* was born:

> If a definition of idealism as a sense of obligation to conform to an
> abstract conception of absolute fitness of conduct is of any use to any
> member of the audience, he or she may quote it as the one given by
> myself.

While this is clear enough, it contains a vaguely implied disclaimer that is
made explicit in the ensuing paragraph:

> Having concluded with a definition, I must add that if my critics expect
> me to be bound by it, or feel apprehensive of being bound to it by me,
> they do me a double injustice. As it is impossible to say exactly what one
> means, it follows that it is impossible to mean exactly what one says.[2]

The definition is omitted entirely from the *Quintessence,* although nearly
everything said there (with an important exception) is in harmony with
it. In fact, he explicitly refuses there to "deal in definitions," and his
suggestion that those made uncomfortable by the term realist "associate
it, not with Zola and Maupassant, but with Plato" is less than completely
satisfying.[3] About all it tells us is that a realist is not to be confused with a
pessimist or a cynic.

If Shaw himself retreated so quickly from defining idealism and realism after his hesitant first attempt, critics must proceed here with caution. Carpenter's book on the first ten plays, although devoted entirely to
Shaw's attack on idealism, wisely (if unfortunately for us) abstains from

definitions.[4] Alfred Turco is more hardy, and he provides at least a starting point for our understanding of this difficult concept. He begins by rhetorically asking: "What, according to Shaw, is an ideal? An illusion. A pretense. A lie." But that is only at the simplest level; at heart the Shavian concept of an ideal reflects Shaw's belief in "the primacy of the concrete over the abstract." As Turco explains it,

> If on the simplest level an ideal is a pretense or convention, and on a deeper level an ideal is an absolute or principle, then on the deepest level an ideal becomes any abstraction that attempts to constrict what Shaw sees as life's concrete particularity.[5]

But there is more to it than this, and the additional element is crucial to a complete understanding of Shaw's philosophical stance. The authority is Shaw himself, who was much more explicit as to what idealism is *not* than as to what it is:

> One or two persons with whom I have discussed the matter seem to have supposed that idealism stands and falls with generalization, abstraction, typification, and cognate methods of thought. This of course would be absurd, although no doubt it is in trying to work these methods that people fall into the mistakings which I call idealism. For instance, it would be interesting to obtain a generalization of feminine beauty of the English type by making a composite photograph from all the pretty women in the country. But if you proceeded to denounce as ugly every woman who did not resemble the photograph, and to take exception to her taste in dress on the ground that her bonnet, however becoming to herself, was un-suited to the face in the photograph, that would be idealism; but obviously a denunciation of such idealism would not be denunciation of composite photography.[6]

So it is a mistake simply to equate idealism with abstraction, but it is a confusion to which Shaw himself contributed. The error is the natural result of an attempt to reconcile two disparate notions that Shaw invokes with the name of idealism. Most of the time the context suggests Shaw's retracted definition: an arbitrary standard of behavior, particularly one imposed in opposition to the individual will. But if that is all he meant, it is hard to imagine why he did not simply say so. Shaw was not one to write obscurely merely to appear mysterious. That he had more in mind is clear at the beginning of the chapter on Ideals and Idealists. Ideals are described as "masks" with which Man "in his infancy of helplessness and terror" covers inexorable facts which he could not bear to face in their naked reality. The chief of these "ideals" was established when he fixed the mask of personal immortality on the face of Death. . . . The masks were his ideals, as he called them; and what, he would ask, would life be without ideals? Thus he became an idealist, and remained so until he dared to begin pulling the masks off and looking the spectres in the face—dared, that is, to be more and more a realist.[7]

Obviously, belief in personal immortality does not constitute an arbitrary standard of behavior. Shaw insists on the illusory aspect of ideals, not merely their violation of individual will. The point is important because it is the crucial difference between the realist and the idealist. They both may have the same aspirations, both may be social and moral reformers, and both may be reaching for the same noble goals; but one is willing to look at the facts without illusion and the other is not. Both, in some sense, can be called idealists—a fact which creates some confusion:

If the existing facts, with their masks on, are to be called ideals, and the future possibilities which the masks depict are also to be called ideals—if, again, the man who is defending existing institutions by maintaining their identity with their masks is to be confounded under one name with the man who is striving to realize the future possibilities by tearing the mask and the thing masked asunder, then the position cannot be intelligibly described by moral pen.[8]

Similar as they are, their single difference causes them to behave in vastly different ways. To further complicate the matter, a person can be a realist on one subject and an idealist on another; and the progress toward a kind of realism can take the form of a successive discarding of old ideals and their replacement by new ones. This, according to Shaw, is the Ibsen position; it is also the point at which the Shavian view diverges from Ibsen's. He told the Fabian Society that Ibsen

admits freely that he is an idealist like his fellowmen; and that all he wants to insist on is the need for constantly renewing our ideals, throwing out the stale as we take in the fresh; recognizing that the truth of yesterday is the superstition of today; . . . But I, being more Ibsenite than Ibsen, do not admit that every unfulfilled intention is an aspiration towards an ideal. I do not consider London Bridge the ideal of the Bayswater omnibus; nor do I regard my umbrella as a stepping stone to my ideal of a dry hat.[9]

It is important when looking at the *Quintessence* to remember that Shaw really was writing about Ibsenism, not Shavianism, and to be quite careful in distilling pure Shaw out of Shaw's Ibsen. Shaw agrees with Ibsen that ideals can be useful and even progressive. The *Quintessence* has references to the positive side of ideals. "Ideals," he says, "are sometimes beneficent, and their repudiation sometimes cruel. For ideals are in practice not so much matters of conscience as excuses for doing what we like."[10] The process by which a beneficial, revolutionary ideal becomes a conventional and tyrannous one is described in the original Ibsen lecture:

> Some day a man says "I will not fight a duel." "You are bound to" reply the neighbors. "I dont care: I dont want to; and I wont" says the man; and when the neighbors discover that he is not struck dead for his temerity, nor Society dissolved by it, they follow his example, and presently persuade themselves that they abstain from duelling on principle. Again, there comes a time when the young lady whose mother would rather see her die than working for a living, faces that contingency and applies herself to mathematics with a view to teaching in a High School. And no sooner has she thus driven her will clean through her duty to her parents and to her sex, than she tries to impose the same method of self assertion on all other women as a matter of principle, whether they have any bent towards mathematics or not.[11]

Thus does the tool of the will become its mortal enemy. But while Shaw acknowledges the possible benefits provided by ideals, he insists that they are all illusions and thus capable of impeding progress. He makes this clear in his remarkable essay "The Illusions of Socialism." He starts by describing, out of the many kinds of illusions, two particular types: flattering illusions and necessary ones; but later in the essay it becomes clear that they overlap considerably. In fact, he has chosen those labels because they represent different aspects of Socialist illusions, which are "flattering" insofar as they portray the Socialist as morally superior to his enemies and "necessary" to the extent that they stimulate people's interest in the cause sufficiently to work hard for it. One could as easily (glancing back at idealist illusions) speak of "fearful" and "hopeful" illusions in order to distinguish between those that mask fearsome realities and those that decorate unrealized but beneficial possibilities. But on further examination these appear to overlap as well, for when those under the spell of Socialist illusions are confronted with a piece of Socialism as a "raw reality," they react much as does the Idealist of Marriage when presented with the truth about that Holy Institution. Some merely dismiss the concrete step toward Socialism as fraudulent because it does not resemble their dreams, but others "will violently denounce it, and brand its advocates as frauds, traitors, and so on." Some, no doubt, will simply lose interest when they recognize, like a bride and groom after the honeymoon, that reality is indeed prosaic. So the same illusion can serve some as a stimulus for enthusiasm and others as a shield against what they dare not face. Socialism, "for ninety-nine out of every hundred . . . ardent young Socialists," is idealism, in virtually the exact same sense as that word is used in *The Quintessence of Ibsenism*.[12]

Can we now define idealism (and thus take a long step toward defining Shavian realism)? Having pointed out how others have stumbled who have entered this rocky field, I wish to tread gingerly myself, but I think we can at least make the path a bit smoother. In the closing sentences of his Preface to the *Pleasant Plays*, Shaw suggests that his business is to dramatize the consequences "of our persistent attempts to found our institutions on the ideals suggested to our imaginations by our half-satisfied passions."[13] The essence of idealism would seem to lie in illusions that are either self-imposed or else clung to as if they had been; it is the inclination to act as if our passions—our values and desires—had *objective* as well as *subjective* reality. Shavian realism recognizes the importance—and the reality—of those desires when it stresses the primacy of the individual will, but it refuses to use them in the fabrication of imaginary things (which we call ideals) *outside* ourselves. At heart, the realist's secret is a simple knack for always making the distinction between what is inside and what is outside, while insisting on the importance—and the *reality*—of each.

This talent is simple, but it is also exceedingly rare. Of course, we can all claim to be realists with respect to those ideals we happen not to share. We can, that is, if we forget that the "Philistines," who make up seventy percent of the population, are quite as free from deluding ideals as is the one in a thousand who is called a realist. We should beware of feeling smugly superior to nineteenth-century ideals that have become as antiquated as the laced corsets and buttoned shoes with which we associate them. We should also beware of viewing Shaw's abstract categories with idealist eyes. His "composite photography" should not become an arbitrary standard for judgment. The Philistines, who, let us remember, received their unfortunate label from offended idealists, are guilty only of satisfaction with the present; the idealists Shaw attacked may have been deluded, but they need not have been fools; and although those ideals, like those idealists, are dead, idealism is not. A glance at any week's political news should be enough to satisfy that point. Shaw, on the other hand, was a lifelong realist to a degree that was—and still is—distinctly abnormal.

That raises another important distinction between these illuminating if somewhat arbitrary categories used by Shaw. At one level the distinctions between the groups can be made rather clearly: the idealist differs from the Philistine as well as the realist in not being able to face the facts, and the Philistine differs from both realist and idealist in being genuinely satisfied with things as they are. The realist can accept things as they are despite his aspiration for something greater. On another level, Philistine and idealist are labels that might well be exchanged depending on the issue in question, while realism is a pervasive, if peculiar, way of looking at the world. The Philistine on the subject of marriage (in Shaw's example) might well be an idealist with respect to, say, patriotism, but the realist is apt always to be a realist—although idealism can be so seductive that no one is utterly immune.[14] And realism is the quintessence of Shaw just as, according to Shaw, a constant striving to refine and revise ideals is the quintessence of Ibsen.

The realist point of view is so unusual that it requires further explanation. In the Preface to the *Unpleasant Plays* Shaw relates how a test of his eyesight provided him with a sudden revelation about himself. He was told that he was highly unusual and fortunate in having "normal" vision, vision which confers "the power of seeing things accurately." He immediately concluded that his "mind's eye, like [his] body's, was 'normal': it saw things differently from other people's eyes, and saw them better" (1:12–13). He was a realist, in other words, whose mind's eye was unobscured by illusion. Despite the old saw about the one-eyed man in the land of the blind, Shaw found that his condition could be disabling in many lines of endeavor, yet it superbly qualified him as a humorist: "All I had to do was open my normal eyes, and with my utmost literary skill put the case exactly as it struck me, or describe the thing exactly as I saw it, to be applauded as the most humorously extravagant paradoxer in London" (1:14). But times and ideals change; illusions once so fiercely defended went out of fashion, and persons of ordinary vision who had been idealists (or would have been had they been born earlier) became Philistines—at least with respect to old ideals. Looking back, they saw things as Shaw had seen them earlier, and they proclaimed him a great reformer. They began to take him seriously. Then the Great War began; Shaw looked at it, described it with his realist's eyes, and was promptly denounced as a traitor. Even his defenders felt that he had made a grave error; *Common Sense About the War*, it was pleaded, was a "mistake," but "intelligently read, [it] vibrates with patriotism, and it proudly proclaims the essential rightness of the struggle in which Great Britain is now engaged."[15]

On that issue as well, time has caught up with Bernard Shaw, but there are still many ways in which Shaw's "normal" but rare vision has puzzled critics. To avoid the natural confusion of Philistine vision with realist vision (noted above) that occurs when discussing unfashionable ideals, it is necessary to observe how a realist sees more universally held ideals. One such ideal is Economic Justice, which, although a popular notion, is as much a figment as any other illusion. Of course there are innumerable versions of what Economic Justice means in practice, but they are all based on the illusory notion that it is possible to determine how much a given individual "deserves." The Republican businessman who thinks it outrageous that a loose-living actress can have ten times his own income and the Socialist who seeks to give workers the wage they deserve are both worshipers at the altar of Economic Justice. This is not a matter of true and false Justice; it is only different people wanting wealth to be distributed in different ways and both projecting their desires onto a screen they both call Justice. Shaw was a socialist who passionately wanted to eliminate the degrading and debilitating effects of poverty and the destructive effects of institutionalized economic anarchy; he was also a realist who knew that no one "deserves" anything. He reasoned that the ends he desired demanded central distribution of wealth, and that meant devising a formula to determine the amount of each share. At this point the idealist seeks to divine the nature of Economic Justice because it is unthinkable to him that the "formula" could be anything else. Shaw merely observed that once you have taken the decision away from the caprice of the marketplace, there is no sensible reason why any one individual should have any more than any other, no matter how offensive that might be to those whose sense of worth depends on knowing that their income is greater than those they deem inferior. Thus Shaw declared that Socialism is "a state of society in which the entire income of the country is divided between all the people in exactly equal shares, without regard to their industry, their character, or any other consideration except the consideration that they are living human beings.[16]

There is no such thing as Economic Justice because there is no such thing as Justice—at all. There are only various more or less arbitrary and conventional ways of dealing with conflicts betweeen individuals in a given community. Since there are no independent scales—apart from each person's own preference—for weighing one individual's "worth" or "deserts" against another's, it is sensible to treat them all equally, to grant them moral as well as social and economic equality. This is what Shaw argues in his Preface to *Major Barbara*. Acceptance of moral equality leads him to moral tolerance, and tolerance runs smack into the inescapable existence of what Shaw calls "impracticable people," people whose behavior cannot be tolerated by any sane society. In the society that Shaw envisioned, such people could "without inhumanity be handed over to the law, and made to understand that a State which is too humane to punish will also be too thrifty to waste the life of honest men in watching or restraining them" (3:60). Bluntly stated, prisons would be abolished and criminals simply, but as humanely as possible, be killed. Few people are willing to take this proposition seriously. A common reaction to it is that it would lead to wholesale slaughter like that perpetrated by the Nazis; but this conclusion is quite as hysterical as declaring that to tell the truth about marriage would mean the destruction of the family and universal debauchery. There is no reason why such a system could not incorporate all our present safeguards against unreasonable incursions of the state on individual lives; it would unquestionably have an additional and powerful safeguard: each of us, as members of this society, would have to accept that we were collectively inflicting mortal injury on a fellow citizen and not observing an independent "Justice" being performed upon a "criminal." The illusion of Justice not only flatters us that the injury is something "right" and "good," but relieves us of the responsibility: the demands of harsh Justice, not our benevolent selves, are to blame. It is worth keeping this in mind when comparing Shaw's proposal to the views of those opposed to the death penalty. It is not impossible that those who claim lengthy prison terms to be more humane than death are grasping for the same illusion that impelled Creon to entomb Antigone alive rather than stone her as he had promised—a thin ruse through which weak consciences are shielded by strong imaginations; it is possible that prisons are preferred to death chambers because prisons are virtual oubliettes—they allow us to forget about their human contents and absolve ourselves of responsibility. If we are reminded of the reality, we can soothe our consciences with talk of "prison reform" and "improving rehabilitation." Of course, the squeamish humanitarian who cannot bear the idea of killing anyone may genuinely believe prison to be a benign alternative, and not merely be willing to accept prison because its brutality is easier to ignore; that cannot be determined here. At all events Shaw's proposal has the virtue of facing the fact that an injury is indeed an injury, however necessary it may be deemed. It is the proposal of a realist.

This extended look at Shaw's habit of mind was necessary, although our subject is the nature of Shavian *dramatic* realism, because this temperament is rare enough to warrant illustration and because it is essentially what Shaw meant when he referred to himself as a realist playwright. When he alluded to "the consequences, sometimes terrible, sometimes ludicrous, of our persistent attempts to found our institutions on the ideals suggested to our imaginations by our half-satisfied passions," he opposed it to his own interest in "a genuinely scientific natural history" (1:385). He objected strenuously in a letter to Augustin Hamon against "thesis hunting" in *Candida:*

> My plays are studies in the natural history of mankind: I am simply a
> dramatic Buffon or St Hilaire. When you read Buffon's description of
> the Horse you do not begin to ask whether Buffon regarded the Horse as
> a triumph of speed, or a triumph of traction power, or a triumph of
> fidelity; you understand that he is simply trying to shew you what sort of
> animal a horse is. Well, in Candida I am simply trying to shew you the
> sort of animal the people in Candida are. I take a great interest in animals
> of that sort, just as Buffon did in animals in general; and I write for the
> gratification of people who share my interest."[17]

If people suspect Shaw of being disingenuous or ironical in this and
similar passages, it is because he appears to be placing himself alongside
Zola and Becque, yet his plays are obviously quite different. But Shaw
thought he was *more* a realist than either French writer, and he thought
so precisely because he rejected their rather dismal view of the world.
The surprising truth is that Shaw's realism was inseparable from the
"fact . . . that, with reasonably sound specimens, the more intimately I
know people the better I like them." He summed up his argument in "A
Dramatic Realist to His Critics" by declaring that *Arms and the Man* is "a
play the whole novelty of which lies in the fact that it is void of malice to
my fellow creatures, and laboriously exact as to all essential facts."[18] In
the *Quintessence* he equates "the inevitable return to nature" with the
elimination of heroes and villains, an observation which has become
something of a cliché of modern criticism.[19] But for Shaw it goes deeper
than that. Unfortunately, when most critics reject villains and heroes,
they are really only rejecting those they find *unconvincing;* Shaw did not
believe in the existence of "good" or "bad" people at all. In a letter to
William Archer he declared that in the matter of promoting realism in
opposition to ideals he had gone beyond Ibsen, "who is by old habit a
pessimist. My whole secret is that I have got clean through the old categories of good & evil, and no longer use them even for dramatic effect."[20]

   The difference between a demand that portraits of good and bad
people meet the high standards of perceptive, intelligent, and skeptical
critics, and the utter elimination of "the old categories of good & evil," is
more subtle than one might think. It was essential to Shaw not merely
that we judge people (in life or fiction) evenhandedly but rather that we
dispense with such judgments entirely. Consider this passage from *The
Quintessence:*

> When you have called Mrs. Alving an emancipated woman or an unprin-
> cipled one, Alving a debauchee or a victim of society, Nora a fearless and
> noble-hearted woman or a shocking little liar and an unnatural mother,
> Helmer a selfish hound or a model husband and father, according to

your bias, you have said something which is at once true and false, and in both cases perfectly idle.[21]

It should be clear by now that what Shaw is attacking here is not generalization but the confusion of judgment with observation. To call anyone either a "selfish hound" or "a model husband" is to ascribe to objective reality your own subjective attitudes, to confound what is inside with what is outside. It is to go beyond the description of objective reality and divide it into the illusory categories of good and evil.

That is what Shaw refuses to do. He accepts only a "realist morality," one which never asks "Is he good or bad?" but only "What are the effects of his actions?" He is perfectly aware that the effect of some people's actions is quite appalling. His "optimism" does not consist of having "faith" in the "essential goodness" of mankind, in the sentimental eighteenth-century way; he merely observes that, generally speaking, the better he knows people, the better he likes them. This may sound suspiciously naïve to the average high-brow intellectual, weaned as he is on existential despair, but it is greatly advantageous to a dramatist. It allows him to create characters without judging them. Shaw's method is the same as that of an actor he praised for creating his part "like a true actor, by the simple but very unusual method of playing it from its own point of view."[22] This has become standard in modern acting classes, where the "suspension of judgment" is considered an essential part of basic technique. If critics had a bit more of this same type of training, they might have less difficulty with Shaw's plays, for Shaw's realism, which is the heart of his playwriting technique, is first of all the ability to create characters from their own point of view. It is secondly the ability to look facts in the face without having to mask them with figments woven of wishful thinking. It has nothing to do with creating the illusion of a cinematic record of real events—Candid Camera realism. Thus *Major Barbara,* frankly presented as a social and religious parable, is as good an example of Shavian realism as is, say, *Candida.*

Candida, however, provides an excellent demonstration of the nature of Shaw's idiosyncratic but eminently sensible form of realism. If a poll were to be taken today and knowledgeable critics asked to name Shaw's most "realistic" play, *Candida* would certainly end up near the top of the rating. Louis Crompton, for instance, calls it "a resolutely naturalistic play."[23] By itself, however, this would prove nothing. A poll of critics taken ninety years ago, similar but for the inclusion of other contemporary playwrights, might have suggested that any play by Shaw was about as realistic as *The Mikado,* while the pinnacle of English naturalism was probably *The Second Mrs. Tanqueray,* a play which Shaw, concurring with modern critics, thought false and conventional. No doubt the current critics are right and the older critics wrong; but as Shaw said in a different context, "a very ordinary person may now be of opinion that the earth is round without necessarily being a greater man than Saint Augustine, who believed it to be flat."[24] The best evidence that *Candida* is a genuinely realistic play is actually the extraordinary diversity of opinion recorded by intelligent observers since it first appeared. William Archer, referring in 1899 to Shaw's parable of his abnormally normal vision, wrote of Shaw,

> He looks at life through an exceedingly abnormal temperament, and has convinced himself that it is the one absolutely normal temperament in the world. . . . How far Mr. Shaw is from possessing that objectivity of vision which he claims may be judged from the ease with which any reader of the least critical faculty could reconstruct from these plays *[Pleasant and Unpleasant]* the character and opinions of their author.[25]

Archer proceeds confidently to explain that while the views of Shakespeare and Ibsen are hidden behind the canvas of their works, Shaw has painted a vivid self-portrait in his. We still hear the cliché that all Shaw's characters are really thinly disguised Shaws, despite the ease with which that assertion is shown to be false, but even those who make that claim cannot agree as to who the real Shaw was. This endures in spite of the fact that Shaw, unlike Ibsen and Shakespeare, wrote volumes of expository prose explaining his opinions. At least some of the critics of the 1904 production of *Candida* thought the play merely a pulpit from which Shaw could "expound his cynical philosophy." They stamped it an exercise in "social satire," although one called the satire "aimless," presumably because he could not determine quite what or whom was being hit.[26] More astute observers have seen satire in the piece; Carpenter detects an attack on clergymen, partly, it is true, because Shaw once called Morell the "butt" of the play. Shaw's comment is unfortunately misleading because the play is not an "attack" on Morell, clergymen, or anyone else. While it certainly does, as Carpenter demonstrates, attack idealism, it does a good deal more: it promotes realism; and its positive function is more important than its negative one. It represents an important innovation in the author's realistic technique and the advent of a peculiarly Shavian realism.

As often noted, *Candida* was very closely linked in its author's mind with *A Doll's House,* and it also has a close family resemblance to other plays of Ibsen, notably *The Lady from the Sea* and *Little Eyolf.*[27] The plot of

Shaw's play is actually much closer to that of *The Lady from the Sea* than to *A Doll's House*. Why, then, did Shaw so firmly link it to Ibsen's earlier play? His own answer was that "Morell is really nothing but Helmer getting fair play,"[28] and that "the play is a counterblast to Ibsen's *Doll's House,* showing that in the real typical doll's house it is the man who is the doll."[29] The last remark was made in 1944, long after Nora's cause was thought to have won the day, but that was hardly the case in 1894. Why would Shaw, having written four plays aimed at exposing the lying delusions with which a smugly complacent society shielded itself from unpleasant truths, want now to see that *Helmer* got fair play? Why would the author of "The Womanly Woman" want to provide "a counterblast to Ibsen's *Doll House*"? There is a hint in the closing paragraphs of the original *Quintessence* when Shaw warns his readers not to "think that the cases of Nora and Mrs Elvsted are meant to establish a golden rule for women who wish to be 'emancipated': the said golden rule being simply, Run away from your husband."[30] This, he notes, is a mistake made by both Ibsenites and anti-Ibsenites. It is also one that could lead the anti-Ibsenites to use *A Doll's House* as evidence for their cause: "Imagine what would happen if marriage laws were liberalized," they could say; "All women would become Noras, and the family would be a thing of the past!" As Crompton so clearly points out, *Candida,* like a number of Shaw's other plays, aims to show that freedom does not mean chaos, and if all compulsion attached to marriage were removed, "the great majority would remain together for the same reason they had in the past— because they *want* to."[31]

Candida means more than this as well. It is in a sense the point at which Shavianism firmly separates itself from Ibsenism and strikes out on its own.[32] The difference is both philosophical and technical. The philosophical difference is the difference between realism (Shavianism) and the constant search for better ideals (Ibsenism). The technical difference is suggested in Shaw's remark (made a few months before he began *Candida*) that, unlike Ibsen, he *no longer* used the "categories of good & evil" even "for dramatic effect." How such categories could be used for "effect" is suggested by his assertion that the new school of drama founded by Ibsen

> will trick the spectator into forming a meanly false judgment, and then convict him of it in the next act, often to his grievous mortification. When you despise something you ought to take off your hat to, or admire and imitate something you ought to loathe, you cannot resist the dramatist who knows how to touch these morbid spots in you and make you see that they are morbid.[33]

This, Carpenter shows us, is a technique Shaw himself uses in the *Unpleasant Plays*.[34] He also uses a less extreme version of it in *Arms and the Man:* the judgments that the audience is originally led to form of Sergius, Raina, and Bluntschli are quite different from those with which it leaves the theater. But the technique is, as Shaw discovered, a hazardous one for a "realist" playwright. It was not his intention that the audience should conclude by "loathing" Sergius, or by attacking Raina as a "liar" and a "minx."[35] It is not enough merely to confuse people as to who is admirable and who contemptible; the goal is to teach them to drop such illusory categories and to "respect reality" (1:385). So in *Candida* Shaw dropped the technique altogether, although critics have never stopped trying to force it back on the play.

On the other hand, there are few of Ibsen's plays in which that technique is more in evidence than *A Doll's House*. Krogstad enters as a classic villain but leaves with our sympathy and concern; Helmer seems an ideal father and husband until he is exposed as shallow, insensitive, and trivial; and Nora, who is introduced as empty-headed and frivolous, is ultimately revealed to be intelligent, resourceful, and endowed with the highest ideals of anyone in the play. The three major characters in Shaw's play are introduced as admirable and remain admirable to the very end. Even Morell, the "butt" of the piece, will lose the sympathy of the audience only if wretchedly played. In the same way, all three have distinctly unheroic moments. Both men often look ridiculous, and the extreme variety of critical reaction to the character of Candida speaks for itself. Morell *is* "Helmer getting fair play," and Candida too, in an important sense, is Nora given fair play, for instead of being presented as a silly woman transformed into a heroic one—one illusory ideal substituted for another—she is a strikingly convincing portrait of a real person. The proof of that last assertion—if it is needed—lies in the varied judgments of her from critics and spectators: they have been left free by the playwright to judge her, as they might a real person, according to their own biases. That is, they may apply their idealist standards to "real" characters as they habitually do to real people, but they are wrong to speculate whether their judgment is the same as the playwright's. Shaw's own view was surely that whether you call Candida a philistine or a saint, a "sentimental prostitute" or the epitome of motherhood, "you have said something which is at once true and false, and in both cases perfectly idle."

It is understandable that critics should have spent so much time trying to divine Shaw's attitude toward his characters, to determine which "side" he is on, for the manipulation of audience sympathy is one of the primary techniques by which authors convey their meaning. But in this case the message to the critics—obviously a difficult one to get across—is to "learn to respect reality, which would include the beneficial exercise of respecting themselves" (1:385). It is not for nothing that Shaw puts the moral (to the limited extent that the play can be so neatly summed up) in the mouth of his "butt," Morell, when he tells Burgess to be true to himself: "God made you what I call a scoundrel as He made me what you call a fool. It was not for me to quarrel with His handiwork in the one case more than in the other."[36]

Thus *Candida* is a "realist" drama not merely in technique, but in theme. That is, it is not so much anti-ideal as pro-reality; it affirms rather than attacks. The "astonishing, many-sided objectivity" that Eric Bentley marvels at is precisely its point.[37] It is true that Morell and Marchbanks are stripped of their illusions, but these are not masks to hide the brutal facts of a diseased social system, as in the *Unpleasant Plays,* or the self-denying enemies of the will with which Sergius torments himself; they are rather those "beneficent" ideals that are mostly "excuses for doing what we like." If Morell's ideal marriage is shattered, it is that he may learn to value the real one.

In Ibsen's play the reality exposed is petty and insubstantial, but the symbol of Nora's shattered idealism, the "miracle" she dreaded and hoped for, is resurrected at the end of the play as the "greatest miracle of all," the half-despairing hope for a "true marriage."[38] It is a case of "The ideal is dead, long live the ideal." She had mistaken a tawdry reality for a glorious ideal; now she courageously abandons both in order to seek the genuine ideal. *Candida* is a "counterblast" to *A Doll's House* in that it shows that reality itself can sometimes be accepted without cynicism, that it may be worthy of "respect" even if it fails to meet some ideal of what it should be.

But what, then, of Marchbanks? His exit at the end of the play, like that of Nora, can be seen as a repudiation of the domestic reality accepted (albeit on a new and more honest basis) by Candida and her husband. Like Nora, he rejects that reality once his illusions are stripped away, but only after it is made clear that he is doing not what is *absolutely* right, but what is right for *him.* The assertion of the poet's vision does not require the denigration of the parson's. That does not mean that they are precisely equal. Whatever else Shaw may have meant by suggesting that *Candida* was an attempt to "distil the quintessential drama from pre-Raphaelitism," it would seem from the context that he found himself as a playwright who had rejected the easiest source of dramatic conflict—the opposition of good and ill—and was seeking a conflict for dramatization that *does not falsify what he took to be an underlying and fundamental unity.* He sought conflict without heroes and villains—even those who surprise the audience by exchanging roles. Marchbanks represents one aspect of that

conflicted unity: "the first broken, nervous, stumbling attempts to formu-
late its own revolt against itself as it develops into something higher"
(1:373). Note that Shaw says "develops into something higher." He is
hesitant to assert the supremacy of Marchbanks's vision, but merely suggests that it possibly points to a higher way. It is irrelevant that Shaw
undoubtedly shared at least something of the young poet's vision. He
had found a dramatic conflict corresponding to the genuine conflict of
our existence, the unending struggle of life to become something better
than itself. In *Candida* Shaw first achieved a dramatic technique fully in
harmony with his philosophy, first found a form of dramatic conflict that
avoids the Manachean fallacy of seeing the world as a struggle between
perfect good and perfect evil without falling into the Optimistic fallacy
that all is for the best in the best of all possible worlds.

The assumption that we can promote the "better" merely by identifying and destroying the "worse" will only hinder our progress. In a Fabian
lecture of 1910 the teetotaling Shaw rejected the appropriateness of
trying to breed out even "tuberculosis, epilepsy, dipsomania, and lunacy"
in the quest for the Superman, who

> may be tuberculous from top to toe; he is quite likely to be a controlled
> epileptic; his sole diet may be overproof spirit; and he will certainly be as
> mad as a hatter from our point of view. We really know nothing about
> him. Our worse failures today may be simply first attempts at him, and
> our greatest successes the final perfection of the type that is passing
> away.[39]

Evenhanded objectivity is not an aesthetic principle with Shaw, but a
philosophic one. For once you have asserted the primacy of the will, on
the grounds amply developed in the *Quintessence,* and adopted the rigor-
ous principles of realism, you are led inevitably to moral equality, since
there is no logical way to give any individual will preference over another. This doctrine may be "optimistic," because it puts its faith in
human will, but it is not simple pollyannaism, for it raises extremely
difficult philosophical and ethical questions, questions that are examined
in depth in plays like *John Bull's Other Island* and *Major Barbara.*

Shaw's own form of dramatic realism, although most people will never
feel quite comfortable with calling it that, is really more deserving of the
name than either the everyday use of the term—"impressionistic"
realism—or the "scientific" realism of Zola. When we use the term casu-
ally and impressionistically, we do nothing but compare what we see to
the template of our biases. Works that are scorned as conventional and
artificial today were acclaimed as masterworks of realism yesterday.

Zola's naturalism tried to avoid precisely that problem by striving to be scientific, but Zola did not naïvely think, despite his use of some unfortunate expressions, that art could ever really duplicate the scientific laboratory; he knew that "a work will never be more than a corner of nature seen through a temperament." The reliability of that temperament, then, becomes all important: for the work to have the necessary "moral impersonality" the naturalist must be "only a stenographer who forbids himself to judge or to draw conclusions. He confines himself to the strict role of a scientist who exposes facts."[40] Yet Zola's "facts" were constantly colored by his assumptions about the "scientific" nature of reality—the assumptions of pessimistic deterministic materialism. Shaw's own "abnormal temperament," as well as his sharply contrasting worldview, was arguably more "realistic"—less clouded by unwarranted assumptions—because it simply asks to observe the actions taken by individual wills, making no assumptions about the factors that cause the will to be manifest. The theory of the Life Force is no more (and no less) provable than that of scientism, but the dramatist who holds it is compelled to allow the will to speak for itself.

Of course, to people who are convinced that any form of optimism is unrealistic, and that an honest view invariably shows the world to be corrupt, human nature degraded, and the human condition absurd, there is no answer except to invite them to try being as objective as Shaw and see what they really find. They will not accept the challenge because they will be convinced that they already see the world more clearly than anyone. It cannot be determined logically whether they are right or are desperately clinging, like Molière's Alceste, to their right to rail at mankind. At all events, vigilantly critical optimism and hopeless despair are both something in the nature of self-fulfilling prophecies. If art is to resume its traditional role of responsibility to the world, and not to become increasingly self-absorbed, self-consuming, and self-destructive, Shaw's hopeful, critical, and ever-demanding realism may well be worth another look.

Notes

1. E.g., Bernard F. Dukore, *Bernard Shaw, Playwright: Aspects of Shavian Drama* (Columbia: University of Missouri Press, 1973), p. 10, and John Gassner, "Bernard Shaw and the Making of the Modern Mind," *Bernard Shaw's Plays: Major Barbara; Heartbreak House; Saint*

Joan; Too True to Be Good, ed. Warren Sylvester Smith (New York: W. W. Norton, 1970), p. 295. Louis Crompton is less hesitant in calling Shaw's method naturalistic, but confines his remarks primarily to character drawing in *Shaw the Dramatist* (Lincoln: University of Nebraska Press, 1969), p. vi.

2. "Fragments of a Fabian Lecture 1890," *Shaw and Ibsen: Bernard Shaw's* Quintessence of Ibsenism *and Related Writings,* ed. J. L. Wisenthal (Toronto: University of Toronto Press, 1979), pp. 95–96.

3. Ibid., p. 122.

4. Charles A. Carpenter, *Bernard Shaw and the Art of Destroying Ideals* (Madison: University of Wisconsin Press, 1969).

5. Alfred Turco, Jr., *Shaw's Moral Vision: The Self and Salvation* (Ithaca: Cornell University Press, 1976), pp. 24, 30, 34. Others have come to similar conclusions. See Wisenthal, *Shaw and Ibsen,* p. 30.

6. "Fragments," p. 95.

7. *The Quintessence of Ibsenism: Shaw and Ibsen,* p. 118.

8. Ibid., p. 121.

9. "Fragments," pp. 94–95.

10. *Quintessence,* p. 177.

11. "Fragments," p. 83.

12. "The Illusions of Socialism," *Selected Non-Dramatic Writings,* ed. Dan H. Laurence (Boston: Houghton Mifflin, 1965), pp. 406–7.

13. Preface to *Plays Pleasant,* in *The Bodley Head Bernard Shaw: Collected Plays with Their Prefaces* (London: Max Reinhardt, 1970–74), 1:385. All subsequent references to the plays and their prefaces are to this edition.

14. Shaw himself was not entirely immune. It is hard to avoid the conclusion that his view of the dictators who loomed so large in the 1930s was influenced by his own vision of what they "ought" to be.

15. John Palmer, "George Bernard Shaw: Harlequin or Patriot?" *George Bernard Shaw: A Critical Survey,* ed. Louis Kronenberger (Cleveland: World, 1953), p. 57.

16. "The Simple Truth about Socialism," *The Road to Equality: Ten Unpublished Lectures and Essays, 1884–1918,* ed. Louis Crompton (Boston: Beacon, 1971), p. 155.

17. *Collected Letters: 1898–1910,* ed. Dan H. Laurence (London: Max Reinhardt, 1972), p. 668.

18. "A Dramatic Realist to His Critics," *Selected Non-Dramatic Writings,* p. 326.

19. *Quintessence,* p. 214.

20. *Collected Letters: 1874–1897,* ed. Dan H. Laurence (New York: Dodd, Mead, 1965), p. 427.

21. *Quintessence,* pp. 197–98.

22. *Our Theatres in the Nineties* (London: Constable, 1954), 2:3.

23. Crompton, p. 29.

24. "Illusions," p. 422.

25. William Archer, *Study & Stage: A Year-Book of Criticism* (London: Grant Richards, 1899), p. 3.

26. Quoted in Irving McKee, "Bernard Shaw's Beginnings on the London Stage," *PMLA* 72 (1959), 478.

27. The similarities have been discussed by several commentators, especially Dukore (pp. 54–60) and Wisenthal (pp. 60–64).

28. *Collected Letters: 1874–1897,* p. 612.

29. "Shaw Reveals Who Was Candida," *Bodley Head Bernard Shaw,* 1:603.

30. *Quintessence,* p. 201.

31. Crompton, p. 44

32. There are of course many differences between the plays of Ibsen and the first four plays of Shaw. I am referring here only to Ibsenism as defined by Shaw.

33. *Quintessence,* p. 183.

34. Carpenter, p. 16.

35. "Dramatic Realist," p. 325.

36. *Candida,* 1:530. This is not the only time Shaw placed an appropriate version of a fundamental Shavian idea into the mouth of a "butt." Sergius declares, "Oh, give me the man who will defy to the death any power on earth or in heaven that sets itself up against his own will and conscience; he alone is the brave man" (1:454); and it is Lomax who brightly asserts that "there is a certain amount of tosh about this notion of wickedness. It doesnt work" (3:175).

37. Eric Bentley, *The Playwright as Thinker: A Study of Drama in Modern Times* (New York: Harcourt, Brace & World, 1967), p. 135.

38. Henrik Ibsen, *A Doll's House. Four Major Plays,* trans. Rolf Fjelde (New York: Signet-NAL, 1965), p. 114.

39. "Simple Truth," p. 186.

40. Emile Zola, "Naturalism in the Theatre," *Documents of Modern Literary Realism,* ed. George J. Becker (Princeton: Princeton University Press, 1963), pp. 198, 209.

Bernard Shaw

CIVILIZATION AND THE SOLDIER

Listed as item C1354 in the Laurence Bibliography, this essay appeared in The Humane Review, *1 (January 1901), 298–315, but has had no U.S. publication. Shaw examines English attitudes toward the British Empire and then discusses devastating actions by the English military during the Boer War. Some of his comments anticipate* Back to Methuselah *by two decades. At one point he contends that English civilization requires "the substitution for these artless grown-up children of a quite different sort of Englishman," and later he implies an early view of Creative Evolution that would help to inform his "metabiological pentateuch": "I am a great believer in life: my ancestors developed thumbs sooner than perish for want of them; and my contemporaries have developed County Councils sooner than go back to the woods. . . . Let the nations that grovel before institutions, the worshipping nations, the loyal nations, the pious nations, the respectable nations perish: the race is imperishable."*

In the last days before the war, I fell a-musing one afternoon, rocked into reverie in my deck chair on the bosom, gently heaving, of the Ionian Sea. Let me to back to that moment and recall my holiday thoughts. I am surrounded by respectable English people. It is a fine morning; and for the moment the bosom, gently heaving, soothes them into a peaceful contentment with their guide books. They were in Syracuse yesterday, and to-morrow they will be in Athens; so for once they read Art and History, until the bosom, gently heaving, steals their senses and closes their eyes. They are not bad people, these, as people go. I, the solitary Humanitarian, regard them as a sort of friendly savages, and watch them eating slaughtered animals, drinking spirits, gambling in sweepstakes on the distance run by the ship since noon yesterday and always reserving a tiny little third prize for their gods (ten shillings to the Marine Charities) to buy indulgence for the sin of betting, reading children's stories which they recommend to you as awfully clever novels, coming to dinner in shirts daubed white with starch to symbolize cleanliness as an Indian's face is daubed with vermilion to symbolize bravery, and finishing the evening in the smoking room. I really like them because they never kill anything but time; for though they certainly put that to a very lingering death with deck games which would have bored Robinson Crusoe, and with toy racecourses and amateur betting rings, yet they have no guns: there are no bleeding gulls or gasping fish to make the voyage horrible: their only shots are snapshots with the Kodak; and any wildness that is still untamed in them they work off, under the pretext of dancing and round games, by nocturnal rompings, in which the garment of gentility, always so thin and so laboriously held on by British folk, gets torn to shreds and sometimes drops off altogether.

In the afternoons and evenings a band, representing a great English steamship company's notion of high-class modern orchestral music, and consisting, to be precise, of two violins, a double bass, a cornet and a piano, plays gallops, waltzes, and selections from The Runaway Girl, The Geisha, and other musical farces of the day, except on Sundays, when The Runaway Girl is suppressed, and the cornet player, giving them The Lost Chord, deeply affects them. Songs about lovers waiting by the river also touch them; and when God Save the Queen concludes the concert they spring to their feet with enthusiasm, because it expresses the emotion stirred in them by the belief that England must be greater than any other country because they were born in it.

In any other place than this cradle and grave of many civilizations we should not seem ridiculous. Transport us on magic carpet to an English country town, and we shall appear persons of importance; moneyed, travelled, substantial Englishmen of good credit and standing. But here, on the bosom, gently heaving, that makes so light of us, our absurd ephemerality will not hide itself decently. We believe, every man of us, that we shall endure to the end, our Empire growing ever greater, until the Last Judgment shall be enacted—probably in Westminster Abbey—and the millennium inaugurated by the extension of British rule to the entire universe. We are ploughing the fields of Neptune from tomb to tomb of perished civilizations, leaving our boots nightly to the cabin steward that he may brush from them the dust of subtle Greek, forceful Roman, and pious Saracen, wearing on our faces meanwhile the modest gravity with which the eternal contemplates the temporal. Why did they perish, these peoples who can hardly have solaced their voyages with cruder pastimes than The Runaway Girl and sweepstakes on the run, and who certainly wore cleanly and seemly clothes instead of shirts muddied with starch and shoes clogged with pipeclay or noisome with blacking? The answer is simple. They were not English.

Alas! such answers carry no conviction to me, who am not only an

Irishman, looking at them with the completest detachment of national sentiment, but also what they call a cynic: that is to say, a person who cannot look at life as a countryman looks at a melodrama. Nothing is more clear to me than that English civilization is at the end of its tether, and that the tether can only be lengthened by the substitution for these artless grown-up children of a quite different sort of Englishman. In nothing are my travelling companions more boyish and girlish than in their freedom from all such misgivings. In their hearts they do not believe that Cæsar, with all his genius, Socrates with all his wit, or Saladin with all his chivalry, could have made five thousand a year for himself in Sheffield or Manchester. Not that they are specifically arrogant: on the contrary, they are specifically modest even to abjectness. They admit the Frenchman a finer logician, the German a deeper philosopher, the Italian a tunefuller musician, the Turk a hardier soldier, the Jew a keener financier. There is no specific quality you can name in respect of which they will not humbly allow precedence to some nation which has no more of it than themselves. Ten years ago they would have made one reservation, setting up against their confessed inferiority in wit, manners, learning, and the fine arts, an unapproachable superiority in cricket. To-day their humility is complete: they yield the willow to the Australian, and worship the supreme cricketer in the person of an Indian prince. Is such humility natural? Yes; for they believe that they can afford it ten times over. Are they not Englishmen? They justify themselves not by works but by faith: their personal qualities are to them but filthy rags: their salvation is that they are English. Just as I myself, slower than a horse, weaker than an elephant, duller eyed than an eagle, inferior at a hundred points to bird, beast, insect and reptile, yet do not doubt that I shall prevail against them; so do these my shipmates conceive themselves, as Englishmen, superior to all other mankind, how clever soever it may be. Therefore they are sure that the perils which have wrecked past civilizations will not wreck theirs, whatever envious foreigners and matricidal colonists may wish, and vainly try to believe, to the contrary.

And still the bosom, gently heaving, dandles the passing Englishman, having dandled many races with the same dreams. It is smiling to itself, this sunny Ionian sea; and for the life of me I cannot help smiling too.

Yet I am no historical fatalist either; and if a million civilizations had perished amid ripples of sunny Ionian laughter, I should still not admit that *my* civilization cannot weather the Cape of Good Hope. I grant to the Ionian Neptune that the Englishman's conceit is foolish, and trebly foolish his notion that faith in the destiny of his country can make him strong as well as adventurous. I grant that all nations have the same conceit, and that when I land presently on the Piræus my Greek guide, dragging me through an intolerable waste and disorder of shattered columns amid chirrups of "How interesting!" will talk of what "we" did at Salamis and Thermopylæ as if the spring tide of the Periclean age were still flowing. I grant that history cannot show us a single civilization that has survived the imperialist stage of democratic capitalism. I grant that in this very ship, with the band playing the National Anthem on a quarter deck open, without distinction of class, to every man and woman with a pocket full of sovereigns, and the grimy proletarian gasping and sweating for his pittance in the stokehold below, there is evidence for Neptune that the fatal hour is at hand for England. I grant that the ship sails through a deadly mist of illusion, in which the power of riches to ruin a country appears to each rich person only as a beneficent power of his own to purchase righteousness by doing good; in which the man who is afraid of his fellow to the point of killing him appears brave, and the man just who outdoes the criminal in cruelty; in which the fear of poverty has so swallowed up all other fears that the pursuit of success develops heroism by mere stress of fundamental cowardice; in which the very millions of money that seem to multiply in the struggle are as unreal as the Arabian magician's gold, and represent nothing but a future power of robbing the poor; in which, once for all, the moral fatuity symptomatic of the mortal diseases of the bygone civilizations reappears with deadly punctuality as the day draws nigh in which we must in our turn go under or else attain a higher degree of social organization than the race, even at its best, has ever yet attained.

But when all this, and much more, is admitted, what then? Shall we be logical, and, by committing suicide, save ourselves the humiliation and fruitless misery of going from bad to worse? Or shall we pretend that suicide is cowardly, and sit shaking our heads mournfully over Shakespearean poetry of the "Out, out, brief candle" order in the intervals of eating our share of the general plunder or tamely suffering our share of the general oppression? Clearly, those of us who have more than a farthing flicker of vitality will never surrender either way. Even were no way out discoverable, the thoroughly live man would remember that when the perfectly logical conclusion is reached, it still remains to be considered whether that conclusion is valid or whether it is merely a reduction to absurdity of the axioms and postulates from which it starts. Demonstrate to me that life is religiously, morally, scientifically, politically, philosophically and practically not worth going on with, and I *must* reply, So much the worse, not for life, but for what you call religion, science, politics, philosophy, and the current practice of the art of living. There is something wrong with these things if they lead to nihilistic conclusions. If you are shocked, and ask me whether I am prepared to throw them away merely because they do not flatter my selfish clinging to life, I reply, Yes, like so many buckets of dirty water, if necessary. When my friends who know what an excellent heart I have, explain that I do not mean *true* religion, *true* morality, and so on, I allow the pious excuse to those who are comforted by it as a soldier under fire is comforted by the shelter of a clump of rushes; but in truth I care nothing for your institutions, sacred or profane: what interests me is pure natural history. I am a great believer in life: my ancestors developed thumbs sooner than perish for want of them; and my contemporaries have developed County Councils sooner than go back to the woods. And shall I despair of evolving a practicable Commonwealth, of six-fingered men if necessary, because Babylon and Alexandria, Carthage and Rome, let their constitutions be enfeebled by institution-idolatry and pessimistic poetry? I think not. Let the nations that grovel before institutions, the worshipping nations, the loyal nations, the pious nations, the respectable nations perish: the race is imperishable.

And is not England pious, loyal, respectable? I fear so. All that means cowardice. Do not tell me that yonder young British officer with the new Victoria Cross is a brave man: he has chanced bullets, because chancing bullets is a British institution; but ask him to walk down Bond Street at five on a May afternoon in this grey collar of mine and you shall see him blench. And so, on the bosom, gently heaving, I salute the survivors of civilizations, the kindred of Prometheus, the defiers of prohibitions, the thoughtfree, the self-respecters, the critics of the gods.

Now that I am on firm earth again, and a year of war has elapsed, I find myself more than ever impressed with History's lesson that Empires, like men, are mortal, and a permanent political individuality, like a permanent personal one, an impossibility. For Empire is upon England now, and England has not the nerve for it. Her old Promethean fire is burnt out; and she grovels before all the idols and all the institutions. Grovels flattest, too, before that woodenest of all idols, the soldier, and that most foolish of all institutions, the army. Drops, if you please, upon some poor thriftless lad loafing about Trafalgar Square; talks him, in the confidence trick manner, into exchanging his boasted English freedom and manhood for a shilling; dresses him in a uniform; teaches him a few of the obsolete tricks which amuse German kinglets and Russian grand dukes on the parade ground; and then falls down and worships him as the embodiment of the noblest qualities of the British race, until it is time to throw him back into the street again, where, on his asking one of his worshippers for a job, the worshipper promptly refuses to employ him because he was a soldier. Will the Fate that makes Empires by allotting

Governments to them that can govern, give an Empire to a people that behaves in this silly manner? I doubt it; for it is Justice that is blind, not Destiny.

Let us look back a little over the expiring century. All through it, Empire has been stealing upon us as steadily as the hand of a clock, with invisible but inevitable motion. From time to time we notice that the hand is nearer the hour than before; and each time we sweat with terror. Mostly the hand has taken the form of Russia advancing towards India. And how we have dreaded Russia! What anarchy of mountain tribes intent only on blood feuds has been too disastrous? what despotism of fierce Amirs too cruel for us to cherish, if only it served as "a buffer state" between us and the rival civilization we dreaded? Think of it! England cheering every reciter of Tennyson's foolish lines about the most casual blunder in the Crimean war, and at the same time clinging to the knees of the Amir of Afghanistan to save her from coming face to face with Russia. Imagine an Empire that dares not man its own ramparts! that hides behind a moat full of "barbarians"! that dares not say, Civilization shall cover the whole earth: its frontiers shall be the posts where its guards shall relieve one another! Well, that pusillanimous thing is the British Empire in north-west India. And in the south east those two great evangelists of civilization, England and France, have solemnly agreed by treaty to maintain a strip of "barbarism" between their frontiers, so mortally afraid are they of meeting face to face. Wonderful "imperial instinct"! Buffer states at one end of the scale, dog muzzles at the other; between, the whole gamut of human cowardice, with "l'honneur de l'armée" and "our gallant Tommies" for keynote. And yet this poor trembling creature, Man, cannot rest or retreat, and must brag and dare—must even seek concrete danger as a relief from superstitious fear, just as men sometimes commit suicide to escape from the dread of death.

To the ordinary civilian, unconscious of the burden of Empire (except for the Income Tax): to whom, indeed, the Empire is a mere toast like Lovely Woman or Auld Lang Syne or any other emotional overflow pipe, all this has no meaning. But the statesman at the Foreign Office is bewildered; and the soldier at the front is mad with fear. From the newest general, with the mortally apprehensive eyes and the nostrils strained to scent danger, to the oldest one, with his blarney for the private and his little dish of carefully cooked successes for the Government at election times, all sense of proportion in measures, all foresight in public action, all heed to common human obligations are obliterated. If the enemy is a fanatic, dig up his dead prophet, mutilate the corpse and wreck the tomb, not in mere ferocity and brutality (for these would not matter more than the day's police court record matters), but, if you please, in cool policy! Here are the official religions of Europe, all standing upon faith in the prophet whom the Jews spat upon, scourged, mocked, crucified, and derisively asked why he, who professed to save other people, did not save himself! Every insult, every torment, every demonstration of the mere helpless humanity of the victim, has since become a Station of the Cross; and millions of Europeans travel from Station to Station on their knees, with their faith deepening at every Station. And here is your European "Christian" general, inferring from all this, that the way to destroy the prestige of the Mahdi is to add to it the sorrows of martyrdom, and fortify it with the horror, the pity, the generous indignation, the devotion which outlast by centuries the straw fire of mere militarist and nationalist enthusiasm. What an eye that general must have for history and for human nature! An English general too! Did not the English dig up Cromwell, whom they always hated, and still hate, for imposing on them the one virtue they cannot forgive—the virtue of respecting freedom of conscience? What harm has the digging up ever done Cromwell? is he any the less known to be the greatest of modern English princes? did the childish attack on his corpse revolt his contemporary Pepys, good royalist and true blue British snob as he was, any less that it revolted the Whig Macaulay 200 years later?

And yet this masterstroke of military stone-blindness was well received by us, and has now set the fashion in war. At first, our local civil diplomatist could not bring himself to endorse the mutilation, though, not having the courage to denounce it, he left it to be inferred that his approval of the bombardment of the tomb extended to the decapitation of the corpse. The House of Commons soon shewed him how superfluous his scruples were. It swept away Mr. Morley's protest with three times three for the general in the gallery; and now tomb desecration is *de rigueur* in British and Oriental warfare. The Boxers have torn up the British cemetery in Pekin. We retort by arranging to strike a decisive blow at China by desecrating the tombs of the Ming dynasty. And nobody in England even laughs. The nation delightedly thinks that it is standing no sentimental nonsense, but is going about its business in a serious, long-headed, practical way. If a French general were to threaten to bring England to her knees by smashing the tombs in Westminster Abbey, we should shake with derisive merriment. But the English general who believed in this method of subduing the Soudan is heaped with honors and sent to South Africa, where, on the field of Paardeburg, he is too excited to be persuaded that Cronje cannot do impossibilities to him, and presents us with a long roll of widows and orphans as the fruit of his strategy.

Unfortunately, the public understands no military quality except the personal courage of the company officer; and even that is not distinguished from the common pugnacity of the street scrapper. We may say in church that "the fear of the Lord is the beginning of wisdom," and admit, if hard pressed in argument, that a man without fear is no more to be desired that a man without honesty or any other quality of heedfulness; but none the less we console ourselves for all our blunders and disgraces by "the bravery of our soldiers" as set forth in war correspondence carefully edited by themselves. No doubt our soldiers fight fiercely enough: there is nothing new in the fact that Man is the most dangerous of the animals. But we are not likely to conquer the earth by a quality which we hold only in common with all its inhabitants. Our soldiers can hardly suppose themselves to be braver than the Dervishes whom they annihilated at from 2,000 to 600 yards distance. The Boers, who altogether decline to await charges or expose themselves to any avoidable peril, and have, in fact, made a frank display of civilian timidity, have beaten our soldiers over and over again, and would clearly have wiped us off the map of South Africa if they had been able to match our numbers and our money. The pluck of our officers is equally irrelevant to the Imperial question. All the court pageantry of hall-marking heroes with Victoria Crosses—quite as mechanical a business as the distribution of birthday honors—cannot place our officers in point of bravery above the Khalifa and his chiefs, who, when they were defeated, sat down on their carpets and waited for our soldiery to bayonet them, which, to judge by the significant absence of any details in the reports, was, we may conclude, pretty thoroughly done.

Pluck, then, may be left out of the question: public opinion can always create as much of that ruffianly virtue as it demands. What public opinion cannot create, and what in fact it misunderstands, discredits, and sulkily resents, is the strength of mind that disdains its common passions and penetrates to the realities behind its foolish fusses and self-conceits. Soldiering does not seem to encourage this quality. The general who will ride about under fire without—shall we say preoccupation?—will commit any atrocity to avoid being defeated, and will carry political cowardice—the only sort of cowardice that really matters in a general—to its uttermost extremity. Lord Roberts, who wears a Victoria Cross, no doubt did his duty when he was a company officer without flinching. He is cleverer than most military men and more humane. He has written an enormously popular book, in which he has testified to the folly of the flogging system, and frankly let out the fact that the stupidity and mendacity which provoked the Indian Mutiny were not, as Mr. Kipling imagines, merely the faults of those formidable qualities which make the

Englishman of romance invincible in an emergency, but the natural defects of that want of character and competence which showed itself in all directions when the explosion occurred, and which led to the quiet dropping of so many military duffers when it was over. The Empire would have been wrecked then but for the work of a few exceptional men who saved the situation, and diverted public attention from the majority who were quite unequal to the occasion. Yet the historian of these significant events, this clever, shrewd, rather kindly old soldier, our idolized "Bobs," when left in an enemy's country dependent on a flimsy railway line of communication as long as from Paris to St. Petersburg, loses every feeling except the dread of having that line broken, and orders that whenever it is attacked, the farmhouses for miles round shall be solemnly burnt.

There are two ways of regarding this step. It is clear to the non-military mind that to burn a Boer militiaman's farm when you have failed to shoot him is to convert him into a desperado with nothing to lose and an unpardonable injury to avenge. It is to give your civilian enemy the cardinal soldierly qualification of homelessness. It is to ruin the country you have just declared part of the Empire. It is to provoke the one real danger to the British Empire in the South African situation: the danger of a general rising of the Cape Dutch under the influence of a wave of indignation. It is to force the Home Government, which you have just saved by your victories, to capitulate at the first brush with the Opposition, struck down by a single letter from a burnt farm sent by Mr. Morley to the *Times*. That is the general human point of view.

But from the military point of view, it is simply war reduced by the brute force of facts from the visions of Jingo romance to its own real essence, which is, destruction of the enemy. It is plain enough that Lord Roberts, if he could be driven from his entrenchments of rhetoric and blarney to a sincere defence, would say: "I devastate because I am a soldier, and devastation is a soldier's business. I did not make this war. The choice between the two methods of peace and war was not made by me, but by you, the nation. You must take the consequences of your choice. You knew perfectly well that the peaceful method meant humanity, undisturbed firesides, harvests left to the reaper and cattle undisturbed on the field. You knew equally well that war meant murder and devastation, ruin and misery, plague, pestilence, and famine. You choose war and sent me to carry out your choice. I have done so; and I shall not pretend to concern myself about the people who suppose that a general's duties are the same as an archbishop's. Of all the operations of war, none is better known than the devastation of an enemy's country in order that he may find no supplies in it. The nerve to do it is the quality that

distinguishes the capable general from the city missionary and the chival-
rous counter-jumper who prates about defenceless women and children
as if the morality of killing depended on age and sex, or the tunic of a
soldier were any more bullet proof than the apron of a perambulator. As
long as I have to hold my line of communication against a hostile force, I
shall not leave a farm standing that can supply a man of that force with a
meal, or harbor a woman or child that can give him news of my movements and pass on messages for him."

All that is perfectly reasonable. And, as such, it is the *reductio-ad-
absurdum* of the glory of war and of the bravery of the soldier. War is an
orgie of crime based on the determination of the soldier to stick at
nothing to bring it to an end and get out of daily danger of being shot.
Every soldier confesses this: his pet paradox is that clemency is mistaken
kindness—that the true mercy is to bring the war to an end at any
sacrifice. So it is, once you have begun it, *and if you are in the enemy's
territories and do not intend to make them your own;* but a better way is not to
begin it. If you disagree, and do begin it, believing in war as a school of
manliness, then you should strive to perpetuate it by all means in your
power. "Of life and freedom is he alone worthy," said Goethe, "who daily
conquers both." Goethe was no soldier. The soldier always begs to be
allowed to kill everybody who could possibly kill him in order that he
may sheathe his sword for ever. And who shall blame him? But it is one
thing not to blame a poor bedevilled, but logical, military fellow creature
who pays with his skin for the murderous arrogance of the fat citizens
who skulk on their tight little island behind the guns of the fleet, clamor-
ing for the blood of their neighbours. It is quite another to make his
bedevilled logic the policy of your Empire.

The truth is, that the abler a man is as a soldier, the more unfit he is
for civil statesmanship. With all Wellington's Irish common sense and his
experienced contempt for soldiers and dislike for officers, he was a
greater failure as a statesman than any man of his ability could possibly
have been without a military training. Cromwell, who, like Cæsar, picked
up the trade of general as an amateur in middle age, and swept before
him the military professionalism of Europe after a few months' practice,
was involved in irremediable errors by discovering how easy it was to
achieve military successes, without discovering at the same time that, like
most easy achievements, they were worse than useless for the settlement
of social questions. No man who has learnt a short and apparently effec-
tual way of disposing of political difficulties will ever have patience to
forego that method. Cromwell's way with Ireland, Napoleon's way with
Europe, is finally every capable soldier's way everywhere. A soldier has

no other policy; and to make him your counsellor is to relinquish all choice of policy.

One of the reasons, then, why the modern statesman must stand out stiffly against the crowd (especially the well-dressed crowd) is that to the crowd the soldier is always a hero. He need not even be a conquering hero. He may not only burn farms, he may actually do the very things he burns farms in his terror of: that is, get defeated; and yet he is idolized. When Roberts and Kitchener return, they will find no acclamations louder than have already greeted Buller and White. Sir Charles Warren, a distinguished officer who, when he undertook civil duties as chief of the London police in the eighties, began by maltreating our dogs in his dread of hydrophobia, and ended by breaking our heads in his dread of revolution, would, if he returned to London, be as wildly cheered as if Spion Kop had been another Waterloo.

Indeed, when we come from the general theory of militarism and its effects to the actual proceedings of the nation and the army to-day, the discussion loses all its dignity. Lord Rosebery tells us, on the excellent authority of Napoleon, who observed it in others before he proved it in his own person, that even the best generals last only six years. We have to keep them for thirty. The British officer cannot control his men without special laws to enslave them; and even with these laws he demands a censorship of the press, nominally to keep news from the enemy (who seldom seems at a loss for it) but really to keep news of his mistakes from reaching home. When it does leak out, we, the public, hasten to encourage the officer in folly and the private in blackguardism. We excuse the devastation of the Transvaal (*our* Transvaal) on the ground that ammunition has exploded in the burning farms (an excellent reason for searching them, but not for burning them); and we raise a clamor for the heads of the Chinese Princes who were patriotic enough to back the Boxers against us. We also want to have Chinese cities razed to the ground. It has dawned on us after some weeks that the heathen Chinese have not the very faintest intention of complying with these Christian requirements; but we cannot disclaim either the infamy of having made them or the humiliation, from our own weak-man-putting-down-his-foot point of view, of failing to enforce them.

We still, however, retain our sense of the sacredness of a lady's bedroom. When we burn a farm, and the lady of the house asks where she is to sleep, we convey her to the nearest town and take rooms for her at a hotel. And so our melodrama, after all our expenditure in red fire and real blood, ends as comic opera.

It is our folly, not our cruelty, that is the measure of our danger; for, though useless cruelty is not a bad measure of folly, political success is quite compatible with a great deal of incidental cruelty. A king who works hard and intelligently at his craft of kingship may indulge in a personal taste for cruelty with impunity. James II., who lost his kingdom, was cruel, but not crueller than Louis XI., who built up his. Peter of Russia was monstrously cruel, as coarse a blackguard as any Hooligan in London and a poltroon into the bargain; but he founded modern Russia. Charles I. was less cruel than Peter—indeed he was by comparison an amiable and sensible person—and he was one of the few really genuine martyrs in history; but he lost his head and Cromwell kept his. An Imperial policy has to succeed; and it cannot be proved either that cruelty never succeeds or that humanity always does. Humanity is neither a commercial nor a political speculation, but a condition of noble life. Those to whom that is no recommendation—ourselves just at present, for instance—have no reason to be humanitarians. Therefore I leave humanity out of the argument.

Further, I am no pro-Boer, and have, in fact, been vigorously reviled for my impartiality as between President Mauser and Emperor Lee-Metford, and my conviction that a political reconstruction of South Africa, involving the absorption of the Transvaal Republic in a larger political organization, was inevitable, and, like most political reconstructions, likely to be precipitated finally by a violent blow from without. Mr. Kruger unhappily staked his position on violence. From the moment when he bought his first cartridge, he stepped into the arena with the other cartridge buyers. His doing so was not surprising; for he had invaded and seized the Transvaal by explosive force, and meant to establish himself there by explosive force. We are now trying to drive him out by explosive force, with what prospects of final success, or even escape from the risk of being ourselves driven out by a united Afrikanderdom, neither I nor anybody in this press-censored country can tell. At all events, there is no humanitarian side in the quarrel, however vehemently our factions may exploit it as a pretext for virtuous indignation. The English principle that no man should do wrong unless he is provoked is cited to justify the Boers in drawing the sword and the British in trying to make them perish by it. Not accepting the principle, I care nothing for such recriminations. I know that war will never cease whilst either the Jingo temper or the pro-Boer temper governs us.

What will win in the race for Empire is the courage to look realities in the face and the energy to adapt social organization to the needs of the modern conscience, and so substitute a fruitful life for a fool's paradise. In what part of the British Empire these qualities are to be found at present (if in any) I know not: I have certainly not observed them lately in England. The war has stirred us up; but nothing has come to the surface so far but the commonest bumptiousness of spirit, the most provincial donnishness of thought. Sir Alfred Milner is, I think, the most representative Englishman now living; and Sir Alfred Milner reminds me of nothing but the most hopeless type of schoolmaster. But it is too painful to deal with the personalities of the hour: let me seek the same moral in a few boasted mechanical trivialities of our time. Take the telephone, for example. It came 20 years ago, and we still tie the wires to chimneys, unable to adapt our cities to it, even to the extent of putting up poles in the streets. The bicycle was perfected fifteen years ago, and still no house provides accommodation for it. Mr. H. G. Wells has just made magazine-reading London shriek with laughter over the cycle drill book issued by the War Office. Mr. William Clarke notes the decay of our industrial supremacy and our easy money-soothed descent into the position of a pleasure resort for the rich Americans whose employees make the twopenny-tube railways which we, from lack of adaptability in our engineering firms, have been unable to make ourselves. After all, why should we take the toilsome line which is no longer the line of least resistance? It is hard to learn how to make the twopenny tube: it is easy to touch the hat to the American shareholder and take his tip. That is why all forms of flunkeyism are reviving and flourishing here. They do not hurt our self-respect as the old social distinctions did; for we really worship money and like to see it in places attainable by ourselves, whereas our deference to rank, character and genius was always more or less a sham. As an incidental result, however, we are become tedious as a subject of literature; and I find myself yawning as I try to pursue it.

Yes: there is no denying it: the evidence goes to prove, so far, that this island is done for as the centre of the Empire. Imperial Federation, if it comes, may retain it as a park for holiday tours and pilgrimages to historic monuments; and it may leave us our House of Commons as Head Ranger (like George of Hyde Park), and even some ghost of our army as park keepers; but it will probably either take the serious business of the Empire out of our fat and nerveless fingers, or make some potentate a present of us, like Heligoland.

In a few centuries, the Ionian sea will still laugh in the southern sun; and on its bosom, gently heaving, the shadows of airships (of Chinese manufacture, run by International Federations as State lines) will flit towards the white cliffed island where a once famous nation will live by letting lodgings. I cannot foresee whether national frontiers, those last ditches of dog-in-the-mangerism, shall by then have been wholly filled up; but I am sure that until that comes to pass, the supremacy will fall to the Power on which it shall first dawn that the soldier, the man-machine, the fighting automaton, the thing that does not reason and does not fear death, the projectile on horseback, the walking weight in the butt of the bayonet, the creature with five senses and neither moral rights nor moral duties, is a worse imposture than Kempelen's automaton; for the man that was hid behind the sham machinery of that famous humbug could at least play chess, whereas the poor hungry fellow inside the khaki frame can only betray himself by eating chocolate and keeping the box to be pawned when he is discharged, and finds that nobody will employ a sham automaton. And as to the unfortunate officers who through congenital deficiency of perception or excess of imagination are duped into pretending to work the automaton when they are young, and dare not refuse to keep up the imposture when they are old; who, believed to be heroes by romantic young ladies and sporting hansom cabmen, are known to be mostly duffers by the accidentally capable among their commanders, just in proportion as their counsels and terrors prevail with a State will that State lose its nerve, the one being a symptom of the other.

But Englishmen will not believe all this: they believe in nothing but the soldier, who is a positive nuisance, the gentleman, who is a comparative nuisance, and the lady, who is a superlative nuisance. And so I think the world will tire at last of the Englishman's stupidity and send him back to his hovel, like the fisherman in the fairy tale who wanted to be lord of the sun and moon because his simpler virtues had been rewarded by a success or two. I am sorry; for I have wasted much good advice on him, and believed greatly even in his stupidity; for since English stupidity is steadfast, and Irish cleverness is treacherous, I thought that if the traitor lent his brains to the blockhead, and the blockhead his steadfastness to the traitor, they might between them do something. But it was a dream: the blockhead is still stupid (witness the Transvaal) and the traitor is still unstable (witness the fate of Mr. Horace Plunkett); and the dram of ale— the quotation is obscure and somewhat musty; but it will serve.

Michael J. Holland

SHAW'S SHORT FICTION: A PATH TO DRAMA

Writing did not always come easily to GBS. During his early years in London, the young Shaw tried his hand at a number of different types of writing while serving his literary apprenticeship. One genre he experimented with was short fiction, which has received very little comment compared with his novels. Shaw's short fiction illustrates the creative development of a natural dramatist. Many later plays would refine material that initially appeared in these early efforts.

Shaw wrote enough short fiction to collect some of it in volume six of his Collected Edition, *Short Stories, Scraps and Shavings* (1932). This eclectic material, in addition to some lost or misplaced items, reveals that Shaw's short fiction fits into three distinct groups. The first consists of his earliest, and most awkward, efforts. These stories are predominantly narrative, in imitation of most popular literature of the late Victorian era. Shaw once confessed (*CL,* 28 January 1928) that his earliest attempts at fiction were "monstrous exploits" he attributed to a Dublin neighbor named Dowling: "I made him a character in an endless tale of impossible adventures which I used to tell to a boy named Bellhouse." The second category indicates a progression to subjects of greater political or social interest, as well as a stylistic progression from narration to dialogue. The final group consists of stories written after Shaw had become a well-known playwright. These were largely occasional pieces and contain subject matter or elements that were not intended for dramatic presentation. All these works, however, contain elements that would find their way into Shaw's most famous plays.

The first extant story, "The Miraculous Revenge," displays the influence of Victorian writers of fiction, especially Charles Dickens. In 1878 Shaw had planned a novel, *The Legg Papers,* based upon *The Pickwick Papers.*[1] The intended cast of characters—the Reverend Epaminondas

Gentleflower, Jupiter Beedleby, Friday Morgan Legg—indicates Dickensian influence. Zeno Legge, the protagonist and narrator of "Revenge," is all that remains of those early plans. A satire on Irish Catholicism and its penchant for miracles, the tale was first published in the March 1885 issue of *Time* magazine after having made the rounds of publishers' offices since 1881.[2] It was republished without authorization in 1921 by the Appeal Publishing Company of Girard, Kansas, before Shaw included it in his Collected Edition of 1932.[3] The plot concerns Zeno's visit to his uncle the Archbishop of Dublin, a letter Zeno sends to the Archbishop from a small village where he is investigating a supposed miracle, the conclusion of Legge's village stay, and his own postscript to the story.

Shaw's tale is flawed from the outset by the exaggerated characterization of the protagonist Zeno. His erratic behavior and abrupt mood shifts make him an unreliable first-person narrator. Young Zeno plays the piano in his hotel drawing room after one in the morning, pounds loudly on his uncle's door shortly before dawn, and fervently pledges to join the Catholic Church when a statue of the Virgin Mary causes him to sob uncontrollably. Readers have no choice but to agree with his uncle, who justifies sending Zeno to a village as his spy because the youth is "too crazy to excite the suspicion of those whom you may have to watch."[4] Yet Zeno's apparent madness makes the story almost impossible to follow. Since he is the only source of information, we never really know how much is true and how much is imagined by the narrator.

The confusing narrative of "Revenge" may also have been paralleled in "The Brand of Cain," a manuscript lost in late 1884. Shaw had submitted it to *Temple Bar* magazine in December 1879, only to have it rejected by the publisher George Bentley in a 5 March 1880 letter. Bentley was kind enough to offer some constructive criticism to the aspiring author, insisting that "the photographer's character must not be too exaggerated in regard to his nervousness. This is overdone when he photographs the woman.[5] Shaw wrote back the same day to thank Bentley. Shaw concluded that he must have "missed . . . aim" if his attempt at creating ambiguity through an unreliable narrative voice had resulted only in an awkward effort to churn out a conventional romance.[6] St. John Ervine's comments on Shaw's first novel reflect both the weaknesses and the strengths found in "Revenge": GBS "lacked the gift of narrative, and was, therefore, not a novelist. He had, supremely, the gift of dialogue and was, therefore, a dramatist."[7] The young writer's "gift for dialogue" emerges in a brief sequence with an Irish ferryman. Shaw's early attempt to capture colloquial dialogue anticipates his characterization of Alfred Doolittle in *Pygmalion:*

Faith, it never was as good as it mightabeen. The people that comes from the south side can see Billy's grave—Lord have mercy on him!—across the wather; and they think bad of payin a penny to put a stone over him. It's them that lives towrst Dublin that makes the journey. Your honor is the third Ive brought from south to north this blessed day.[8]

The religious ejaculations, the parenthetical phrase blessing the sinner, the words spelled to simulate pronunciation (*wather, towrst*), and the deferential form of address display the author's ear for idiomatic speech. Shaw's use of the apostrophe in "it's," in contrast to his own idiosyncratic views on punctuation, may have been a concession to the editor of *Time* magazine. The tale's ironical conclusion also displays the author's paradoxical sense of humor. Zeno discredits the priest, but only by proving the veracity of the miracle to his listeners. Shaw's creation of an article from the *Times* which recounts how the priest was declared a fraud lends some credence to Zeno's account. Shaw would turn to this device frequently to avoid appearing too heavy-handed with his authorial voice.

Shaw adopted the narrative guise of a newspaper reporter for "The St. James's Hall Mystery," a story composed in February 1879, which Shaw never published. The plot concerns the sudden appearance of Mozart's ghost during an evening recital at St. James's Hall. The ghost's comments satirize musical pedants whose obsession with the technical details of performance stifles the beauty and spirit of the music. Shaw's narrative purpose was clear: to establish a detached, objective narrator to describe the incident so that readers would not be confused about actual events. Unfortunately, the reporter succeeds at the expense of the story's pace. Mozart's ghost does not appear until the fifth page of a thirteen-page manuscript. The twenty-two-year-old Shaw uses the same sort of conclusion found in "Revenge," a newspaper account. Here it is less effective, abruptly ending the story one short paragraph after the ghost has disappeared. Possibly responding to Bentley's advice, Shaw created a dry, objective manuscript that buries both his humorous barbs and his fine characterization of the ghost.

Mozart's ghost is a Shavian triumph in embryo. His confrontational persona anticipates John Tanner and Andrew Undershaft. The ghost dominates the action through his lively monologue, drawing upon Shaw's critical knowledge of music. Throughout the concert, the ghost regularly violates Victorian etiquette, loudly referring to the string section as "three parts scrape, and one part tone," before falling asleep during the piece's repetition.[9] After praising the performance of the female harpsichordist, the ghost rapturously whispers, "Aloysia!" When the critic who has accompanied him asks whether his wife's name was Constance, the ghost "blushed and said nothing, but addressed himself to the hearing of the concerto."[10] GBS enjoys playing with the historical assertion that Mozart may have been romantically involved with his sister-in-law Aloysia. The scope and humor of the ghost dominate this story, much as Shavian supermen would dominate subsequent works. The ghost is the only character provided with extensive dialogue. The ghost defines himself.

The muscial pedants, personified by the critic and the arranger's associates, are satirized through the third-person account of the newspaperman. A more experienced Shaw would allow his buffoons to speak for themselves, as in *The Doctor's Dilemma* (1906). After Mozart insults the conductor, the man's friends defend him by insisting "that they would reject any piece of music bearing his name as spurious, if it were not calculated to confound rather than to amuse them."[11] This deftly humorous touch is buried in a prose paragraph in the journalist's distant commentary. When a music critic contemptuously refers to the harpsichordist as an "amateur" while unknowingly talking to her husband, Shaw allows a piece of comic confusion to remain untapped. "Mystery" is one instance where narrative control has stifled a young writer's inherent ear for speech and submerged his comic sensibilities.

Shaw's last fully narrative story was "Don Giovanni Explains," a predecessor of *Man and Superman* (1902) that has been identified as a fictionalized account of his affair with Jenny Patterson.[12] He began writing this story on 25 July 1887 as a possible offering for *Unwin's Annual*.[13] By 2 August, he had completed and revised the story, but could not find a publisher for it. In November he offered the story to *Longmans,* but it was again rejected. Contemporary editors, possibly sensing a scandal behind the story, were unwilling to publish it.[14] In spite of its cold reception, Shaw liked the tale. His diary for 6 December 1889 notes, "Got out my old Don Giovanni story for [H. W.] Massingham; read it; and was greatly pleased with it."[15] This may explain why, although still then unpublished, he included it in his 1932 Collected Edition.

In order to create a believable narrative persona, Shaw invents an intelligent woman of artistic sensibilities with an avid interest in "good music, good books, botany, farming, and teaching children."[16] This female GBS stresses her overwhelming appeal to all males, yet lacks interest in their attentions. By overstating her position, Shaw can now present the ghost of Don Juan as "a man who spends his time running from amorous women, and whose reputation as a lover is based on the fabrications of his servant and the wish fulfilment slanders of slighted females."[17] Indeed, when the young woman falls in love with the Don's ghost, we see the attitude that would later be espoused in *Man and Superman,* "that the female was the driving sexual force in the universe and the male her nearly passive victim."[18]

"Don Giovanni Explains" consists of four segments: the young girl's account of her background, her critique of the opera, the tale of the ghost, and the young girl's reaction. Shaw's reliance on narrative, only briefly resorting to dialogue, stifles our interest and makes the girl's profession of love at the end less credible than convenient. The ghost's story, a detailed reminiscence of his life, seems implausibly long. An older, more experienced Shaw would use other characters' interjections to break up the speeches of his main figures. Don Giovanni's ghost is too obviously on a soapbox, preaching the author's theories. While "Don Giovanni" is much more interesting and easier to follow than either "Revenge" or "Mystery," the story is still too clearly contrived.

The tale's anticipation of the Life Force theory is its real strength. *Man and Superman* offers only a more polished presentation. The Don's ghost of the tale describes himself as a "Spanish nobleman, much more highly evolved than most of my contemporaries,"[19] just as the Don Juan of the play possesses more of the Life Force than do any of his peers. The Don's friend who wishes to marry Dona Ana is the unfortunate Ottavio, while the hapless Octavius desires Ann Whitefield in *Man and Superman.* The story and the play present the same view of heaven and hell: places where the dead are free to come and go of their own volition. The play's third act is a carefully thought-out description of the Shavian universe created in this story. Shaw's creative process included turning set speeches from the story into the fast-paced dialogue of the play.[20] The most significant distinction between "Don Giovanni Explains" and *Man and Superman* concerns organization—the play is the work of a writer more sure of his tools.

Much of this early short fiction contains detailed references to music that display the knowledge and background of a professional critic. Zeno Legge plays the piano and describes a sudden depression he experiences as "a coarse threatening sound in my ears like that of the clarionets whose sustained low notes darken the woodland in 'Der Freischutz.' "[21] The use of Mozart's ghost in "Mystery" to criticize the pompous musical concerts performed at St. James's Hall parallels the use of the young girl in "Don Giovanni" to criticize the amateurs reinforcing the orchestra. Shaw was drawing upon the experiences that had first trained him to write and initially exposed his need to create fiction.

Shaw's first job as a writer began in November 1876, when G. J. Vandeleur Lee, the musical conductor who had trained Shaw's mother and sister, asked the youth to ghost-write musical criticism for a satirical

London weekly called *The Hornet.* This enterprise lasted only eleven months, but exposed Shaw to professional writing. By 1885, William Archer had helped GBS advance his career by obtaining Shaw's appointment as a critic for the *Dramatic Review.*[22] These experiences provided the background needed to create Corno di Bassetto, the impudent critic-of-all trades who brought Shaw to public notice in the music columns of the *London Star* in 1888.

An examination of Shaw's musical criticsm for the *Star* illustrates his compulsion to dramatize, even while producing nonfiction. Bassetto may be his first fully successful fictional persona. The 21 February 1889 review opens with a humorous conversation between Corno and his editor T. P. O'Connor, who wants his temperamental reviewer to visit an East End production. Shaw describes the editor, "throwing himself back in his chair and arranging his moustache with the diamond which sparkles at the end of his pen-handle," in an aside that provides precise stage directions.[23] His use of the prosaic "deuce knows where" in O'Connor's mouth shows that GBS has already learned how "speeches can be made to seem colloquial if they are spoken conversationally and not oracularly."[24] The appeal to Bassetto's vanity compels him to review the concert. Shaw would revert to dialogue openings repeatedly to display the personality of Bassetto.[25]

Shaw was not above exaggerating real events to create a humorous narrative. The final paragraph of his 12 February 1890 review describes Bassetto's attempts to imitate a dance step he had witnessed on stage that evening. After Bassetto falls on the pavement in the early hours of the morning, a policeman picks him up on the assumption that the critic is drunk. Once the reviewer has explained, the policeman tries the step himself, with no more success. Eventually they are joined by a police inspector, a milkman, and a postman. Shaw's reference to "Fitzroy Square," his actual address, adds a touch of authenticity to the piece.

Shaw's earliest story to display prominent dialogue as support for the narrative emerges from even earlier musical experiences. "The Serenade" was first referred to in a 27 June 1882 diary entry.[26] It was eventually published in November 1885 by the *Magazine of Music,* and later included in *Short Stories, Scraps and Shavings.* Forty-year-old Colonel Green makes a credible narrator as he describes the musical gymnastics he goes through to win the hand of a beautiful, refined singer named Linda Fitznightingale. The story possesses an ironical twist, much like "Mystery" and "Revenge," but succeeds because of some well-placed dialogue and a trustworthy narrator.

"The Serenade" works because Shaw dramatizes, rather than describes, humorous incidents. The opening demonstrates Green's egotis-

tical concern for his "entertainment," while briefly mentioning Fitznightingale and the young rival Porcharlester. Green disparages the young
officer's "effeminate baritone voice" before Shaw establishes their conflict.[27] Porcharlester describes the colonel as "fidgety"; Green retorts by
characterizing his opponent's behavior as boyish and immature. Green's
unwillingness to disagree with Linda emerges when she asks whether he
likes Schubert's Serenade. He stumbles, "Hm! well, the fact is—Do *you*
like it," verbalizing his hesitancy.[28] When he hums the notes to show her
that he knows it, Miss Fitznightingale agrees, "it is a little like that,"
advising readers of the colonel's limited vocal skills.[29]

Shaw's use of the horn instructor's cockney accent to create humor
stems from autobiography. The instructor tells the colonel that he lacks
the lips needed to play the horn. Matthew Edward McNulty, a childhood
friend of Shaw, recalled in his memoirs that GBS had been told the same
thing when he tried to learn the clarinet in Dublin.[30] Shaw's caustic
comments may reflect unpleasant memories. In "The Serenade," the
teacher advises Green to give up the horn only after "he pocketed the
five guineas" that was his fee.[31] He also anticipates the story's ironical
conclusion when he says that "the 'orn resembles the human voice,"
much as the Irish ferryman of "Revenge" unconsciously provides Zeno
with the information that allows him to discredit the priest. Another
minor character, the drunken clarinet player who misses his cue in
Green's show, recalls a drunken clarinet player in *Love Among The Artists*,
a novel Shaw had completed in 1881, but would not serialize until 1887–
88 in *Our Corner*.

The strength of "The Serenade" lies in a taut narrative which makes
the ironical conclusion more plausible. Shaw concentrates on natural,
realistic details to place his readers at the scene. Green exclaims credibly
that "the mouthpiece of my instrument was like ice; and my lips were
stiff and chilly" when he plays his nocturnal serenade.[32] Shaw has substituted a letter from Linda to Porcharlester as the denouement, in place of
the newspaper accounts concluding both "Mystery" and "Revenge." The
epistle is more immediate and dramatic. The colonel's pursuit of Linda
Fitznightingale ends with two terse paragraphs, in direct contrast to
Green's volubility at the opening. Shaw is refining his fictional techniques, using familiar material which he could handle confidently.

Shaw's increasing involvement with the Fabians led him to move beyond music to try his hand at political satire with a fictional thread. His
diary entry for 9 March 1887 dates his writing of "Shutting Up An
Individualist" for *To-Day Magazine*, where it appeared that April.[33] He
hid behind the anagramatic pseudonym "Redbarn Wash" and never
publicly acknowledged this comic dialogue, which takes place aboard a

third-class carriage of the Metropolitan Railway between an idealistic socialist and a comfortable, self-satisfied skeptic. "Shutting Up" criticizes the various socialist parties' lack of practical accomplishments by describing the groups' varied beliefs and interspersing the reactions of a wry opponent. Shaw uses a cockney accent for the old gentleman antagonist which highlights the author's ear for speech. H. M. Hyndman becomes "Yndman," and the monocled Hubert Bland turns into "A hoverbearing gent with an [sic] heye-glass."[34] Shaw also pokes fun at himself and his own group, the Fabians. The old man labels them "genteel socialists" who only invite their opponents to meetings so they can attack contemporary values. He evinces even less respect for "Bunnard Shorr, wot noone regards as serious."[35] The story is chiefly of interest for its emphasis upon dialogue to carry all the action, and upon humor to show the shortcomings of pure idealism.

Political satire was also the focus of his next published tale, "A County Councillor's Dream," for the double number of *The Star* on Thursday, 17 January 1889. The story seems to have been timed for the London County Council Election, at which Shaw voted on that same day.[36] GBS took great pride in being able to vote, a privilege he had been unable to exercise until November 1888, since election rules listed him as his mother's lodger and not as a head of a household.[37] "Dream" is a futuristic vision, probably inspired by Shaw's reading of Edward Bellamy's *Looking Backward, 2000–1887* (1888). The narrator is a complacent old vestryman hoping to be reelected to his local Board of Works. He falls asleep the night before the contest and dreams he has been transported to London of A.D. 3000, where the inhabitants see him as a "BLOATED AND SOMEWHAT UNPLEASANT TYPE common to the 19th century."[38] After viewing the advantages of the future, he is convinced of his own ineptitude.

"Dream" points to techniques that Shaw would later use in some of his most memorable plays. He uses a dream frame to tell the story, beginning with a speech of the vestryman's before the County Council that turns into a futuristic London Bridge scene. This transition is belabored and abrupt. The dream ends suddenly when the candidate throws himself into the water from the same bridge, only to find himself on the floor of his own bedroom. Shaw would refine his technique and present dream elements in some later plays. When writing the futuristic sections of *Back to Methuselah* in 1918, GBS may have recalled elements of "Dream." In the play he resurrects technological advances like the photophone for communication and the pneumatic tube for rapid transit. The communities of both the play and "Dream" represent a utopian vision of well-preserved people who lead much longer, more pleasant lives. "Dream's" optimistic vision includes a sparkling clear Thames river and a society that has done away with market transactions. These are the kind of specific improvements Shaw would always envision for the future.

On a rhetorical level, "Dream" contains a harangue directed against the vestryman and his society which displays the techniques a later Shaw would reserve for the title figure in *Candida* and Dick Dudgeon in *The Devil's Disciple*. The representative from the future tells the vestryman,

> Your color blindness, your obtuseness of palate, your insensibility to stimuli, and your sloth in responding to those coarse enough to be felt by you, your incapacity for dealing with abstract conceptions, your egotisms, your love of notoriety, your greediness, your dulness, your complacent imbecility, your superstition, and, in short, your stupidity, are
> PRODIGIOUS AND UNIQUE.[39]

Shaw achieves a repetitive cataloguing effect he would use later in his plays, while avoiding the appearance of wordiness. As St. John Ervine would later observe about Shaw's mature style, the prolix sentence, "swift and tightly packed . . . carefully and deliberately made," typifies him at his best.[40]

Shaw's increasing tendency to use dialogue in place of narrative in his early fiction reaches its culmination in his sequel to *A Doll's House*. In the January 1890 issue of *The English Illustrated Magazine*, Walter Besant published his "representative middle class evangelical verdict" on Henrik Ibsen's play.[41] While most of his contemporaries chose to ignore Besant's "forgotten production,"[42] Shaw wrote a rejoinder to what he characterized as "Besant's nonsense."[43] On 4 January 1890 Shaw met Edward Aveling and promised he would furnish a response for *Time* magazine. He quickly dashed off his fictional riposte by 7 January, reading it that evening to Henry and Kate Salt.[44] By the 13th he was correcting the final proofs for a work that J. L. Wisenthal has suggested "could well have been one of the ways in which Ibsen led Shaw to the beginning of his career as a dramatist."[45]

In a 28 January letter to the actor Charles Charrington (husband of actress Janet Achurch), Shaw complained of the poor returns he had received from *Cashel Byron's Profession* and his other fictional writings. Referring to the "dramatic form" of "Still After the Doll's House," Shaw declared, "My next effort in fiction—if I ever have time to make one— will be a play."[46] "Still After the Doll's House" is designed as a dialogue between Nora and Krogstad the moneylender. Shaw dispenses with the narrative voice after an opening paragraph that describes Nora's "indignation" and provides a description of the setting. This passage follows

the style of stage directions in a play. Nora dominates the interview with
Krogstad, anticipating the aggressive Violet Robinson's confrontations
with men in *Man and Superman*. As he had in the condemnation of the
vestryman in "Dream," Shaw uses tightly controlled parallelism in a dia-
tribe directed at the banker:

> You have clung to your respectability; but your heart has not been nar-
> row enough to make you content with it. You have hankered after our
> wider life; but your heart has not been large enough to make you join
> us.[47]

The sustained nature of the dialogue shows that its author has learned
how to create dramatic tension in a physically static environment. Like
the ghost of Don Giovanni from Shaw's story three years earlier, Nora
bears the burden of social disapproval for the actions and assumptions of
others, and identifies their mutual hypocrisy. "Still After the Doll's
House" is strained in its hasty attempt to respond to Besant, but Nora is a
predecessor of aggressive women like Vivie Warren. In 1892 Shaw realized his playwriting boast to Charrington, completing *Widowers' Houses*
for J. T. Grein's Independent Theatre Company. With the move to
drama established, Shaw had found his medium.

Shaw would return to short fiction only to present subject matter not
conducive to dramatic presentation. These works are largely occasional
pieces, expressing Shaw's views on a wide variety of topics. His opinion
of London theaters that pandered to the pretentious tastes of his society
is offered in "The Theatre of the Future," a farce published in the
February 1905 *Grand Magazine*. Shaw satirizes his contemporaries by
setting the tale five years into the future. GBS is drawing upon his own
critical comments as Corno di Bassetto sixteen years earlier, when he had
raged at the "plutocratic power" of the "excessively rich people" who
supported opera at Covent Garden and turned the concerts into their
own "fashionable post-prandial resort" at the expense of the music.[48]

Shaw's imaginary theater world of London 1910 is a bleak place. The
theater owners offer only bland melodramas for wealthy, titled people
who are admitted to the shows by invitation. "Theatre" is about the
destruction of this cartel by Gerald Bridges, a millionaire who "read the
Elizabethan dramatists in the spirit of Charles Lamb" and loved "rhetorical balderdash."[49] He initiates a "cash-for-admission" theater that takes
business from its competitors until they are forced to follow his lead. A
third-person narrator distances the audience from Bridges so that GBS
can ridicule the free market system which allowed this character to stumble onto his wealth. Shaw's primary theme, that good theater requires

the lively performance of thought-provoking material, recalls his attack on the pedants in "Mystery."

"Theatre" demonstrates Shaw's tendency to fall into habits formed in his earliest fiction. The story's conclusion summarizes the theater's success "in a few observations, and an extract from the theatrical advertisements of the time."[50] Like the letter in "Serenade" and the newspaper accounts in "Mystery" and "Revenge," Shaw is still using outside authorities to bolster his own narrative. The most effective passages in "Theatre" are two dialogue exchanges, the first between an assistant manager and a wealthy patron and the second between the same assistant and Bridges. Both are lively, witty debates which identify the state of the theater while illustrating Bridges's intentions. As in "Doll's House," Shaw writes most persuasively when not bound by the conventions of narrative.

Within this satire Shaw reveals his own idea for a future play. Bridges's Theater announces that Algernon Swinburne is rewriting Henry VI, especially "the Joan of Arc scenes from the point of view, not only of what Shakespeare undoubtedly ought to have written, but of the *entente cordiale* between this country and France."[51] In a 1913 letter to the actress Mrs. Patrick Campbell, GBS expressed his indignation at Shakespeare's treament of The Maid in Henry VI while insisting he would eventually write his own version of events.[52] This comment has usually been accepted as the genesis of Shaw's famous Saint Joan (1923), even though the author had expressed interest in a play on that subject the same year "Theatre" was published.[53] Two letters to actress Eleanor Robson from August and December 1905 show GBS apologizing for not insisting that she play the lead in Major Barbara. As a token of respect, Shaw explains that he has urged George Tyler, the American theatrical manager, to encourage a prominent poet to write "a Joan of Arc play" as a vehicle to display her talents.[54] Thus Shaw may have formed his characterization of the 1923 Saint Joan from ideas first publicly expressed in "Theater of the Future," eighteen years earlier.

Shaw aired his political views through the publication of another satire, "Death of An Old Revolutionary Hero," in The Clarion of March 1905. This story supports a long-held Shavian political dictum, the idea that "compromise was the law of political life."[55] "Death" satirizes the utopian zealotry of Shaw's Fabian peers in a style that recalls "Shutting Up." Shaw must have realized that this treatment of the theme is more effective, for he included "Death" in Short Stories, Scraps and Shavings. He uses himself as first-person narrator to demonstrate that principles of absolute morality impede all attempts at reform.

"Death" is effective satire because Shaw limits himself to a single purpose and creates a dominant character imbued with Falstaffian bluster.

In Joe Budgett, Shaw presents a mock-heroic figure who possesses "the lion-like mane of white hair [and] the firmly closed mouth with its muscles developed by half a century of public speaking" which typify a demagogue.[56] Joe entrusted "all his business affairs to his faithful wife" while he spent his time speaking for political causes.[57] He had claimed to be on his deathbed since the age of seventy-five, never rising from his bed "except to address a meeting or attend a Socialist Congress."[58] "Death" makes much use of dialogue when Shaw recalls goading the old worker into a fury by breaking his clock after an argument over the futility of Budgett's methods. These observations work against the protagonist because readers share the author's perspective—that Budgett is a meddling old fool who creates more problems than he solves. Shaw has learned from his mistakes in "The Brand of Cain" and "Revenge." The tongue-in-cheek exposé of "Death" displays marvelous control of the narrative.

GBS next turned to short fiction in the summer of 1907 to satirize traditional Christian perceptions of the afterlife in "Aerial Football: The New Game." The story is notable for its similarity to a tale by Mark Twain. Shaw had been introduced to the author of *Huckleberry Finn* by Archibald Henderson on 3 July 1907. The two writers commended each other's works in general terms, but spoke of no specific projects either might have had in progress. When GBS published "Aerial Football" in *The Neolith* issue of November 1907, Twain noted its similarity to his own "The Late Rev. Sam Jones's Reception in Heaven," an unpublished short story he had written in 1890.[59] Shaw dated his story 31 July 1907 when he republished it in *Short Stories, Scraps and Shavings*, only adding to the critical conjecture of why the stories are so similar.

"Aerial Football" also possesses an interesting publishing history. In addition to its British publication in *The Neolith,* the story was presented in *Collier's Weekly* on 23 November 1907. When the editors of *Collier's* subsequently presented GBS with a $1,000 prize for writing the best story for that quarter, he angrily responded in a February 1908 letter, calling the check an insult. "If it was the best," argued the irate writer, "what right have they to stamp their own contributors publicly as inferior when they have taken steps to secure the result beforehand by paying a special price to a special writer?"[60] GBS returned the check and retained his integrity.

"Aerial Football" possesses the cyclical unity of a framed story, contrasting the violence and confusion of earth with the serenity of heaven. The tale begins with a carriage accident that results in the deaths of the two protagonists. Shaw solves the problem that had plagued "A County Councillor's Dream"—the abrupt shift from Victorian London to the world of the future—by paralleling the death of Mrs. Hairns with that of a bishop, contrasting the fear of the charwoman with the arrogance of the churchman. Quickly paced dialogue between a medical student, cab driver, and footman explains the accident to readers before focusing the narrative on Mrs. Hairns by locating her at "the foot of a hill with a city on the top."[61] The remaining action takes place at the gates of heaven until both the bishop and Mrs. Hairns have entered the city. Stanley Weintraub argues that the incident of the horse "Chipper," who carries Mrs. Hairns to the gates of heaven because he recalled an unconscious act of kindness she had done him, may have furnished GBS with the idea of the ruffian soldier in *Saint Joan*'s epilogue. In the play the infantry-man receives an annual holiday in heaven for "an impulsive act that had had no moral meaning to him."[62] The bishop enters heaven only after he has shed the pompous social conventions of earth by playing aerial foot-ball with the angels. Once both characters' fates have been resolved, Shaw uses the voice of the medical student to pull his audience back to earth and to the reality of death.

Shaw's last significant short story, "The Emperor and the Little Girl," grew out of the tragedy of World War I. He had written the tale to be part of a gift book that would raise funds for a Belgian children's charity, the Vestiare Marie Josef. Instead, when the woman "who had solicited the story was reluctant to bury it in a gift book, [she] sold it instead—for the charity—to Mrs. Whitelaw Reid of the *New York Tribune* for £400."[63] The story appeared in that paper's Sunday magazine on 22 October 1916 and was later reprinted in *Short Stories, Scraps and Shavings*. GBS once categorized "The Emperor" as " 'a children's story,' [although] it was a hyper adult story."[64] It depicts a meeting between the German Kaiser and a little girl in the midst of no-man's-land between the lines. Shaw exhibits firm control of the narrative voice in a work that speaks out against both German imperialism and English war fervor.

Shaw's clever manipulation of the narrative displays the subtlety he had striven toward in "The Brand of Cain." The detached third-person narrator provides a brief introductory passage about "no man's land" before limiting himself to the perspective of the Kaiser. Shaw's simple, direct explanation of the soldier's risks—"If they shewed their heads for a moment: bang! they were shot"—is both startling and disturbing.[65] This voice allows the author to translate the Kaiser's oft-repeated com-ment, "Ich habe es nicht gewollt" as " 'It is not my doing' . . . just what you say when you are scolded for doing something wrong."[66] Such direct moralizing is effective within the context of the story because it is unex-pected. Shaw has found a method of delivering editorial comments and guiding his readers' interpretations without appearing too obvious.

GBS uses three scenes of dialogue to divide the meeting between the Kaiser and the little girl into an introduction, a climax, and a conclusion. The opening dialogue articulates the actual horrors of war. The little girl describes the bombing of her father's farm by German, French, and English armies, for Shaw views war as a devastator which produces no heroes. The Kaiser objects to the little girl calling a German soldier "Boche," yet later claims that Englishmen never tell the truth. His reactions demonstrate that national chauvinism and prejudice are the natural by-products of war.[67] The climax occurs when a shell bursts, freeing the little girl and a number of soldiers from a violent world. The nominally agnostic GBS would often use the motivation of an afterlife when he wanted to lambaste materialists of his own age. The concluding sequence consists of a brief exchange between the Kaiser and his guards. In his sorrow and anger at having lost contact with the little girl, the Emperor swears at his soldiers. Among themselves, they mutter that he must be drunk. Shaw refrains from commenting on these remarks, allowing the readers to reach their own conclusions. This tactic deflates any final pretensions to grandeur that the Kaiser may have possessed. We leave the story seeing a broken old man, rendered far more pathetic than Joe Budgett.

"The Emperor and the Little Girl" anticipates techniques that Shaw would soon refine for *Saint Joan*. The careful, deliberate introduction plants the the idea that the little girl's appearance may be a dream-vision. The narrator refers to those who might "fancy that wonderful kinds of people will come out of the blacknesses and have adventures with them,"[68] an incongruous statement about "no man's land" unless it is meant to foreshadow the child's appearance. Like Saint Joan, the little girl is an innocent who speaks wisdom that comes from the heart. After being hit by the shell, she becomes a disembodied voice, much like that used for the epilogue to the play. In the drama's final sequence, Joan's disembodied voice brings self-wisdom to another tired, old ruler (King Charles VII). Just as the little girl is set free by the shell which kills her, Joan of the play is set free by the fire. Shaw had learned many lessons from his short fiction, adapting his earlier material to a dramatic medium.

Bernard Shaw's short fiction shows a young author working to master the craft of writing. The early works display a writer struggling with narrative voice. His ear for detail allowed him to create vivid characters, like the Irish ferryman in "Revenge" or Mozart's ghost in "Mystery," but the narrative within these stories suffers from either the wild exaggeration of Zeno Legge or the lack of involvement of the nondescript newspaperman. Shaw's own newspaper criticism for both the *Dramatic Review* and *The Star* displays his compulsion to fictionalize actual events. This drive led to the creation of self-characterizations like Corno di Bassetto and political arguments in the guise of stories like "Shutting Up An Individualist." "Still After the Doll's House" gave Shaw the confidence to complete *Widowers' Houses* and produce *Mrs Warren's Profession,* secure in his ability to create powerful dramatic scenes. After 1890, GBS resorted to short fiction only when he wanted to reach a particular audience, as in "The Theatre of the Future," or depict events that could not be dramatized, as in "Aerial Football." Shaw's short fiction marks an important early chapter in the development of a great playwright.

Notes

1. Bernard Shaw, *Collected Letters, 1874–1897,* ed. Dan H. Laurence (New York: Dodd, Mead, 1965), p. 21. Apparently Shaw added an *e* to *Legge* when composing the short story.
2. Bernard Shaw, *The Diaries, 1885–1897,* ed. Stanley Weintraub (University Park: The Pennsylvania State University Press, 1986), 1:58.
3. Dan H. Laurence, *Bernard Shaw: A Bibliography* (Oxford: Clarendon Press, 1983), 1:150.
4. Bernard Shaw, *The Collected Works, Volume VI: Short Stories, Scraps and Shavings* (New York: William H. Wise, 1932), p. 38.
5. *Collected Letters,* p. 29.
6. Ibid., p. 30.
7. St. John Ervine, *Bernard Shaw: His Life, Work, and Friends* (New York: William Morrow, 1956), p. 71.
8. *Collected Works,* VI:43.
9. Jerald E. Bringle, "The St. James's Hall Mystery," *Bulletin of Research in the Humanities 3 (1978), 276.*
10. Ibid., p. 277.
11. Ibid., p. 278.
12. Stanley Weintraub, *The Unexpected Shaw: Biographical Approaches to G. B. S. and His Work* (New York: Frederick Ungar, 1982), p. 30.
13. *The Diaries,* 1:287.
14. Ibid.
15. Ibid., p. 566.
16. *The Collected Works,* VI:95
17. Stanley Weintraub, "Genesis of a Play: Two Early Approaches to *Man and Superman,*" in *Shaw: Seven Critical Essays,* ed. Norman Rosenblood (Toronto: University of Toronto Press, 1971), p. 26.
18. Margot Peters, "As Lonely as God," *The Genius of Shaw,* ed. Michael Holroyd (New York: Holt, Rinehart and Winston, 1979), p. 190.
19. *The Collected Works,* VI:102.
20. Weintraub, "Genesis of a Play," p. 29.
21. *The Collected Works,* VI:42.

22. *The Diaries*, 1:53.

23. *London Music In 1888–89 As Heard by Corno di Bassetto (Later known as Bernard Shaw) With Some Further Autobiographical Particulars* (London: Constable, 1937), p. 63.

24. Ervine, p. 72.

25. See, for example, "Agathe Backer-Gröndahl" (13 July 1889), *London Music*, p. 161.

26. *The Diaries*.1:32.

27. *The Collected Works*, VI:205.

28. Ibid., p. 202.

29. Ibid.

30. B. C. Rosset, *Shaw of Dublin: The Formative Years* (University Park: The Pennsylvania State University Press, 1964), p. 12.

31. *The Collected Works*, VI:205.

32. Ibid., p. 207.

33. *The Diaries*, 1:249.

34. Bernard Shaw, "A 'Redbarn Wash' Adventure," *The Shaw Review* 23 (January 1980), 28.

35. Ibid.

36. *The Diaries*, 1:459.

37. Ibid., p. 9.

38. Bernard Shaw, "Two Pieces from *The Star*," *SHAW: The Annual of Bernard Shaw Studies* 6 (1986), 161. This story was never collected by Shaw and is not cited in the Laurence *Bibliography*.

39. Ibid., p. 164.

40. Ervine, p. 73.

41. *Collected Letters*, p. 239.

42. J. L. Wisenthal, ed., *Shaw and Ibsen: Bernard Shaw's* The Quintessence of Ibsenism *and Related Writings* (Toronto: University of Toronto Press, 1979), p. 155.

43. *The Diaries*, 1:577.

44. Ibid., p. 578.

45. Wisenthal, p. 8.

46. *Collected Letters*, p. 241.

47. *The Collected Works*, VI:132.

48. *London Music* (26 July 1889), p. 171.

49. *The Collected Works*, VI:58.

50. Ibid., p. 76.

51. Ibid., p. 77.

52. Alan Dent, ed., *Bernard Shaw and Mrs. Patrick Campbell: Their Correspondence* (London: Victor Gollancz, 1952), p. 163.

53. Weintraub, *The Unexpected Shaw*, p. 185.

54. Bernard Shaw, *Collected Letters, 1898–1910*, ed. Dan H. Laurence (New York: Dodd, Mead, 1972), pp. 550, 587.

55. J. Percy Smith, *The Unrepentant Pilgrim: A Study of the Development of Bernard Shaw* (Boston: Houghton Mifflin, 1965), p. 116.

56. *The Collected Works*, VI:192.

57. Ibid.

58. Ibid., p. 191.

59. Rodelle Weintraub, " 'Mental Telegraphy?': Mark Twain on G. B. S.," *The Shaw Review* 17 (May 1974), 68.

60. *Collected Letters, 1898–1910*, p. 758.

61. *The Collected Works*, VI:4.

62. Weintraub, *The Unexpected Shaw*, p. 185.

63. Stanley Weintraub, *Journey to Heartbreak: The Crucible Years of Bernard Shaw 1914–1918* (New York: Weybright and Talley, 1971), p. 204.

64. Ibid.

65. *The Collected Works*, VI:15.

66. Ibid., p. 17.

67. Ibid., p. 18.

68. Ibid., p. 15.

Lee W. Saperstein

THE ORKNEYS REVISITED

Some months before a family trip to Scotland, the Isle of Skye, and the Orkneys, I mentioned to a colleague our intended itinerary. He, being most interested in the works of Bernard Shaw, responded a few days later with a note and an enclosure: "You may be interested in reading GBS's description of travelling in Scotland and the Orkneys." No sooner was it read than the work became an essential part of the plans of our trip.

A good trip requires a good guide. The anticipation is heightened by reading about the potential places to visit, to stay, and at which to eat. For me, the realization comes as a pleasure and not as a disappointment when the planning is properly guided. Hence, I was incredibly grateful for Shaw's unpublished essay, because it gave me an insight to the Orkneys different from that of the *Blue Guide to Scotland*.[1] The *Blue Guide* is invaluable, but it contains no human asides as Shaw's essay does.

After returning from our trip, my colleague asked me how the essay, which Shaw wrote in August 1925 for private circulation to members of the Royal Automobile Club, stood the test of time. "Remarkably well," was my reply, both because Shaw was extremely percipient and, just as important, because in many ways time had stood still on the Orkneys. His description, mainly of items of interest to motorists—hotels, roads, ferries, principal sights—remained valid. Save one, none of his items had been bulldozed or paved over or remade into a cubist box. The only thing missing is "a stupendous smell of herrings, and a pall of smoke from the steam trawlers and colliers in the harbor," with which he declared that Wick (a town on the east coast of Scotland, seventeen miles south of John o'Groats) is "afflicted." The old fishing harbors now serve mainly pleasure craft. Indulge me, I told my colleague, and I will set my thoughts on paper.

Since I am a better traveler than I am a literary analyst, I can describe only in the most naïve of terms Shaw's essay, which was on seven and one-half double-spaced typewritten pages. It begins by describing the approach to the north Scottish port of Thurso in one page, takes three pages to describe the Orkneys, three more for the Shetlands, and then wraps it up with some generalizations on climate ("mild, . . . and . . . markedly southern in character") and clothing, the traveling season, the possible ordeal of traveling by ferry, the opportunities for naturalists and sportsmen, respectively, to observe or to catch wildlife, and the general demeanor of the people.

Times change and so does the ferry, which is now capable of carrying tourist coaches (more on the ferry anon). The Orkneys thrive on tourism; the incidence of resettling by people seeking the tranquil life has now reached a volume that causes native Orcadians to fear for their heritage. Nonetheless, Shaw remains correct; the people were "pleasant," as well as candid and surprisingly free from hostility. Given the history of domination by the Vikings and the Danes and then the Scots (even today, the antiquities in the museums in the Orkneys are often reproductions of those that have been acquired by the Museum of Antiquities in Edinburgh), I wondered whether there would not be resentment of outsiders that is often found in other island paradises. While the newspaper may carry stories on Orcadian desire for limited self-determination—a devolution from both Scotland and the United Kingdom—nothing but open pleasantness was directed to me and my family.

Just as Shaw wrote, "The crossing to Orkney is made from Thurso, a quiet, easygoing, rather attractive seaside town, with the hotels of about the same modest pretensions." Thurso is on the northern coast of Scotland, between Dunnet Head, a high peninsula of cliffs, affording marvelous sea views to the Orkneys (but only when it is clear, which is rare). It is the truly northernmost point of island Britain, being a mile or two further north than John o'Groats, and Dounreay ("experimental industrial nuclear power research centre, begun in 1954. There is a visitor exhibition." *Blue Guide to Scotland,* p. 373). We approached Thurso from the west and departed it to the south so that our journey picked up Shaw's recommendations at the end. Indeed, we have almost no recollection of arriving at the ferry because we were so late. I had overestimated the speed that can be maintained on northern Scottish roads and, consequently, arrived at the ferry with less than ten minutes to spare. Anyone who expects to travel faster than thirty miles per hour average is mad; we averaged forty-two. As Shaw pointed out, "The best way to Thurso is by the road that goes to the left out of the main north road in the middle of Lybster [from A9 take A895]. It passes a fine set of standing stones by a lake. The coast road by John o'Groats is tedious."

We can agree with Shaw that "the coast road by John o'Groats is tedious," but John o'Groats's notoriety as the destination of most cross-Britain endurance car races caused us to visit it anyway. Shaw's observation of "an uninteresting hotel" is doubly valid today. However, we did note the existence of a passenger—no cars—ferry service to the Orkneys. Not having taken it, I can make no comment on its reliability. On the way south, we stayed at the Portland Arms Hotel in Lybster, where we dined on fresh salmon and drank some local whiskey (*Old Pulteney*, named for a district in Wick, and *Clynelish*, a malt distilled in Brora originally by the Duke of Sutherland of Dunrobin Castle, and which I found most palatable). We stayed in a room, described by the landlord "as the one with the bed." Presumably, all rooms had a bed of some sort, but this one was a huge canopied affair that was so high off the floor that one's feet dangled when sitting on the edge of the mattress.

> The Orkney mail boat does not ply from Thurso town, but from a little port a mile and a half to the north in Thurso bay, named Scrabster. It is a small but powerful boat, with a first class cabin and separate ladies' cabin, not spacious, but enough for about twenty passengers at full length. . . . The charges are high. . . . Therefore it depends on the length of stay whether it is worth while to take the car across or leave it in Thurso and hire on the islands. . . .

> The voyage is not always rough; but even on calm days certain moments (when the tide races clash) are trying for bad sailors. Inside Scapa Flow it is smoother.

Shaw further tells us that the boat to the Orkneys is named the *St. Ola* and then proceeds for almost a page to give details of route and schedule and whether or not cars could be driven onto the boat or would have to be lifted by slings. Apparently drive-on, drive-off could occur only at high tide. In Shaw's day, the boat went to the east of the island of Hoy, past Flotta Island, and docked first at the southern port of Kirkwall (Scapa Pier), where it discharged its cars, and then went on to Stromness, which was its overnight terminus.

The sight of a modern blue P & O ferry sitting at Scrabster ("a little port a mile and a half to the north in Thurso Bay") Pier made us wonder about the aptness of Shaw's description. We should never have feared. Strip away the mechanical trappings and we had a boat, still named the *St. Ola*, that, above its vehicle decks, had an enclosed passenger deck with a forward reading and lounging cabin—the equivalent of the ladies cabin—and an aft lounge with bar and snack cafeteria, and above that an open observation deck. It is easy to pick out Shaw's bad sailors; they are the white, pudgy ones who are stoking up at the snack bar while the ferry is still and moored. Filling those white plastic bags that were to be found in reserve everywhere takes a lot of energy; it is best to be prepared.

Perhaps it is because Flotta is now the terminus for the undersea oil pipeline from the off-shore wells in the North Sea; perhaps it is because the south Kirkwall harbor cannot accommodate the *St. Ola;* or perhaps, simply, today's ferry is stable enough to go directly to Stromness on a shorter route. For whatever reason, the ferry goes to the west of Hoy on its way to the main island of the Orkneys, named, appropriately enough, Mainland. Most of the journey is spent steaming past the magnificent cliffs of Hoy. The red sandstone must carry a vertical plane of weakness in it for the cliffs are sheer. Where the sea has worn through the base of a promontory, there are dramatic sea caves. The "Old Man of Hoy" is one such promontory where the sea cave has collapsed, leaving an isolated stack of stone standing alone 450 feet into the air. Two miles farther north, as the ferry comes about to the east, it passes St. John's Head, which, at 1,140 feet, is the highest sheer cliff in Britain. Thence, we entered the famed Scapa Flow, haven for the British Fleet in two World Wars, where ships of the vanquished Kaiser's navy lie at the bottom, scuttled by their officers in 1919 rather than turned over to British sovereignty. Scapa Flow is also where a German U-boat sneaked through supposedly impregnable defenses to sink the *H.M.S. Royal Oak* in 1939, and where Britain's oil wealth now passes on its way to market. We entered from the western end of Scapa Flow, close to Stromness, which has an adequate drive-on, drive-off pier, rather than from the south and east as had Shaw.

The modern sailing schedule varies by the day of the week, with anywhere from one to three sailings a day. The prospective traveler should book well in advance, particularly if taking a car, through P & O Ferries, Orkney and Shetland Services, New Pier, Stromness. As in Shaw's day, it remains expensive. There is now scheduled air service to Kirkwall.

Both Kirkwall hotels described by Shaw now have lifts, yet little else appears to have changed. The Kirkwall Hotel, where we stayed, was truly "most comfortable" and even had showers that worked well (a rarity for modern Britain). We peeked into the Stromness Hotel, and the lobby, as described by Shaw, was dark. The public bar is on the ground floor; the dining room and reception are on the first floor.

In discussing the Pentland Hotel in Thurso, which is still there, Shaw describes the service as mixed: "The attendance is unsophisticated and to some extent idiotic; but the atmosphere is obliging and homely; and one is happy enough there." I wouldn't change a word in switching the description to the Kirkwall Hotel.

We accepted Shaw's enthusiasm for the Kirkwall Hotel and stayed there. We also hired a car from the hotel for a day of car-borne sightseeing; Kirkwall itself is easily encountered on foot from the hotel. I would like to compare notes with someone who has stayed in Stromness. That town is prettily sited; it is close to many of Mainland's ancient monuments; and it now has "internal attractions." A local museum is devoted to Stromness's natural life, its maritime history, and, particularly, the history of the German Fleet—its scuttling and then subsequent salvage for scrap metal. There are taxis and rental cars on the quay adjacent to the ferry pier; the bus for Kirkwall leaves from in front of the Stromness Hotel, which faces the P & O Ferries' waiting room, the taxi rank, and the harbor.

The only sour note about the Kirkwall Hotel was the state of its cuisine. Thank Heavens for Baikie's Restaurant in Finstown, which was able to serve broiled salmon that was succulent rather than sere and desiccated. On the other hand, our waitress in the hotel was worth the journey. "Unsophisticated and to some extent idiotic," she chattered to us gaily, indeed almost in Gaelic, as she served us our barely edible meal, fussed over the positioning of the third-rate cutlery as if it were solid silver, and never failed to make the pleasantries associated with fine eating. Her enthusiasm for life, the Orkneys, and the success of not only our holiday but also that of all those dining more than overcame her consumptive cough and the state of the food.

In reserving our rooms at Kirkwall, I had developed a sense of warmth for "L. Daly, Partner," because of an exchange of correspondence which, in the most straightforward but friendly fashion, informed me of ferry times, the availability of the rental car, and the existence of the public bus from Stromness to Kirkwall. For the sake of propriety, I quickly rearranged my thoughts when I discovered that my correspondent was the attentive young lady behind the desk. When I did meet Mr. Daly, he told me, "I sign lots of letters." As I worked my way diligently through each of the Orcadian whiskies (*Highland Park,* distilled in Kirkwall, may be available in the United States), Daly began to tell me of life in the Orkneys, of the concern for overdevelopment and for oversettling by well-to-do dropouts escaping the pressures of the modern commerical world. Yet he was not an Orcadian but a mainland Scot, albeit Gaelic speaking, who also had sought a refuge in the Orkneys. Clearly, his professional interest, and the hotel's profit center, was in its two bars—the Public, entered from the street by a side entrance, and the hotel's lounge. Thin and spare as he was,

I could understand his lack of interest in the quality of food. He won our hearts, however, when he provided the guests of the hotel with live entertainment by the Orkney's Strathspey and Reel Society. Approximately a dozen violins, a bass, a concertina, an electric keyboard, and the occasional vocalist filled one end of the hotel lounge and regaled us with Scottish country music, interspersed with introductions and the rare joke. Shaw's initial directions plus "L. Daly's" warmth had steered us right.

> Kirkwall, a cathedral city, is much more interesting than Stromness, and much larger; but Stromness is more convenient for expeditions by motor boat to Hoy, and commands Scapa Flow, on which Kirkwall turns its back. Kirkwall has excellent shops, one of the finest cathedrals in Britain, a delightful situation, and is a quite comfortable and pleasant place for a halt of a week. Much more so, for instance, than Inverness. The pictures of ancient lanes, too narrow for wheeled traffic, give as absurd a notion of it as photographs of the old London city courts give of Fleet Street. . . . With a car the whole main island can be explored lazily in two or three days.

All this description of Kirkwall is true today. My family all bought sweaters (hand loomed with occasional hand knitting for decorated parts) for very modest prices from Annette's, one of the "excellent" shops, which is devoted solely to knitwear. The cathedral, dedicated to the martyred St. Magnus, is built of the local reddish sandstone in a mostly Norman style. Small intricate carvings on the interior fabric are reproduced as silver jewelry available in another of the "excellent" shops. Kirkwall's main shopping street (Bridge Street leading to Albert Street, which becomes Broad Street) appears to go inland from Harbour Street, on which stands the Kirkwall Hotel. An excellent pamphlet, "Kirkwall Heritage Guide," published by the Kirkwall and St. Ola Community Council (available from the Tourist Office on Broad Street), showed how the infilling of the Peerie Sea, the ancient natural harbor, had caused this street to become removed from the harbor. A day or more could be spent examining the twenty-one sites listed in the Heritage Guide. Albert Street is narrow and makes no distinction between sidewalk and roadway. Although traffic is restricted, the occasional car does move slowly along it. Hence Shaw's allegation that a picture can give an "absurd notion" is both right and wrong. He is right in that the automobile is well accommodated by spacious parking lots only one-half block from Albert Street; thus a photograph of this street could convey the notion that all streets are medievally narrow. He is wrong in that Albert Street and the main street in Stromness really do exist, are narrow, do convey a sense of the medieval past, and are very much a part of the reality of the Orkneys.

We stayed in Kirkwall for two nights. Shaw's "halt of a week" may be too long for the casual tourist and far too brief for a serious student of the islands. Although Kirkwall has several restaurants, only the saving Baikie's was open on Sunday night. It was obvious, from the coming and going of several motor launches, that it was relatively easy to reach other islands of the Orkneys. Several passengers sensibly carried bicycles onto the launches. The cabins were closed and the boats small compared with the *St. Ola*. With the Orcadian penchant for smoking, the bad sailor could have a rough time on these boats.

We spent a day crisscrossing Mainland, going from Skara Brae, a stone-age village, to the Brough of Birsay, on which sits a Viking village, to the late sixteenth-century Earl's Palace at Birsay, to the World War II fortifications of the Churchill Causeways, which were built to link South Ronaldsay with Mainland and to close off the route taken by the U-boat that sunk the *Royal Oak*. We also stopped at two ceremonial stone circles, Ring of Brodgar and Stones of Stenness, and at two stone-age tombs, Maes Howe and Unstan Chambered Tombs. The number of stops was made possible by the impatience of my children to be off to the next site and the length of the July day in the far north. Shaw makes no mention of these antiquities, which is a shame, for I would like to have his impressions. However, his essay was written for the motorist of the Royal Automobile Club and, I presume, was directed to problems of the trip and not intended as another guidebook. For myself, the *Blue Guide,* the "Heritage Guide," and *The Ancient Monuments of Orkney,*[2] along with the Ordnance Survey map of "Orkney—Mainland" (Sheet 6, 1:50,000, 1976), gave all I could digest or that we could possibly visit.

Shaw goes on to say that "Shetland is nine hours by sea from Orkney." Alas for a daughter whose very soul hungered for a Shetland sweater, bought in the Shetlands, this is no longer so. The ferries for Lerwick, the main city of the Shetlands, leave from Aberdeen. So as we left Stromness and picked up our car at Scrabster, even though we were visiting places described by Shaw—Thurso, Dunnet Head, Wick, and Lybster—I felt that we were parting, for he was on his way to the Shetland Islands.

My remembrances of the Orkneys are plentiful. Certainly there are the books, maps, and indeed photographs, but there is also the realization that every time I have broiled salmon I will see the waitress at Baikie's trotting in her efforts to fetch our food. A glass of whiskey, particularly if strongly flavored like *Highland Park,* will bring me a conversation with L. Daly, Partner, or the anonymous landlord at the Portland Arms. A piece of shortbread instantly returns me to the enameled pale green-blue and somewhat shabby interior of the tea shop on Albert Street, where tea for four and a plate of baked goodies perched precipitously on the smallest table it has ever been my pleasure to try to put my knees under. Shaw's guide created the anticipation. The timelessness of the Orkneys made the realization and the remembrance true to his description and thus pleasurable.

Notes

1. John Tomes, ed. *Blue Guide to Scotland,* 8th edition (London: Ernest Benn, 1980), 451 pp., 16 maps.
2. Anna and Graham Ritchie, *The Ancient Monuments of Orkney* (Edinburgh: Her Majesty's Stationery Office, 1978), 82 pp., 1 map.

Bernard Shaw

ORKNEY AND SHETLAND

PRIVATE. For [Royal Automobile] Club members only

—Orkney and Shetland—

—Information for Motorists—

The crossing to Orkney is made from Thurso, a quiet, easygoing, rather attractive seaside town, with the hotels of about the same modest pretensions. The Pentland Hotel is comfortably kept in a domestic way by the two Miss Harpers. The food is not contract food. It is marketed personally by one of the ladies, who is also a first rate plain cook. The attendance is unsophisticated and to some extent idiotic; but the atmosphere is obliging and homely; and one is happy enough there. The garage, two or three minutes drive away, has lock-up cages. There is a motor omnibus and a car for hire. Charges very reasonable.

The best way to Thurso is by the road that goes to the left out of the main north road in the middle of Lybster. It passes a fine set of standing stones by a lake. The coast road by John o'Groats is tedious. There is nothing at John's but an uninteresting hotel, with a common table for lunch. Dunnet Head and John o'Groats can be explored by excursion from Thurso, also Wick, which has a quite important hotel, the Station, but is afflicted with a stupendous smell of herrings, and a pall of smoke from the steam trawlers and colliers in the harbor. The harbor, however, is a sight worth seeing. At the first milestone south of Wick a lane goes round seaward to an old castle, the situation of which is as fascinating as that of Dunnottar. They call it the Old Man of Wick. It is possible to get from Wick to Orkney by sea; but this hardly concerns motorists. Wick is "dry" in the American sense: that is, compulsorily teetotal.

The Orkney mail boat does not ply from Thurso town, but from a little port a mile and a half to the north in Thurso bay, named Scrabster. It is a small but powerful boat, with a first class cabin and separate ladies' cabin, not spacious, but enough for about twenty passengers at full length. When the tide serves it can take, at a pinch, three small open cars, or a big and a little one. But there are periods of five days together during which the captain will not book full sized closed cars, as they are too heavy for the slings. When slinging has to be resorted to instead of driving on and off, disc wheels are said to be objectionable. Everything is at owner's risk; and the charges are high: £4-6-0 for cars over one ton up to two each way. Therefore it depends on the length of stay whether it is worth while to take the car across or leave it in Thurso and hire on the islands.

The distance to Orkney as the crow flies seems nothing; but the tides in the Pentland Firth are so fierce that the boat has to make a circuit of thirty miles (often bringing it within a stone's throw of Dunnet Head, by the way) to get round Hoy into Scapa Flow. It takes three hours to get to Scapa pier for Kirkwall (2 miles off), and another hour to get to its final destination, Stromness. Cars for Stromness are landed at Scapa, and do the rest of the journey by road, fifteen miles fast driving. The roads are much better than one expects.

The voyage is not always rough; but even on calm days certain moments (when the tide races clash) are trying for bad sailors. Inside Scapa Flow it is smoother.

The boat, called the St Ola (1862), Captain Swanson, starts from Stromness every morning at 8; leaves Scapa where cars embark at 9.45; and is due at Scrabster at 12.30. It leaves Scrabster for Scapa and Stromness daily at 2, unless the mails, for which it must wait, are late: but if the mails come earlier it does not undertake to wait even until 2. Cars are told to be at the pier at 12.30; and previous booking is much insisted on; but unless a full complement of booked cars turn up there is a chance up to the last moment, as they are a happy-go-lucky folk in these latitudes. Owners of full sized cars, which are beyond the lifting capacity of the slings, must remember, however, that unless they ascertain from the captain of the St Ola when the tide will enable him to bring them back, they may find themselves marooned on Orkney for five days.

The St Ola will not take even a booked car in very bad weather; and in that case the car will have to wait for the next unbooked turn.

Cars may get a bit scratched. The arrangements are much more primitive than at Folkstone.

The hotels in Orkney are run very capably by Mr John Mackay, Senior, of Stromness. Stromness is very fascinating as you approach it by sea; but it has no internal attractions whatever. The hotel is, according to Orkney standards, important: local publications describe it as magnificent. It looks as if it had been lifted out of the middle of Birmingham; and except that it is profusely decorated with stuffed sea-birds, its inside carries out the impression. No expense has been spared on it; but parts of it are ill planned as to daylight; and it is very much the sort of hotel that was considered first rate in 1850 on the mainland, except that there is electric light. There is no lift. The food and plain cooking are good, and the attendance friendly and sufficient.

The Kirkwall Hotel, built in 1890, is on the quay overlooking the harbor to the north, 40 minutes walk from Scapa pier, where the St Ola touches (Kirkwall has two sea fronts being on an isthmus). The boats for Lerwick in Shetland sail from the harbor. The hotel is a big one for Orkney, pleasanter and better planned inside than the Stromness Hotel, and equally efficient. It needs only a lift to be one of the most comfortable hotels in the extreme north.

The Standing Stones Hotel (same proprietor) is a new hotel for fishermen on the Stennis lake between Kirkwall and Stromness. It is a bungalow with two storeys, and looks very neat. It is close to the Meashowe and the Standing Stones.

Kirkwall, a cathedral city, is much more interesting than Stromness, and much larger; but Stromness is more convenient for expeditions by motor boat to Hoy, and commands Scapa Flow, on which Kirkwall turns its back. Kirkwall has excellent shops, one of the finest cathedrals in Britain, a delightful situation, and is a quite comfortable and pleasant place for a halt of a week. Much more so, for instance, than Inverness. The pictures of ancient lanes, too narrow for wheeled traffic, give as absurd a notion of it as photographs of the old London city courts give of Fleet Street.

There are no signposts on the island, and no hotels or refreshment houses except as aforesaid at Stromness, Stennis, and Kirkwall. With a car the whole main island can be explored lazily in two or three days.

—SHETLAND—

Shetland is nine hours by sea from Orkney in fine weather (this is the minimum); and the first thing to be grasped in making arrangements is that it is not connected by a daily service, like Orkney. A letter posted in London to catch the night express will be delivered regularly in Stromness or Kirkwall 50 hours later: but it may have to wait there a day or two for a boat to take it to Shetland. A sailing list must be obtained from the North of Scotland and Orkney and Shetland Steam Navigation Company, Matthew's Quay, Aberdeen (James McCallum, Manager). There are two routes, the east from Kirkwall to Lerwick, the west from

Stromness to Scalloway. There are three boats a week, at the beginning and end, between Kirkwall and Lerwick, and one in the middle between Stromness and Scalloway. The biggest and newest boat is the St Magnus; but it is dangerously top heavy in bad weather for want of sufficient cargo. The St Ninon is dirty; the Sonnival is only a steam yacht; and the St Rognvald is, on the whole, the best boat.

The regular hotel accommodation in Shetland, recklessly described by the North of Scotland Steam Navigation Co in its sailing lists, and by the hotel proprietors in their booklets, as "first rate," is very poor indeed. The Company's hotel, the St Magnus at Hillswick, 36 miles from Lerwick, is a seaside two-storeyed bungalow built in 1900 for the purpose, and seems to be the only hotel that members of the R.A.C. would consider modern and civilized. It is a season hotel, crowded, and not particularly clean.

As the tourist approaches the jetty at Lerwick from the sea he sees to his right an imposing architectural facade inscribed in golden letters Grand Hotel, and to his left what looks like a dismal old warehouse inscribed in black and white *Queen's Hotel*. But the architectural facade belongs to a block of shops on the upper floors of which a hotel has established itself; and the old warehouse is the ancient principal hotel of the town. In spite of its express declaration to the contrary, it is right down on the smoking funnels of the multitude of trawlers which spend their week ends in the harbor, and is serenaded by screaming seagulls and honking steamer sirens, no place in Lerwick old town (and the Queen's Hotel is in the thick of the old town) being out of their range. The house is a well designed and cheerfully lighted big private house built probably in the XVIII century; and the proprietor (Mr Sherman) and his wife are most friendly; but the place is old and incurably musty; the cooking is plain to the verge of ugliness and is clearly not done in aluminum saucepans; the bedding is penitential; and the sanitary accommodation, though quite clean, is on the private house scale. However, this last drawback is common to all old hotels in the north of Scotland, dating as they do from the period when bathrooms were luxuries, and indoor closets questionable innovations unused by ladies. Such a hotel as the Liverpool Adelphi, in the modern part of which every bedroom has its own separate bath and lavatory etc., would seem an inconceivable extravagance in Scotland.

At Scalloway, the port for the west coast steamers, there are two hotels: one poor and the other poorer, which is a pity, as Scalloway is quiet and very pretty, whereas the old town of Lerwick, where the hotels are, is an unrestful and rather crowded herring port and market.

To take a car from Orkney to Shetland and back costs £7 each way for cars weighing over one ton, up to two tons. One ton cars cost £4-10-0 each way. Comfortable Sedan Fords carrying three passengers can be hired from Canson Brothers of Lerwick at rates which work out at about 9½d a mile. These Fords jog along at about 20 miles an hour (no doubt the drivers earn a bonus by economising petrol); but as all the roads are mountain roads a fast car could not do much more. From these figures the motorist can calculate whether it is worth while to take his car with him to Shetland.

The drives are very attractive. The whole island is a narrow zig-zag between the North Sea and the Atlantic, with many mountain lakes in the peat moorland. The fiords (called voes) and bays occur every quarter of an hour, either from the east or the west; and they are all beauty spots.

The drawback is the lack of hotels and the poorness of those which have survived the island going "dry" two years ago. When this happened the abler hotel keepers cleared out, knowing that they could not tide over the winter without their bars. The hotels either closed; so that the map cannot be depended on, or else were taken by retired ship stewards and other innocents who have bitten off more than they can chew.

However, there are houses which will give you a very good plain lunch, especially if you wire beforehand that you are coming. The only drink available (except water) is buttermilk; but the food is good. They will even put you up in a simple way for a week at the seaside. Thus, when you make the western excursion to Reawick, you telegraph to Miss Robertson, Reawick House; and she will be ready for your luncheon party. For the southern excursion to Jarlshof and Sumburgh wire to Mr. Walter Flaws, Spiggie, Dunrossness. In the north there is the Steamboat Company's hotel at Millswick, already described. There is a house at Balta Sound on the east coast opened two years ago by some ladies. The probable tendency will be for these houses to develop into regular hotels for tourists under the "dry" system. The hotel at Walls has been closed for two years.

There are no signposts in Shetland. Without a hired native chauffeur, one must drive by the map. There is more activity in roadmaking than might be expected: for example Loch Spiggie has a road right round it; and the road skirting Ronas Voe from the Hollander's Grave eastward to the Whaling Station is quite as good as the roads colored as practicable.

—Orkney and Shetland—

The climate in both islands is mild, and, compared with that of the Scottish Midlands, markedly southern in character. As there is no dry heat clothing should be fairly warm; but it is never really cold in the hard northern way, nor unbearably hot in the English way during a heat wave.

The season is from the middle of June to the middle of August. It is light all night during the longest days.

Good sailors should not hesitate for a moment to visit the islands. Bad ones can wait for a smooth day if they are not tied to time. Naturalists will find wild birds galore, and fishermen plenty of sport.

The Shetland people have good looks, good manners, good health (apparently), and soft speech. This is not so striking in Orkney; but the people there are also pleasant folk. As they have not been spoiled by extravagant tourists they are neither servile nor rapacious.

On the whole, within the dates given, a trip to the north of Shetland should include the islands.

August 1925

Howard Ira Einsohn

THE INTELLIGENT READER'S GUIDE TO *THE APPLE CART*

Shaw, a very busy man offstage, often expressed many of the concerns he pursued outside the theater in his plays. A prime example is the kinship between *The Intelligent Woman's Guide to Socialism and Capitalism* (1923–28) and *The Apple Cart* (5 November–29 December 1928), consecutive works whose themes are strikingly similar in that the play dramatizes key points the treatise argues discursively. The similarities indicate that the *Guide* served as a source for *The Apple Cart*, not in the sense that Shaw deliberately mined the *Guide* for ideas he wanted to reiterate in the play, but that the exhausting, protracted creative process of writing the *Guide* had indelibly etched in Shaw's mind the political and economic issues that appeared on the stage in the *The Apple Cart*. The longest and most tightly reasoned prose opus in the canon, the *Guide* occupied the septuagenarian Shaw continually for six years and must have required an enormous expenditure of energy to finish. Given the close temporal proximity of the texts, the *Guide*'s main outlines surely remained a fertile presence for Shaw when he first conceived of Magnus, his Cabinet, and a dissolute England on the verge of self-destruction.

Shaw wrote *The Apple Cart* in less than eight weeks, an unusually brief gestation period. Shaw generally crafted his full-length plays over several months, even years in some instances, before completing them. The uncharacteristic swiftness of the writing suggests that the dramatist was working with material he had considered thoroughly elsewhere, most probably in the *Guide*, as Charles A. Berst has implied. Discussing the relationship between Shaw and Molly Tompkins, Berst attributes part of the reason for *The Apple Cart*'s rapid composition to the play's explicitly political "subject matter": "having been so recently immersed in the politics of *The Intelligent Woman's Guide*, [Shaw] now had an opportunity to vent some of its ideas in a genre congenial to him."[1] Shaw, who had been under pressure to produce something new for the August 1929 opening of the Malvern Festival as soon as he had concluded his "endless book" (the *Guide*), wrote to Molly on the preceding February 2, "I erupted like a volcano and simply hurled out a new play, inspiringly entitled *The Apple Cart*."[2] What "erupted" in this comparatively brief period of volcanic activity was the molten lava of Shaw's massive tome on political economy. The Preface that Shaw later added to the *The Apple Cart* (1930) buttresses the case for regarding the *Guide* as a template for the play. Supplied to enlighten an outraged public that had misconstrued *The Apple Cart* as a radical ideological reversal of Shaw's presumed democratic sympathies, the Preface, clarifying the playwright's aims, contains numerous analogues to the *Guide*.[3]

In the absence of direct corroboration from Shaw, the most compelling evidence that *The Intelligent Woman's Guide* exerted a formative influence on *The Apple Cart* is the marked similarity between them. Three prominent themes in the play—the excesses of capitalism, the weaknesses of democracy, and the inadequacies of parliamentary government—appear in the *Guide*. These give *The Apple Cart* its dramatic tension and conceptual framework. Central elements of the two crucial speeches near the end of Act I, betokening a subterranean layer of Shavian despair beneath the shimmering surface of palace maneuvering, likewise have roots in the *Guide*. Other less obvious motifs of the play, such as the debate between King and Cabinet over England's economic health and the characters of Boanerges and Orinthia, are also integrally related to the *Guide*'s chief preoccupations. These correspondences provide an instructive perspective for enriching our appreciation of *The Apple Cart*. They illuminate how Shaw transformed the discursive arguments of the *Guide* into dramatic arguments for the theater, and they reflect the moral vision that, offstage or on, informed Shaw's abiding outlook on the world.

Shaw fashioned the political crisis Magnus confronts with building blocks he had provided in *The Intelligent Woman's Guide*. Much of the *Guide* condemns the exploitative aspects of capitalism, which Shaw viewed as a serious threat to the survival of civilization (xxxvi; see also xxvi and chapters 40–41). So grave was the perceived danger that the *Guide* likens capitalism to a "runaway car" speeding helplessly out of control toward a "precipice at the foot of which are strewn the ruins of empires" (315). At the same time, the *Guide* reveals Shaw's utter lack of faith in the ability of his nation's political parties—Liberal, Conservative, or Labor—to apply the brakes in time and steer the economy safely in a socialist direction. "The truth is," he wrote, "that none of them can govern: Capitalism runs away with them all. The hopes that we founded on the extension of the franchise . . . have been disappointed as far as controlling Capitalism is concerned, and indeed in many other respects too" (317; see also 452).

Why was democracy impotent in the path of a reckless capitalism? For several reasons, the *Guide* tells us. The process was always dominated by capitalists who gave the ignorant, hapless "majority the vote for the sake of gaining party advantages by popular support" (453). The masses, in turn, were incapable of distinguishing worthy individuals from unworthy ones. When they were not voting for any "fool" who sanctified their "follies" (453), they voted for whom they were told to vote (452). Parliament itself, the putative seat of enlightened government, was obsolete, "as much out of date as instruments for carrying on the public business as a pair of horses for drawing an omnibus" (354; *The Apple Cart* 6:255, 272, Preface). Its members were more interested in getting into office and staying there than in serving the people's needs (348–54; cf. *The Apple Cart* 6:254, Preface); and the entrenched party system forced the king to choose his ministers "from whatever party has a majority in the House of Commons," even though it might be painfully evident "that a more talented Cabinet could be formed by selecting the ablest men from both parties" (348). While supposed statesmen vied for supremacy, the real governing was left to selfish capitalists who bought candidates, elections, and policy decisions favorable to themselves but detrimental to the commonweal.

The convergence of these conditions in post–World War I England, according to the *Guide,* triggered a response that threatened to unravel the social fabric of British society. Desperate voices arose demanding "the abandonment of Parliament and the substitution of a dictatorship" in order to rescue their "livelihood . . . from the purely predatory side of Capitalism" (318; original parentheses omitted). Paradoxically, then, the implementation of democracy resulted in an anguished outcry for its demise. People everywhere, not only in England but throughout Europe, began to look, for deliverance, to any strong leader who promised to save them from the rapacity of capitalism and the do-nothingness of democratic regimes.[4] However, as far as Shaw was concerned, such a reaction could not have come at a worse time. What was needed was not less popular support for government, but more. Only the widespread growth of responsible government, Shaw believed, "can hope to control the Gadarene rush of Capitalism towards the abyss" (317). On reflection, with due allowance for the satirist's customary technique of caricaturing existing tendencies for maximum effect, this is essentially the situation Shaw dramatizes in *The Apple Cart.*[5]

For the all-important struggle in *The Apple Cart,* though only Magnus sees it clearly, is not between a royalist king and a democratic prime

minister (neither characterization is accurate), but between them both as
national leaders and "plutocracy" (6:252, Preface)—between, that is, efficient and responsible government and a capitalism run rampant.[6] At
stake, in the broad sweep of the action, is the survival of England as an
independent and healthy nation. England is menaced by capitalist forces
on two fronts: domestically, by a shaky economy and by Breakages, Limited, a gigantic industrial corporation dedicated to waste and planned
obsolescence, which "has bought and swallowed democracy" and holds all
Britain—ministers, the media, commerce, and industry—"helpless in [its]
grip" (6:253, Preface); and internationally, by the looming presence of the
United States, which is bent on an imperialistic venture to seize the Commonwealth under the pretense of a benign desire for reunification. The
democratically constituted Cabinet, however, emblematic of Parliament
as a whole, blinds itself irresponsibly to the impending dangers.

Instead of uniting with the king in a joint effort to preserve England's
integrity, the one strategy that stands a chance of decelerating "the runaway car of capitalism" before it is too late (*Guide* 314–16), the foolish
ministers try to strip Magnus of any effective power he might wield in
the nation's defense by compelling him to accept an ultimatum prohibit-
ing his active participation in government matters. With little or no help
from a "bungling and squabbling" cadre of ministers (6:307, 311), Magnus has resolved one "crisis" after another (6:286), protecting the people
as much as possible from "corrupt legislation" (6:300) and "the political
encroachments of big business" (6:306) during three years of Labour
Government ineptitude. Yet his obstructionist Cabinet, concerned more
with prerogatives than with remedies, insists on reducing the country's
only hope for salvation to a "complete nullity" (6:363), a "cipher."[7]
Should it succeed in muzzling Magnus, in making him "a dumb king"
(6:316, 317), an "indiarubber stamp" (6:290) whose "sole privilege
[would be] that of being shot at when some victim of misgovernment
resorts to assassination to avenge himself" (6:323), England could not
long survive as a free and prosperous nation. Through a clever tactic,
however, the king triumphs, for the moment at least, "not by exercising
his royal authority, but by threatening to resign and go to the democratic
poll" (6:249, Preface). Magnus prevails precisely because Proteus recognizes that should the adroit, very popular king carry out his threat, he
would "rally the anti-democratic royalist vote against him" and eventually undermine his own position as prime minister (6:249, Preface).

Magnus, however, harbors no ambition to rule England as a tyrant, nor
does he wish to be an "Emperor" (6:356). He knows that "the day of
absolute monarchies is past," and that he cannot govern effectively without a Cabinet (6:364; see also 6:323). Indeed, if necessary, he will abdicate

"to save the [constitutional] monarchy, not to destroy it" (6:365). Here Magnus mirrors the *Guide*'s view that dictatorships, whatever their label, are inherently undesirable forms of government because "in the long run . . . you must have your parliaments and settled constitutions back again" (379). The king also understands what Shaw makes plain in *The Apple Cart*'s Preface, that "modern government is not a one man job; it is too big for that" (6:267). In his long oration to his ministers at the close of the first act, Magnus comments that government service "wears out the strongest man, and even the strongest woman, after a few years" (6:324). This sentiment reprises the *Guide*'s argument that even if some Cromwellian figure could impose his will on the people, "he would be worn out or dead after a few years" (318; see also 381), leaving the pressing problem of how to govern well still unresolved. Despotism, then, is not the answer to the riddle of good government. Neither is democracy satisfactory in its present form. At bottom, it is an unworkable ideal that, as Magnus remarks, renders responsible government impossible (6:320; *Guide* 317–19, 347). Universalizing the franchise on the assumption that everybody can make informed decisions simply paves the way first for political chaos and eventually for authoritarianism.

Democracy, plutocracy, autocracy—none of these elicits Shaw's allegiance. He prefers aristocracy, or as he puts it in the *Guide*, "government by the best qualified" (454). "Government," he says, "demands ability to govern" (454), but nature does not distribute the appropriate skills in equal proportions. Some are, necessarily, better able than others to legislate wisely and justly. Only such individuals should hold elective office. Shaw is not extolling the virtues of the modern aristocracy. On this point Magnus is explicit: "I do not want the old governing class back. It governed so selfishly that the people would have perished if democracy had not swept it out of politics" (6:325; cf. 6:257–58, Preface). It is not the aristocrat as "robber baron" that Shaw desires but, as Eric Bentley observes, the aristocrat as "gentleman."[8] "A real gentleman," the *Guide* says, "is not supposed to sell himself to the highest bidder: he asks his country for sufficient provision and a dignified position in return for the best work he can do for it. A real lady can say no less" (340).[9] Therein lies what Bentley calls "the core of Shavian ethics": "the socialist idea, . . . the gentlemanly idea" that obliges us "to give more than [we] take," a standard of conduct irrevocably opposed to a capitalist morality that requires individuals and nations "to get more than [they] give."[10] On stage, the gentleman-aristocrat comes alive in Magnus. Combining probity and ability in the furtherance of the common good, Magnus is the ideal ruler, an agent of the Life Force who stands "for the eternal against the expedient; for the evolutionary appetite against the day's gluttony" (6:326).[11]

Like the *Guide, The Apple Cart* does not call for an end to participatory democracy and the resuscitation of absolute monarchy.[12] To be sure, government must be representative and consensual, with the governing and governed alike adhering to the aristocratic ethic. But for Shaw, government could never be literally *by* the people. Some have the equipment to govern. Some do not (6:259–61, Preface).[13]

In addition to affirming the *Guide*'s stand against despotism, the lengthy set piece Magnus delivers recapitulates other ideas from the treatise as well. For example, the king's assertion that politics, once the lifeblood of the nation, has become a scorned, neglected vocation desperately in search of worthy practitioners also has unmistakable parallels in the *Guide*. Magnus's complaint that he can no longer "depend on the support of the aristocracy and the cultured bourgeoisie" in ruling (6:323) elaborates the *Guide*'s statement that the old aristocrats "had to make the laws and administer them, doing military work, police work, and government work of all sorts," whereas today "all the chores and duties of the feudal barons are done by paid officials" (166).

Similarly, the *Guide*'s observation that "those who fully understand how heavy are the responsibilities of government and how exhausting its labor are least likely to consider them voluntarily" (455) anticipates Magnus's claim that virtually no one "will touch this drudgery of government, this public work that never ends because we cannot finish one job without creating ten fresh new ones" (6:323). The king ponders why indeed anybody would want a job that is endless, debilitating, and low in pay and esteem, especially if, echoing the *Guide*, it requires one to enter daily "the squalor of the political arena" to do dubious battle "with foolish factions in parliament and with ignorant voters in the constituencies" (6:324). Those who do somehow stumble into politics, Magnus adds, are unequal to the task, since the genuinely capable, as both play and *Guide* indicate, have long since been lured to supposedly greener pastures by capitalist concerns (6:324–25; *Guide* 170–71). In *fin de siècle* England, where the worship of Mammon has supplanted the worship of the common good, few are willing, and fewer are able, to assume the burden of responsible government service.

Magnus also argues in his State of the Kingdom message that, unlike himself, the Cabinet is "dangerously subject" to the "tyranny of popular ignorance and popular poverty" (6:325). He offers two specific reasons for his allegation: the ministers have failed "to take control of the schools," which foster a mentality opposed to progressive socialist reform, and the ministers are dependent on a servile capitalist press, which can mobilize the miseducated citizenry to make or break them politically

(6:325–26). The *Guide* comments extensively on both the schools and the press, providing an explanatory context for the king's remarks.

Magnus asserts that his ministers cannot act autonomously in Parliament primarily because of their failure to revamp a corrupt educational system that perpetuates "superstitions and prejudices that stand like stone walls across every forward path" (6:325). The particulars of these "superstitions and prejudices" are spelled out in the *Guide*. Administered by capitalists, with strong vested interests in maintaining the status quo, schools at every level did not—understandably—teach students "such vital truths about their duty to their country as that they should despise and pursue as criminals all able-bodied adults who do not pull their weight in the social boat" (63). Worse, they defended the undeserved advantages of the affluent by falsely teaching, on the one hand, "that without the idle rich we should all perish for lack of capital and employment" and that "the highest form of government possible for mankind" is an oligarchy of the wealthy in which "the worship of rich idleness" is the chief civic virtue (63–64); and, on the other, that the poor are themselves responsible for their condition (64) and that, as demonstrated by economic theory, "the wages of the poor cannot be raised" (63). Those who dared teach otherwise were "dismissed from their employment and sometimes persecuted for sedition" (63). Fed a steady diet of such "superstitions and prejudices," it is not surprising that the British, particularly the young, whom Shaw regarded as the last remaining hope for redemption, could not distinguish reality from illusion. In Shaw's view, when educators distort the true nature of social relations beyond recognition, when they neglect to inculcate impressionable minds with the values entailed by an aristocratic ethic, stupidity and injustice are likely to predominate in society.

Even so, Shaw would have found the situation less ominous had he perceived that the mighty organ that shapes public opinion, the press, was free to undo the serious damage wrought by his country's educational process. However, here, too, according to the *Guide*, the pernicious influence of rich capitalists was everywhere. Unfortunately, "the Press was not free" (64). In fact, it was little more than a propaganda tool of the wealthy, who either owned the newspapers or advertised in them (64), since "editors and journalists who express[ed] opinions in print that [were] opposed to the interests of the rich [were] dismissed and replaced by subservient ones" (64).[14] Thus, when the newspapers were not publishing "lying advertisements which pretend to prove the worse is the better article" (203), they were hard at work convincing readers that "nationalization," one of the basic tenets of Shavian socialism, "is an unnatural crime which must utterly ruin the country" (105). With a concerted effort they could denounce those who clamored for social and economic reform "as Bolsheviks or whatever other epithet may be in fashion for the moment as a term of the most infamous discredit" (65). Magnus reiterates this perspective, extending it to its logical conclusion, when he reminds his ministers that they are not free agents in the political realm because they "are held in leash by the Press, which can organize against you the ignorance and superstition, the timidity and credulity, the gullibility and prudery, the hating and hunting instinct of the voting mob, and cast you down from power if you utter a word to alarm or displease the adventurers [i.e., capitalists] who have the Press in their pockets" (6:326; see also 6:294).

Indeed, it is just such a fate that one of the few ministers with a semblance of integrity in Magnus's Cabinet dreads the most. Lysistrata, Minister of Power Supplies, is well aware of the grievous disservice Breakages, Limited, is rendering the nation. Still, she is afraid to speak out lest the giant industrial corporation, "with its millions and its newspapers and its fingers in every pie" (6:329), marshal its awesome forces against her. Blowing the whistle on so formidable and ruthless an opponent would achieve nothing save the certainty that she would ultimately "be hounded out of public life" (6:329). As Lysistrata foresees, in the inevitable counterattack that would quickly follow, Breakages would use its newspapers to smear her personally, professionally, and on the basis of her gender (6:329). In the end, she would succumb to the pressure and resign. This would mean the loss of a dedicated public servant when England could least afford it. For Breakages, it would mean the return to business as usual, with impunity. Such is the poisoned power of avaricious capitalists and their obsequious press, as Shaw envisioned it.

The brief debate in Act I between Magnus and the Cabinet over England's economic condition dramatizes portions of the *Guide* in which Shaw discusses the harmful effects of "becom[ing] a parasite on foreign labor" (146). Despite the prevalence of high wages, which the Cabinet members interpret as incontrovertible evidence of the nation's health, Magnus informs them that this seeming prosperity is illusory. Because Britain relies so heavily for her survival on the "tribute" (6:310) paid by poor countries whose cheap labor has been exploited shamefully, unaristocratically, by huge amounts of exported English capital (6:308), the domestic economy is actually so unstable that it could crash at any time. It is overly dependent on external circumstances that could change drastically without warning. What worries Magnus exceedingly is "revolution," not a revolution in England, as his ministers misinterpret his meaning, but a revolution in "those countries on whose tribute we live"

(6:310). "Suppose," he wonders aloud, "it occurs to them to stop paying it!" (6:310). Magnus knows very well what would ensue: the British economy would collapse like a house of cards. The Cabinet, however, is oblivious to the peril. Like the Ritualist Sempronius *père* and his innumerable counterparts, it confuses surface appearance with underlying reality. In the ministers' superficial view, everything is rosy.

This same concern is also raised in the *Guide* when Shaw rhetorically asks capitalists who routinely send "hundreds of millions of pounds" abroad annually to consider the following question: "Suppose the foreign countries stop our supplies either by a revolution followed by flat repudiation of their capitalistic debt, as in Russia, or by taxing and supertaxing income derived from investments, what will become of us then? (34–35). Abhorring loose ends as nature abhors a vacuum, the *Guide* provides the answer: such a nation "becomes too idle and luxurious to be able to compel the foreign countries to pay the tribute on which it lives; and when they cease to feed it, it has lost the art of feeding itself and collapses in the midst of genteel splendor" (146). This is precisely the fear Magnus expresses to his myopic Cabinet.

Instead of achieving as much domestic self-sufficiency as possible by developing her vital industries to the fullest, Magnus's England invested her capital overseas and turned to the manufacture of such luxury items as chocolate creams, Christmas crackers, and golf clubs. So too, in effect, did the England of Shaw's day, and in both cases the result was exactly the same: England left herself extremely vulnerable to outside forces she helped create but over which she had no permanent control. A single sentence from the *Guide* gauges the depth of Shaw's antipathy toward his country's misguided economic policies:

> Nothing in our political history is more appalling than the improvidence with which we have allowed British spare money, desperately needed at home for the full realization of our own powers of production, and for the clearing away of our own disgraceful slum centres of social corruption, to be driven abroad at the rate of two hundred millions every year, loading us with unemployment, draining us by emigration, imposing huge military and naval forces upon us, strengthening the foreign armies of which we are afraid, and providing all sorts of facilities for the foreign industries which destroy our powers of self-support by doing for us what we could and should do as well for ourselves. (144)

With "British capital develop[ing] the world everywhere (except at home)" (144), England's competitors and potential enemies, according to Shaw, grew fat and energetic while the stalwarts in Britain grew lean and lethargic, experiencing decreased production and consumption, high un-employment, increasing inflation, and much poverty. These realities did not bode well for England, yet her leaders persisted in their foolishness.

Magnus's Cabinet refuses to acknowledge the identical problem, nor do the ministers appear especially concerned when the issue of England's overreliance on foreign countries in which she has made substantial capital investments reemerges in the person of the American ambassador, who comes calling with a thinly veiled plan to annex the British Empire. Should England resist, Vanhattan tells Magnus, the United States would "be obliged to boycott you. The two thousand million dollars a year would stop" (6:357), implying that England could not survive as an independent nation under such conditions. The historical irony here is as poignant as it is transparent. The nation that had once colonized much of the globe and enjoyed unparalleled good fortune is herself in imminent danger of being colonized and reduced to ignominious dependence by one of her former colonies. Events outside the theater would soon testify convincingly to Shaw's prescience, for the majesty of England was about to be eclipsed, in large part, by the emergence of the United States as a world leader.

As well as thematic ties between play and treatise, the *Guide* also furnishes the models for characters in *The Apple Cart* who evince different aspects of the Shavian animus toward capitalism and parliamentary democracy in England. Trade Minister Boanerges is clearly the prototypical individual Shaw has in mind when he writes in the *Guide* that "a good many of the ablest and most arbitrary of the leaders of Trade Unionism are resolutely democractic in Labour politics because they know very well that as long as the workers can vote they can make the workers vote as they please. They are democratic, not because of their faith in the judgment, knowledge, and initiative of the masses, but because of their experience of mass ignorance, gullibility, and sheepishness" (452). What is Boanerges's conception of democracy but simply to tell the ignorant, gullible, and sheep-like workers who chime in unison "tell us what to do," to "exercise their vote intelligently by voting for me" (6:295; see also 6:300, 307)? (In the *Guide*, Shaw refers to the British as a "population of sheep" [299].) Like the Trade Union officials the *Guide* describes, Boanerges espouses democracy publicly only "to maintain the system which has kept [him] in power" (451). Privately, he thinks it is a sham.

Boanerges has all the markings of a strong leader, but he is too new to make a significant impact on Cabinet proceedings. In fact, a double recognition occurs between king and trade minister: each perceives the other's political prowess. Granted, Magnus tames the "bull-roarer" (6:286) by flattering him, but his declaration that "no common man could have risen as you have done" is sincere (6:292). The king realizes that, unlike himself, Boanerges has earned his position by merit. Magnus has followed his minister's activities closely; he knows that, should England become a republic, "no man has a better chance of being the first British president than [Boanerges]" (6:293). In turn, Boanerges acknowledges that Magnus is "no fool" and that, had their backgrounds been reversed, the king "would have done pretty well for [himself]" (6:293). This mutual recognition of ability dramatizes Shaw's view that there is no such thing as a ruling class.[15] Boanerges may have been born in the street, literally, and Magnus with a silver spoon in his mouth, yet the former is, potentially, just as capable as the latter. In the Shavian universe, the accidents of birth play no role in politics. Practical wisdom, not rank, is the criterion for holding office. The *Guide* makes the same point, especially in the chapter that stresses the importance of restructuring the democratic process so that only the ablest candidates present themselves to the public (454–55). The accent on competence, on efficiency, on what commentators have called Shaw's pragmatism,[16] manifests the social philosopher's enduring belief that theory is not enough to change the world. Praxis is needed as well. Lofty abstraction must ultimately give way to concrete action; otherwise, one is left with only wishful thinking. Hence the *Guide*'s admonition to practice the aristocratic ethic of giving rather than merely taking, a code that has nothing to do with the privileges of lineage or wealth. But in the materialistic wasteland of *The Apple Cart*, where Magnus alone personifies the ethos of public service, Shaw's vision of a just society in which citizens happily do more than their share is lost on the majority, among whom we must certainly include the king's "mistress."

Orinthia violates one of the cardinal principles of Shavian socialism: Thou shalt not be an idler. An idler, the *Guide* informs us, is not someone who does nothing, but someone who does nothing productive, someone who takes more from the commonweal than he contributes (62). Orinthia is such an idler; she is the antithesis of the Shavian gentlewoman. She performs no socially useful function; she supports herself solely through a state pension; and she says that her feelings of unsurpassable superiority spring from "something nobler than vulgar conceit in having done something" (6:340). She is all talk and no work, and her popularity among the people simply confirms Magnus's observation, addressed to Boanerges, that "talkers are very formidable rivals for popular favor. The multitude understands talk: it does not understand work" (6:295). Orinthia may think of herself as a deity, and many may treat her like one, but she has done nothing to merit such treatment. Indeed, never was anyone's balloon more effectively punctured than when Magnus deflated Orinthia with the quip that "it must be magnificent to have the consciousness of a goddess without ever doing a thing to justify it" (6:340).

Orinthia is a perfect dramatization of the *Guide*'s argument that in capitalist English society "the coveted distinction lady and gentleman" has become nothing but a "detestable parasitic pretension" venerating "persons who never condescend to do anything for themselves that they can possibly put on others without rendering them equivalent service" over the real lady, "who, generously overearning her income, leaves the nation in her debt and the world a better world than she found it" (462–63). This perversion of values, an attempt, Shaw says, to make "Evil: be thou my good" the "national motto," teaches the repugnant doctrine that "working for a livelihood is inferior, derogatory, and disgraceful," that "to live like a drone on the labor and service of others is to be a lady and gentleman," and that "to enrich the country by labor and service is to be base, lowly, vulgar, contemptible . . . " (58–59; see also 399–400). Yet this is precisely the social gospel Orinthia subscribes to wholeheartedly: the "streets" are to be "swept for [her]" by the common people she disdains (female ministers included) so that, without ever having to lift a finger, she can "reign over them" triumphantly (6:341). To her creator, however, such an attitude is anathema. For when idleness epitomizes good citizenship, the end of civilization, the *Guide* says, cannot be far behind (59). Socialists like Shaw, though, proposed an ingenious solution for discouraging the glorification of uselessness: compulsory social service for all able-bodied persons (356–59). This remains a remedy the Orinthias of the world cannot understand.

So self-centered is Orinthia that she cannot fathom selfless behavior. She disparages Magnus's politically active life on the ground that it is a form of "slavery" that, for all its onerous demands and wearisome responsibilities, does not make one "great" (6:340–41). For Orinthia, greatness is a state of being, not a matter of deeds. Her greatness, she claims, exists independently of its expression in action. Magnus takes a different view. He believes that greatness, if it is to be had at all, must be achieved by effort. Otherwise he would not subject himself to the grueling rigors of conscientious kingship. Both credos have a common source in the *Guide*. In contrasting feudal aristocracy with the aristocracy of his own day, Shaw remarks that "Henry IV, who died of overwork, found to his cost how true it was in those days that the greatest among us must be servant to all the rest. Nowadays it is the other way about: the greatest is she to whom all the rest are servants" (166). Magnus is a throwback to Henry IV. Orinthia is in the opposite camp.

Orinthia may embody beauty, pleasure, and romantic love, but for Shaw such values can never become the foundation of a sustainable philosophy of life. They represent a specious happiness that Shaw rejects as ultimately cloying and inimical to human welfare. Like other Shavian heroes in life's service, Magnus seeks the happiness that transcends the circumscribed bounds of the private and the personal to embrace the public and the universal, For this reason, Orinthia can never be more to Magnus than a pleasant diversion, a moment's respite from the ceaseless toils of statecraft, so that, unlike his unfortunate predecessor, he will not die of overwork. Orinthia, then, must content herself with being Magnus's queen in "fairyland" (6:347). There is no place for her in his real world. Thus, from the *Guide's* perspective, the Interlude Scene is not so much Shaw's "revenge" on Stella Campbell,[17] or Shaw's "exorcism" of Molly Tompkins,[18] but Shaw's rejection of useless idlers.

At the same time, Orinthia's flaws should not blind us to her perspicacity. Her keen judgments vividly recall some of the *Guide's* criticisms of the British parliamentary system. She recognizes, for instance, that, like "an overcrowded third class carriage" (6:347), occupied by a "rabble of dowdies and upstarts and intriguers and clowns that think they are governing the country when they are only squabbling with the [king]" (6:345), Magnus's Cabinet is a "disgrace" (6:347). This is an accurate appraisal of the unworthy individuals who hold the highest political offices in the nation and of the deplorable way they conduct the people's business. Had he a choice in the matter, Magnus would surely replace the automatons, the plotters, and the lackeys of Breakages, Limited, in his Cabinet with competent ministers—assuming, of course, he could find some among the multitude of charlatans masquerading as capable legislators. (Presumably he as already exhausted the crop of aspirants the majority party has to offer.) However, as we have seen, English custom forbids so iconoclastic an action. His hands are tied.

Orinthia also recognizes that Proteus, the wily prime minister, is a "poseur," a "greedy schemer," who "humbugs everybody," even "himself" (6:348, 347). "Poseur" aptly describes Proteus—his name refers to the mythical sea deity who changed shape to suit the situation at hand. Analogously, Proteus changes his demeanor and position in order to deal with whatever political issue presents itself. His calculated rages and practiced stormy exits, for example, are designed for effect, to help him, as Orinthia so eloquently puts it, humbug the Cabinet and the king. Moreover, the notion of posing, of affecting attitudes and opinions not genuinely one's own for private gain, suggests the *Guide's* revelation that, to further their careers, British politicians were more likely to vote along party lines than according to conscience (348–49). It is no wonder, then, that in a dramatic turnabout, Proteus rips to shreds the ultimatum he authored when he realizes that Magnus's willingness to upset the apple cart jeopardizes his own ministry. Thus the epithet *poseur* helps us identify Magnus as the true statesman in contrast to the histrionic Proteus, whom it reveals as a mere pretender and unprincipled opportunist.

Despite Magnus's brilliant political coup, the play ends with the fate of England still very much in doubt, for the economy has not been shored up, Breakages, Limited, has not been contained, and the United States has not been dissuaded from pursuing its acquisitive intentions. Far from being a regrettable lapse on the dramatist's part, this inconclusiveness is deliberate: it throws into high relief the Cabinet's complete inability to rise above selfish concerns and to act aristocratically in the best interests of a nation at risk. To remedy such conspicuous inadequacies, as well as to combat the intemperance of capitalism, Shaw had definite reforms in mind. For the latter, Shaw advocated the gradual adoption of Fabian socialism through legislative action (*Guide* chapters 75–76, esp. 76). For the former, he recommended two principal changes: a battery of examinations to test the qualifications of prospective statesmen so that voters could choose among the most qualified candidates and, in lieu of the parliamentary party system, a series of federal legislatures modeled after the committee structure of the municipal governments, with a centralized authority to coordinate the work (*Guide* 454–55 and 350ff.; *The Apple Cart* 6:271–72, Preface).[19] However, in *The Apple Cart*, Shaw was most anxious not to provide solutions but to dramatize the problems[20]—problems that he had treated cogently and at length in *The Intelligent Woman's Guide to Socialism and Capitalism.*

Notes

I am grateful to Alfred Turco, Jr., for his generous comments on earlier drafts of this essay.

All references to *The Intelligent Woman's Guide to Socialism and Capitalism* are to the edition published in New York by Brentano's in 1928 and are cited parenthetically in the text.

All references to *The Apple Cart*, published in English in 1930, are to *The Bodley Head Bernard Shaw* and are cited parenthetically in the text by volume and page numbers.

1. Charles A. Berst, "Passions at Lake Maggiore: Shaw, Molly Tompkins, and Italy, 1921–1950," *Shaw Abroad: The Annual of Bernard Shaw Studies* 5 (1985), 104. For a contrasting point of view, see Margery M. Morgan, *The Shavian Playground: An Exploration of the Art of George Bernard Shaw* (London: Methuen, 1972), p. 307.

2. Berst, p. 104.

3. Shaw himself is partly responsible for his audience's confusion. Although *The Apple Cart* clearly does not repudiate participatory government in favor of absolute monarchy, the dramatist failed to express his views as sharply as he might have. Had the audience come to the play after reading *The Intelligent Woman's Guide,* there would have been no question at all about where Shaw stood on the issues. However, not everyone in attendance opening night could have reasonably been expected to be conversant with the *Guide.* Had Shaw made his position even a little more explicit in *The Apple Cart,* the furor over the play never would have arisen. On Shaw's responsibility in this matter, see Archibald Henderson, *Bernard Shaw: Man of the Century* (1932; New York: Appleton-Century-Crofts, 1956), p. 629 n. 13, and Morgan, p. 504.

4. See also the Preface to *Too True to be Good, The Bodley Head Bernard Shaw* 6:420–21.

5. Although Shaw set *The Apple Cart* in the future, his real targets are contemporary English society in particular and the Western industrialized world in general. See Martin Meisel, *Shaw and the Nineteenth-Century Theater* (Princeton: Princeton University Press, 1968), pp. 397, 399.

6. See also Henderson, p. 632.

7. See Bernard F. Dukore, *Bernard Shaw, Playwright: Aspects of Shavian Drama* (Columbia: University of Missouri Press, 1973), pp. 186–92. Much of my analysis accords with Dukore's excellent discussion of *The Apple Cart.* Dukore, when he suggests sources, links the play to *Man and Superman* and *Heartbreak House;* I link the play to *The Intelligent Woman's Guide.* There is no real disagreement here—just a difference in perspective. "Indeed everything in Shaw," as Eric Bentley points out, "leads to everything else" (*Bernard Shaw* [1947; New York: Limelight Editions, 1985], p. 29).

8. Bentley, p. 24.

9. See also Bentley, pp. 24–25.

10. Bentley, p. 25.

11. For a similar view that emphasizes Magnus's superiority to those around him, see Frederick P. W. McDowell, " 'The Eternal Against the Expedient': Structure and Theme in Shaw's *The Apple Cart,*" *Modern Drama* 2 (1959), 99–113.

12. See also A. M. Gibbs, *The Art and Mind of Shaw: Essays in Criticism* (New York: St. Martin's Press, 1983), pp. 198–99. For a different view, suggesting that *The Apple Cart* inclines toward totalitarianism, see Alfred Turco, Jr.'s revealing interview with Eric Bentley in *Shaw: The Neglected Plays: The Annual of Bernard Shaw Studies* 7 (1987), 18–20. *SHAW* 7 also includes an article on *The Apple Cart* by Barbara Bellow Watson ("The Theater of Love and the Theater of Politics in *The Apple Cart,*" pp. 207–20) that explores Shaw's use of theatrics and artifice in his dramatization of "politics in a parliamentary democracy" (208).

13. In a 1930 interview regarding democracy and *The Apple Cart,* included in vol. 6 of *The Bodley Head Bernard Shaw* (pp. 386–90), Shaw said that "the desideratum is a method of government in which the governed choose their rulers and can change them, but in which only capable persons are eligible for choice or change" (p. 387). What Shaw wanted, then, was not the scrapping of democracy, but its reform, so that only those with ability could compete in the electoral process. Ideally, Shaw preferred legislators who were both able and, in the sense defined, aristocratic. However, if forced to choose between a benevolent but incompetent individual and a competent but ruthless one, he would have seriously considered the latter (p. 387; see also the Preface to *The Millionairess, The Bodley Head Bernard Shaw,* 6:852). For Shaw's final judgment on popular democracy and dictatorship, see Warren Sylvester Smith, "The Search for Good Government: *The Apple Cart, On the Rocks,* and *Geneva,*" *Shaw Review* 21 (January 1978), 30.

14. Compare Magnus's response to Proteus, who has just accused the king of manipulating the press against the Cabinet: "You know that I have no control over the Press. The

Press is in the hands of men much richer than I, who would not insert a single paragraph against their own interests even if it were signed by my own hand and sent to them with a royal command" (6:317).

15. See the interview by G. W. Bishop included in vol. 6 of *The Bodley Head Bernard Shaw*, p. 382.

16. Alfred Turco, Jr., *Shaw's Moral Vision: The Self and Salvation* (Ithaca: Cornell University Press, 1976), pp. 85–92; J. L. Wisenthal, *Shaw and Ibsen: Bernard Shaw's* The Quintessence of Ibsenism *and Related Writings* (Toronto: University of Toronto Press, 1979), p. 10; cf. Wisenthal, *The Marriage of Contraries: Bernard Shaw's Middle Plays* (Cambridge: Harvard University Press, 1974), pp. 3–4.

17. Arnold Silver, *Bernard Shaw: The Darker Side* (Stanford: Stanford University Press, 1982), pp. 265–70.

18. Berst, pp. 104–6.

19. See also William Irvine, *The Universe of G. B. S.* (1949; New York: Russell & Russell, 1966), p. 350, and cf. Smith, pp. 27ff.

20. Cf. Dukore, p. 192.

Leon H. Hugo

THE BLACK GIRL AND SOME LESSER QUESTS: 1932–1934

Shaw wrote his parable about the Black Girl more or less by chance.[1]

He and Charlotte were on holiday in South Africa. They spent the first month of their visit in Cape Town, and then on 8 February 1932 they left to motor to Port Elizabeth, stopping for about a week at the Wilderness, near George, for a private visit.[2] They left the Wilderness on or around 20 February when, somewhere between George and Knysna, Shaw, who was driving, took the car off the road into a ditch. He was unhurt and indignant, blaming the condition of the road for the accident; Charlotte was badly bruised. The projected trip to Port Elizabeth had to be abandoned. They put up at an hotel in Knysna, a small coastal town of the mid-eastern Cape, where they hoped Charlotte would have sufficient peace and quiet to recover from her injuries. Here, for the next four to five weeks, Shaw was to find himself decidedly "off-stage"; and here, while Charlotte was convalescing, he wrote *The Adventures of the Black Girl in Her Search for God*—changed in 1946 to *The Black Girl in Search of God*.

He says in the Preface: "My intention was to write a play in the ordinary course of my business as a playwright; but I found myself writing the story of the black girl instead."[3] This was, on the face of it, a curious decision. *The Black Girl* is a sport in Shaw's work; there is nothing else like it, no religious or other fable, no parable, no black or other girl setting out on any picaresque adventure, anywhere.

Shaw in 1932 was well into his overtly political phase. Religion, though of course never far from the surface of almost everything he said and wrote, had tended to fall away as a specific issue, and it would have been more in keeping with the general tendency of his career had he completed *The Rationalization of Russia,* begun on board ship during the voyage to South Africa, or proceeded on the trail King Magnus had begun to blaze some three years before. But Russia was ignored, never to be rationalized in book form, while Sir Arthur Chavender and other political personages who found themselves on the rocks in the thirties had to wait their turn.[4] The Black Girl had pushed in at the head of the queue, demanding to be heard. What could have induced Shaw to listen compliantly to her?

The South African experience had something to do with it. The fact that he was trapped in an extremely picturesque but (in those days) small, isolated, and somewhat backward coastal town with dense African forest looming over it must have played on his imagination. This was the Black Girl's country, the forest into which she sallied on her quest right there on Shaw's hotel doorstep. Also, some weeks before in Cape Town, he had been attacked in print by a prominent Roman Catholic theologian, Fr. O. R. Vassall-Phillips C.SS.R., who called Shaw an imposter and egolomaniac and, for good measure, "as arrogant and insolent as he is pretentious and crafty." Shaw, in a dignified and restrained reply in the *Cape Argus,* said that all his cards were on the table. But *The Black Girl* could be his attempt at reshuffling the pack and dealing a new hand, at redefining and explaining his point of view for the benefit of Vassall-Phillips and like-minded people.[5]

About five weeks after the accident, on 18 March 1932, he and Charlotte returned to Cape Town. Shaw gave a less than gracious valedictory interview on board ship before sailing. He mentioned *The Black Girl:* "It is not a book at all—it is merely a large pamphlet which an enterprising publisher would make into a book. It deals with a native girl's search for God." He spoke about the "Dutch," as he called the Afrikaners, his cheeky remarks revealing more of his current preoccupations than he may have realized:

> I think they are a fine, upstanding race, particularly well-built and interesting because they have been so long isolated from the world. Outside events have not touched them. The French Revolution and other great developments in Europe have passed them by.
>
> All they need is education. Make them take an interest in things and be intelligent. And, above all, ban the Bible; take the Bible away from them. They depend too much on it.[6]

He said much the same at the conclusion of his and Charlotte's second visit to South Africa in 1935, adding, "I wish someone would make [the Afrikaners] realise that the Bible is an extremely well-written book, but that it should be supplemented by Whittaker['s Almanac]. As a matter of fact, I wrote *The Adventures of the Black Girl in Her Search for God* purely for the advantage of the Boer [i.e., the Afrikaner]."[7] This is GBS at his most outrageous, which means that he should be taken both with a pinch of salt and seriously.

There is a vast divide between Fr. Vassall-Phillips on the one hand and the Afrikaner on the other, but both contributed to the creation of the Black Girl.

A third contribution came from a missionary, Mabel Shaw (no relation), with whom Shaw became acquainted in the late 1920s. According to Shaw, she was "a woman with a craze for self-torture, who broke off her engagement with a clergyman (he died of it) to bury herself in the wilds of Africa and lead negro children to Christ." As Stanley Weintraub has pointed out, the missionary who converts the Black Girl—"a small white woman, not yet thirty: an odd little body . . . a born apostle of love"[8]—is derived from Mabel Shaw.[9] If anything emerges from their brief association, it is Shaw's emphatic rejection of the missionary zeal she represented.

There is a fourth consideration that projects us into the realms of "meta-biology," more or less obligatory in this instance because of Shaw's stance vis-à-vis his friend Dame Laurentia McLachlan. Her repudiation of the book was stern and uncompromising: "the only comfort you could give me would be to withdraw *The Black Girl* from circulation and make public reparation for the dishonour done in it to Almighty God." Shaw's response was to insist that he had been "inspired" to write the book. "You think you believe that God did not not know what he was about when he made me and inspired me to write *The Black Girl*. For what happened was that when my wife was ill in Africa God came to me and said 'These women in Worcester plague me night and day with their prayers for you. What are you good for, anyhow?' So I said I could write a bit but was good for nothing else. God said then 'Take your pen and write what I shall put into your silly head.' "

Similarly, Shaw inscribed the page-proof copy of *The Black Girl* he sent Dame Laurentia:

An Inspiration

which comes in response to the prayers of the nuns

of Stanbrook Abbey

and

in particular

to the prayers of his dear Sister Laurentia

for

Bernard Shaw

"Inspiration" is not forgotten in the Preface; it is there in the very first sentence: "I was inspired to write this tale when I was held up in Knysna for five weeks in the African summer and English winter of 1932."[10] That a private assurance to Dame Laurentia should become a public statement in the published preface is in itself an interesting indication of the way Shaw's mind worked on this issue.

The Nun of Stanbrook, who tells the story of Shaw's friendship with Dame Laurentia, makes much of this "inspiration," insisting that it descended on Shaw when seeing his wife at death's door after the accident. "A man's instinct in such a plight is not to jest but to pray." Here romantic interpretation exceeds the facts of the situation. Shaw made light of Charlotte's injuries, and there was never any question of taking her to hospital. Even so, Shaw would never have used a word like "inspired" lightly. If he says he was "inspired," then he was, or at least believed that this was the best way of explaining how his parable come into existence. If the word mollified Dame Laurentia, whose good opinion meant something to him, so much the better. However, Dame Laurentia was not mollified and refused to reply to Shaw's plea for understanding.[11]

Shaw's "enterprising publisher," Constable, brought out the "pamphlet" in London nine months later, on 5 December 1932. The first American edition, published in New York by Dodd, Mead and Company, followed on 24 February 1933. The American Book-of-the-Month-Club chose it as one of its titles for March. The book had the makings of a best-seller from the beginning, and a best-seller it soon became (by 1930s standards, that is). John Farleigh's wood engravings added special charm to the work.[12]

It had a mixed reception in the press. The more "intellectual" papers were unruffled, granting Shaw his "brilliance" while observing that the Black Girl's quest amounted to a restatement of well-known Shavian themes. The London *Times* commented, "We have heard it before, but it is restated with incisive brilliance in this cameo story"[13] and the *Times Literary Supplement* said much the same, adding, "Quite a number of properly lawn-sleeved Bishops would swallow most of it—so the Black Girl may go on peacefully weeding her garden."[14]

The Right Rev. Cyril Garbett, Bishop of Winchester, was not prepared to swallow any of it. He and other churchmen had, he said, "real cause of complaint against brilliant writers like Shaw who attack Christianity as set forth by its weakest, not its strongest, exponents or who label a construction of their own ignorance on Christianity and then show how easily they can destroy it."[15]

Self-appointed guardians of public morality emerged to condemn both Shaw and the book. The most bizarre of these was Dr. Greene of

Fig. 10. John Farleigh's cover illustration from Constable's edition of *The Black Girl.* Dodd, Mead used the same illustration for the first American edition.

the Wexford Beekeepers' Association, of which, for reasons that baffle surmise, Shaw was a life member. Dr. Greene wished Shaw's name to be removed because of "blasphemous statements" in *The Black Girl.* "On a show of hands," the *Times* reported, "the meeting decided not to hear Dr Greene."[16] The Cambridge Town Council was made of sterner stuff, upholding "by a large majority" the decision of its library committee to ban the book.[17] The London County Council, not to be outdone, excluded the book from schools for being, as the chairman of the subcommittee for books remarked, of "doubtful morals."[18]

It seems inconceivable that the United States should not have produced its crop of protests, but no one anywhere, not even in Boston, appears to have uttered so much as a public cheep, at least not loudly enough to be heard by the *New York Times.*

The Black Girl, like so much else that Shaw wrote or staged, caused widespread reaction. Its success (and notoriety) went well beyond its actual scope and significance in the context of Shaw's works. There was something about it that impinged on the sensibility of the 1930s and beyond; it got under the skin of the period, or at least the kind of skin susceptible to a naked heroine with a knobkerry and a penchant for asking provocative questions about the Bible. Some men and women were sufficiently provoked to take up their pens to respond. They unconsciously revived a subform of literature, the rebutting tract or "reply," echoing the pamphlet "wars" that accompanied religious controversy in sixteenth- and seventeenth-century England, with this difference, that the responses to *The Black Girl* were cast, like the original, in the form of parable.

The first four of the immediate responses were rebuttals of Shaw. The fifth, by Marcus Hyman, was pro-Shavian. They were all ephemeral pieces, but, brought to light after a lapse of more than fifty years, they have period interest, chiefly in showing how variously, and often quaintly, Shaw was regarded at the time. He does not always feature as a "character," but he is a presence in all the responses, as much the focus of attention as the "truth" the assorted protagonists go looking for; and the ways he is portrayed, if viewed as a composite, show him like a Picasso head, multifaceted and multilayered, jester, showman, genius (evil and otherwise), sage, prophet, and mountebank.

We may now turn our attention to these early responses, accompanying their heroes and heroines as they encounter the red-haired Irishman and proceed on their long out-of-print adventures.[19]

C. H. Maxwell's retort, *Adventures of the White Girl in Her Search for God,*[20] was probably the first to appear, coming out four months after *The Black Girl* in March 1933. A reprint and a second edition (a third impression) followed in the same month. It seems to have enjoyed an extraordinary if short-lived success. The publishers made the most of the White Girl's instant fame, managing to print commendations in the second edition, opposite the title page, from a veritable flock of clerics. The Archbishop of York headed the list with a somewhat noncommittal, "I have read it with great appreciation, and hope to have some opportunity of commending it." The Bishop of Ripon wrote, "A charming 'retort courteous' to Mr Bernard Shaw in his own manner. Even he (being an Irishman) will enjoy the rapier play." Among the smaller clerical fry, Canon Guy Rogers drew an analogy that makes one wonder: "Charles Herbert Maxwell's reply to Bernard Shaw is brilliant. He has put on Saul's armour and it fits him like a glove. For wit alone it is worth reading, and for sincerity and feeling I have seen no reply to touch it."

ADVENTURES OF THE WHITE GIRL IN HER SEARCH FOR GOD

Fig. 11. The cover of C. H. Maxwell's early response to Shaw's *The Black Girl,* showing the White Girl with her niblick.

The question is, if Maxwell is David to Shaw's Saul, then who is Goliath? *The Times Literary Supplement* was also complimentary: the White Girl "scores some effective hits with her niblick."[21] (The White Girl engagingly wields her niblick à la the Black Girl and her knobkerry and taps her guide, a paradoxical Irish dramatist, on the head with it whenever he utters a "heresy".)

With such commendations ringing in one's ears, it is a letdown to meet the White Girl, who turns out to be an earnest and lackluster damsel, scarcely representative of the bright young thing of the period and still less any match for the Black Girl. Her companion and ostensible guide, the Irish dramatist, is little better. He gives promise of some entertainment at the beginning; perhaps a flourish or two of that verbal rapier play about which the assorted clerics of England have raved will come our way.

His beard has turned white since he had married the Black Girl, and his only talent lies in standing on his head, which he does pretty well all the time. As he disingenuously explains to the White Girl, people are prepared to pay a lot of money to watch him doing this. He undertakes to show God to the White Girl "and you will see that he is not there" (p. 7), a neat little paradox, if essentially untrue of Shaw's belief about the deity.

Unfortunately, after these displays of wit (to call it that), the reader is treated to a series of less-than-inspired sermons from the mouth of orthodoxy while the White Girl and the Irish dramatist go through the motions of retracing the Black Girl's footsteps. The first encounter is with what the Irish dramatist says is a cruel, bloodthirsty God (who turns out to be sweet and benign), the second with a cunning old god (who turns out to be similarly sweet and benign and actually the same God as before). Aldous Huxley then pitches up carrying a Brave New World on his shoulders, followed in short order by H. G. Wells carrying quite a number of new worlds on his shoulders. Wells is responsible for the only "joke" in the book, a secondhand one at that. "What is that curious ticking noise?" the White Girl wants to know.

> "It is the sound of Mr H.G. Wells changing his mind," replied the dramatist. "Did not Sir James Barrie, when living next door to him at Adelphi Terrace, say that the walls were so thin that every evening he could distinctly hear him changing his mind? Whenever he has done this he produces another world." (p.16)

Next comes an author (unnamed) carrying a great house on his back— the house of the New Morality representing the "new freedom," which, we are earnestly assured, is freedom from the "slave mentality" that bound people to the family unit. This recalls the prevailing critical responses to Shaw's *Getting Married* and *Misalliance* years earlier. The White Girl next meets the dramatist's "conjuror," who turns out not to be a conjuror but the living Christ; thence to Calvary and the rhetoric of salvation, by which time the paradoxical Irish dramatist, who ceased being a factor in the quest a long way back, has gone off on his own, presumably to stand on his head again.

Whatever "brilliance" and "relevance" this "retort courteous" may once have had are now quite lost. It comes to us from the past as an undistinguished little piece, well-intentioned and sincere, but interesting only for its misreading of Shaw.

Dr. W. R. Matthews's (1881–1973) *The Adventures of Gabriel in his Search for Mr. Shaw*—a "modest companion," as the subtitle says, "for Mr. Shaw's *Black Girl*"[22]—appeared in August 1933. Matthews was no mean adversary. Dean of Exeter when he wrote the *Adventures of Gabriel,* he had already made a name for himself as a philosopher-theologian. Later, succeeding the great Inge as Dean of St Paul's, he was to become one of the most honored and respected churchmen of his day.[23] A sense of humor seems to have been among his many gifts.

Celestial beings, he assures the reader in his "Prologue in Heaven," are similarly blest; thus it is that Saint Peter is able to prevail on the Archangel Gabriel to go down to earth to investigate the strange noise coming from a man named Shaw. "Which is . . . the real noise?" Peter wants to know; or, as Gabriel puts it, "Which is the real Shaw?" (p. 13). Arriving on earth, he disguises himself as a private investigator, complete with the "garments of seedy respectability which are the badge of that tribe," and sets out in search of Shaw, discovering eventually the "Shavian wilderness," a "terrain without plan and without tracks" and a "strange confusion of sights and sounds" (pp. 14–15).

Gabriel hesitates. How is he to find the real Shaw in this howling desert? But he enters and in due course finds five different Shaws, the first four illusory, before finally chancing upon the real one.

Shaw No. 1 is beating a big drum. Why, Gabriel wants to know, is he making this din? To draw attention to himself, Shaw No. 1 says. "It's no use having great ideas unless you can get them heard." But isn't this noise inimical to "thinking things out" and "coherence of ideas"? Questioned in this pointed way, Shaw No. 1 becomes abusive: "you will be talking about 'absolute truth' soon! Go away and become a modern man." Irritated, Gabriel breaks the drum and Shaw No. 1 vanishes. "No drum, no Shaw," he concludes. "That means that the Shaw I saw was unreal." (pp. 18–22).

Shaw No. 2 is nearby, sitting on a rustic bench with his arm around a pretty young woman, lecturing her about love. It is, he insists in a loud hectoring voice, the "Life Force . . . making use of us for its own ends"— a better thing, he cheerfully assures Gabriel, than the "old stuff about eternal devotion." Gabriel, being what he is, is properly reticent about offering an opinion but points out that the young woman is fast asleep. Shaw No. 2 leaps up in vexation and fades from sight. Another illusion, obviously, endorsed by the young woman who wakes and says, "I dreamt that a perfect lamb of an old gentleman was making love to me. But, goodness, how the old dear did prose" (pp. 23–29).

On to Shaw No. 3, the enemy of the learned professions. He has tied a judge, a bishop, and a doctor to trees as if to sacrifice them and, watched by an audience of "moonfaced and shy" men and women (no children), proceeds first to insult his audience and then to berate the bishop for being a "dangerous encumbrance":

> You bishops go about preaching a deity whose proper name is "Nobod-
> addy". You probably know very well that the Bible is a collection of
> ancient and now unimportant legends. Yet you never say so. . . . And
> when I write a little tract to show that the myths of your creed are not
> plausible enough to take in an intelligent black girl, either you don't read
> it, or, if you do, you keep very quiet about it. (pp. 34, 37)

He sticks a hatpin into the gaitered shin of the bishop.

The doctor comes next. Shaw No. 3 abuses him as "one of the most
pitiable of creatures . . . who is financially interested in disease" (p. 38).
He is about to stick the hatpin into this creature when Gabriel stops him.
It emerges, however, that the three learned gentlemen are mere wax-
work dummies, made by Shaw No. 3 himself. He explains,

> Whenever I make up a character . . . I make a practice of putting at least
> one human feature into it. It is a point of honour with me. It is not really
> difficult. Just a question of mechanics. (p. 43)

This scene also vanishes into thin air, Shaw No. 3 with it, and Gabriel is
left once more looking for the "real" Shaw. Will it be No. 4, who is
discovered in a high pulpit preaching from a pile of pale green volumes?[24] Of course not. Shaw No. 4 is another figment, who preaches the
gospel of the Life Force with a good deal of proselytizing, not to say tub-
thumping, fervor: "Sweep away the Bible and the principle of Natural
Selection, and you have cleared the ground for the religion of the Life
Force. That is what I proclaim to you. That is the good news which I
bring" (p. 48). Gabriel does not know to which of the recognized heresies
the new gospel belongs and so engages the preacher in discussion which
ends with his accusing Shaw No. 4 of being "nothing but a contradiction
in terms" (p. 54). A dreadful insult, apparently, because it provokes
Shaw No. 4 to emulate his predecessors and vanish.

Still searching, Gabriel enters a miniature world and here, finally, he
discovers the "real" Shaw, a remarkably diminutive Shaw. Gabriel has to
use his magnifying glass to see him. This Shaw admits to having a con-
suming interest in drama, which he sees as a potent instrument of spiri-
tual regeneration. "I have," he says, "sought a firm foundation on which
we can build a life which is noble and secure. . . . I have been filled, too,
with a rage which is hard to control against the unreason and injustice of
human society. . . . When courage and reason could do much, if not all,
to procure a dignified and happy life for the majority of men, I am
overwhelmed by indignation and despair at the cruelty and folly of our
society. Often I laugh so that I shall not weep" (pp. 57–60).

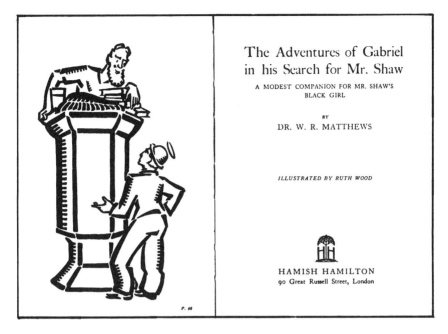

The Adventures of Gabriel
in his Search for Mr. Shaw

A MODEST COMPANION FOR MR. SHAW'S
BLACK GIRL

BY

DR. W. R. MATTHEWS

ILLUSTRATED BY RUTH WOOD

HAMISH HAMILTON
90 Great Russell Street, London

Fig. 12. The frontispiece from W. R. Matthews's *Adventures of Gabriel* shows Gabriel with Shaw No. 4.

Gabriel remarks that these views coincide to a remarkable extent with his own. "But . . . how is it that you are so small?" Shaw No. 5 replies,

> How can I get any bigger . . . while all those other fellows live on me? They consume my substance. There is the fellow who will beat that terrible drum, the one who is always philandering, the one who runs the waxwork show, and, worst of all, the bore who is never happy without his pulpit. They have taken the subsistence which I ought to have had. They have prevented me from growing. (p.60)

Mission accomplished, Gabriel returns to heaven. He has found Mr. Shaw, he tells Peter, "a difficult man to get to know" and "rather on the small side" (p. 62).

The reviewer in the *Times Literary Supplement* did not find the *Adventures of Gabriel* particularly successful. "The present retort from a distinguished theologian is . . . rather a heavy-footed piece of satire."[25] This is ungenerous. The idea of the tract, based on the time-honored principle

of inversion, is fetching, and Gabriel's series of encounters are not without a broad, burlesquing, and occasionally telling humor. The illusory
Shaws are caricatures, of course, and they tend to speak in un-Shavian,
unpolished terms—aggressively, dogmatically, and, worst offense of all,
with little wit and style. The "real" Shaw, on the other hand, speaks with
passion and conviction. Matthews is no stranger to the art of rhetoric,
but, contradictorily, while investing this "real" Shaw with eloquent, even
noble, credibility, he refuses to concede any stature to him or, by extension, to what he says. Those four bullying, blustering figments have not,
and never could have, consumed the "real" Shaw's substance. It is a pity
Matthews would not see this, and a pity Gabriel reported so belittlingly
back to heaven.

In another response, Mr. and Mrs. I. I. Kazi's Brown Girl sets off in
search for God toward the end of 1933, her quest being noted in the
Times Literary Supplement of 15 February, 1934.[26] Thereafter, like the
others, she faded from view, emerging suddenly and rather bizarrely in
Lahore in 1950.[27] Mr. Kazi's local eminence rather than the intrinsic
merit of the book may have prompted this resuscitation.[28]

The authors describe their Brown Girl as a "Companion to the Black
Girl." There is very little companioning in the literal sense. The Black Girl
is mentioned (together with C. H. Maxwell's White Girl, resurrected as a
platinum blonde named "Miss West," whom the Brown Girl has kindly put
through graduate studies in economics and finance). The Black Girl "had
been a student of divinity in her own way, and [the Brown Girl's] sincere
friend. But she had married an Irishman and given up her studies, and
since then [the Brown Girl] saw very little of her" (p. 3).

The Brown Girl is a pampered darling, "the only daughter of an
Eastern potentate of fabulous wealth." She owns a two-seater Rolls Royce
and lives in a "gorgeous flat in Mayfair, wherein she could study, revel
and sin" (pp. 1–2). But she is dissatisfied. "Where is God?" she asks the
one-eyed beggar-woman. She finds her answer in "History," a stern,
hoary-headed fellow who appears to her in a dream. He sends her off on
a kind of Cook's tour of religious beliefs of the past, traveling through
vistas of history, from paganism to various more advanced modes of
theism in both the East and West to comparatively recent forms of religious faith. Civilizations come and go in not very stately procession, and
the Brown Girl is slave, concubine, companion, and interlocutor in more
or less random sequence, receiving as she flits from age to age and sage
to sage crash courses in religious doctrine from, among others, Buddha,
a Pharoah, Moses, the Greeks, Jesus, and Mohammed. A grand vision of
recent and contemporary history follows: the USSR is seen as "a phoenix
rising from the ashes" and the USA as a "great nation in the far west"

which had stopped "drink wholesale" and "recognised the rights of individuals to put an end to matrimonial connections if they so desired" (p.
88). Just when this vision is about to disintegrate, the Black Girl appears,
and there is a touching reunion:

> "Oh, I am so delighted to see you here in this grove!" cried the brown
> girl, kissing her. "I was really getting frightened," and looking at her
> tenderly she continued: "Haven't we reason to thank that great drama-
> tist; but for whom we would not have the pleasure of having you here
> amongst us?" (p. 89)

"But for whom," the Black Girl could and perhaps should have re-
torted, "we would not have had to suffer all this endless prosing." But she
refrains, having no doubt learned the virtue of tact since putting her
knobkerry aside and marrying the Irishman. She says instead that the
White Girl, the platinum blonde Miss West, has fallen out with "my Dramatist Love" because "He told her that she could not find God in the way she
thought; while she claimed to have found God inside everybody" (p. 89).
   The girls enter a vast amphitheater where they find that the authors
have laid on a get-together of great minds for their benefit. For Miss
West's benefit as well, it turns out, for that young lady, faithfully reflect-
ing Mr. and Mrs. Kazi's image of that great nation in the far west, shows
up to promote commercial interests. Thus we have a representative from
each of the three worlds present: the Black Girl representing Africa, the
Brown Girl the East, and the White Girl, obviously, the West, also apparently doubling-up as a look-alike of the well-known actress of that
name—a perplexing compounding of roles. Everyone or practically
everyone who was ever anyone in the first, second, and third worlds
appears on the scene for the edification of the three girls. Within a page
Goethe, Tolstoy, Plato, the Arabian philosopher Ghazali, and Roger
Bacon have spoken, and within another page Hegel and Spinoza. Then
Aristotle . . . Herbert Spencer . . . Karopotkin . . . Carlyle . . . Keats . . .
Shakespeare (a very gloomy Bard) . . . the list goes on and on. But nowhere, regrettably, do the three friends discover a red-haired Irishman.
He is probably at home tending the garden and looking after his
piccaninnies—a pity in a way, for he would assuredly have imparted
verve and vitality to the proceedings. A touch of Shavian irreverence
could have done this dreary book a world of good.
   What all the pronouncements amount to in the end is that theism "is
the natural inborn belief of humanity." This is the contention of the
dust-cover blurb. The book is also alleged to prove that from "Noah
down to Muhammed [sic] every prophet preached Islam in its theistic

aspects." This may be so, but it scarcely makes *The Brown Girl* an effective "companion" to, or development of, Shaw's book. At best, a repeated lament from the prophets we meet, that man, silly man, persists in holding on to outworn creeds, may be seen to echo the theme of *The Black Girl*. As a rebuttal of Shaw, however, which was presumably intended, *The Brown Girl* makes no point at all.

Four Men Seek God, with the subscript "A Reply to a Famous Author's Book," by C. Payne,[29] appeared late in 1934. It was noted in the *Times Literary Supplement* of 13 December 1934; apart from this, it does not seem to have attracted attention. A disclaimer opposite the first page of text declares that "the names and characters in this book are entirely fictitious and refer to no living person." This is true no doubt of the four men, but blatantly untrue of the "famous author" whose infamous book sends them out on their quests. References to this book come thick and fast in the opening chapter:

> It was one of the most exciting and heated debates that one could ever remember, and it lasted long after midnight.
>
> The discussion arose over a famous author's book, which had recently been published—a nauseous book to many minds, yet some of the same train of thought, praised it as high-brow literature. High-brow it certainly was; it awoke more temper and high words than any debate. . . .
>
> "It is against human nature," said Sir George, "and, to my mind, the effect on the minds of the young, and even on some of the elders, will be disastrous. Pure Atheism—if you can call Atheism pure! The outcome of a twisted, tortured mind. I suppose it amuses the author to write such books, and, of course, there are thousands of people who believe in them."
>
> "The reading public of to-day go mad over an author who deliberately flouts God. They say he is courageous, and not afraid of public opinion!" put in Bilston. . . .
>
> "I cannot understand what the author is getting at in his reference to the blacks," argued Sir Archibald. "Certainly, my experience of the black races is different from that of many. As you know, I have spent some years amongst all kinds of blacks and yellows, and, if you treat them properly, they naturally become your slaves. . . . I tell you I think this author must have struck something odd to write a book like that—A Girl in her Search for God."
>
> "I wonder if she found God? The author omits to say that," Blayne queried.
>
> Andrew Bilston immediately answered, "It is quite natural that he omitted that. You must have personal experience of any subject, before you can speak or write about the particular subject, and it is the same with religion. Unless you have religion, how can you write about it? (pp. 3–6)

The "famous author" and his "nauseous book" having thus neatly been put in their place, the elevated and edifying conversation ends with the four friends agreeing to embark on independent quests for God.

Sir George Tomkinson, an eminent scientist, comes first, starting his quest with a dream (dreams and visions are quite a feature of the book) in which he listens to a sermon by a latter-day prophet, a shaggy individual with (so the reader is seriously informed) the mind of a Samson and the appearance of a Joshua, and a line in public confession which closely reflects the "famous author's" godless career in, particularly, its pro-Bolshevik phase. Samson-Joshua inspires Sir George to pursue his quest without delay. His wife humors him, the Bishop retreats in alarm, but his friend Jack, an eminent Harley Street physician (naturally), is prepared to lend a sympathetic ear:

> "What happened last night?" [Jack] asked.
>
> "Only that four of us—the usual four at the club—were debating for hours this last book of The Great Burnet Shore. We were determined to try and prove it right or wrong, and the four of us have made a compact to find God."
>
> Jack laughed, but his laugh soon died away when he saw the seriousness of his friend's face. "All I can say, Sir George, is that you have a big job on. There are so many imitations."
>
> "Do you mean religions or gods?"
>
> "Both!" replied Jack kindly. (pp. 13–14)

So that's who done it—The Great Burnet Shore, no less. Murder will out. Having been warned by Jack, Sir George rapidly disposes of a variety of "imitation gods," among them God in the Virgin and Child as depicted by works of art. (This comes to him in another timely vision, in a railway carriage.) After his wife's sudden death, yet another vision is vouchsafed him, a supernatural odyssey rather, for his ghostly companion takes him whizzing through time and space to view a further series of false gods and religions, not excepting Catholicism, until, in what may be intended as a denunciation of Major Barbara's desertion of the colors, he finds Christ in a humble Salvation Army shelter in the East End of London. All this is too much for George. Death beckons and he summons his three friends to his bedside so that he may testify to having found God. Quite simple, he says. God revealed himself in a vision. This is no surprise, considering the number that came Sir George's way.

Sir George has disposed of most of the "imitation gods" the author can think of, so the quests of the three surviving friends are accordingly shorter. Sir Archibald, a surgeon, also eminent of course, comes next. He muses on the death of his friend George:

> It is one of those mysteries which, I suppose, will never be revealed. . . . To
> the unbelievers, like the author of that book, it would seem that if God was
> a God of Love, He would never allow such things to happen. (pp. 35–36)

The author of that book is not having an easy time of it, but worse is to
come. Sir Archibald, who is "a man of the world," can recognize prosti-
tutes when he sees them, and, being a doctor, he knows everything there
is to know about social diseases. Therefore, "he allowed the women to
pass by. Had he been a disciple of the new moral code, he would have
acted differently" (pp. 41–42). A little while later,

> His mind wandered to those outcasts and street girls. If they had a
> mother and home like he had, they would never be living the life they
> were doing. "Home and good parents are an answer to that author's new
> morality," he said aloud. (p. 43)

Visions do not come to Sir Archibald's aid, but coincidence does. He
rushes to the assistance of a victim of a street accident. Wonder of wonders, it is his sainted mother, come to London to visit him. Sir Archibald
finds God through her, undertaking a retrospective quest through his
childhood with her and becoming as a little child in the process. This
brings the reader to the third friend, the business man, Andrew
Bilston—not apparently a "Sir" but definitely "eminent."
    The God of the previous two quests has revealed himself in a some-
what arbitrary manner but has at least had the backing of biblical authority. Bilston's God is no such purist. Bilston's God is descended from the
deus ex machina and obligingly responds to Bilston's prayer to be saved
from financial ruin by giving him heaps of money. The text does not
invite super-subtleties of interpretation, but the Bilston episode may be
yet another not so subtle swipe at the ethic of *Major Barbara*. Bilston is
described as a rigid Presbyterian, a form of Calvinist. To him, and the
author, the making of money may well be a godly pursuit and that god-
in-a-money-box a sign of divine favor. Was Bodger, one wonders, a
Presbyterian? The ethic would not have found favor in Shavian quarters,
however, least of all in the Perivale St. Andrews to be run by Barbara and
Cusins.
    Coming to the fourth friend, the artist Blayne (not a "Sir" but an
eminent "R.A."), we find ourselves on familiar ground. Blayne has visions. The first, of someone resembling the Christ, sends him out of
London on his quest; later, while painting near a ruined abbey, the same
Christ figure watches with him as the scene changes and the abbey becomes as it was centuries before. The Catholic ceremony they observe

does not celebrate the true God. Christ weeps, and Blayne sees his re-demption in the tears.

The four friends have each found God. All the surviving three need now undertake is a castigation of that "famous author" and his book, which they carry out with the same plodding earnestness (not to say witlessness) with which they have followed their quests:

> "I suggest," said Sir Archibald, opening the subject, "that we go through this book, and try and find out what is actually at the back of the author's mind."
>
> "Is it worth while?" asked Bilston. "Although no doubt it was written with a certain amount of sarcasm and satire, yet out of evil came good. Certainly the four of us, including poor George, would never have faced the question of a personal God if this book had not been written."
>
> "But," put in Blayne, "whatever made an author of such repute pen such expressions?"
>
> "Only this," said Sir Archibald, "it is like a city clerk trying to explain to a farmer how to plough his land."
>
> "You mean," said Blayne, "that he knows little about his subject."
>
> "Precisely," answered Sir Archibald. . . . "You know . . . a man can be a giant in understanding and wisdom as far as this world is concerned, but in his knowledge of God he can be as a dwarf."
>
> "To my mind," said Bilston, "it appears to be like that in this case. He certainly excels in pouring dirty water into the clean, no doubt in the hopes that some miracle will take place. . . . "
>
> "I agree . . . " spoke up Blayne emphatically. "A man has only to have one vision of Christ to feel sorry for anyone who writes such heresy." . . .
>
> "The only good part," reflected Bilston, "was where the woman sought God in a garden. As I read it I hoped that the author would have allowed the seeker to have found the true God there. . . ."
>
> "But don't forget, Bilston," answered Sir Archibald thoughtfully, "that even in a beautiful garden there are weeds and briars and things to destroy, and so it appears to be in this author's mind, though what could have been a beautiful climax is spoiled by the presence of the Irishman. Could the Black Girl have met the missionary who had taught her to seek God, and have related her experiences to him [sic], there would have been a very different ending." (pp. 76–78)

Muddleheadedness, prejudice, misreading of "that book," and an un-derlying fear that cherished beliefs are being threatened, all these emerge. Once again we are confronted with orthodox pieties inexpertly, one might say disastrously, handled. The Great Burnet Shore and his Black Girl emerge unscathed.

Marcus Hyman's *The Adventures of the White Girl in Her Search for Knowl-*

178   LEON H. HUGO

THE ADVENTURES OF THE WHITE
GIRL IN HER SEARCH FOR KNOWLEDGE
MARCUS HYMAN

Fig. 13. The cover
illustration from Marcus
Hyman's pro-Shavian
response to *The Black Girl*.

edge[30] followed hard on the heels of *Four Men Seek God*. The *Times Literary Supplement* reviewed it on 17 January 1935; it was, the reviewer said not very astutely, one of those books that would not have been written but for Shaw's *Black Girl*. Hyman's heroine, Sylvia Swan, is a student at the London School of Physiognomics. Only one student at the School, named George, attracts her, a "tall young Irishman who flaunted a full red beard and kept very much to himself. . . . Sylvia had heard much of his intellectual attainments" (p. 15). One day during a student ramble in Kent she contrives to walk alone with him and is "captivated by his witty and charming conversation." But to her chagrin he shows little interest in her company, preferring to lecture her on the role of Woman in the scheme of things:

"I believe," he said, "that when Adam ate of the fruit of the Tree of Knowledge, he ate the lot leaving none for Eve, who got along much better with more digestible fruit, as do her daughters to this day. And those of them who pretend to thirst after knowledge, like men, are either foolish or perverse. What greater horror could the Devil himself conceive than a blue-stocking, that poor unfortunate creature, neither a man nor a woman, sterilizing the natural feelings within her for intercourse and motherhood, cataloguing facts in her brain, and transforming herself into a living reference book? No woman yet produced anything more original than pleasure and children; and that is as it should be, like it or not. . . . Women seeking Knowledge!" he added, contemptuously. "Pshaw!" (pp. 16–17)

Sylvia is outraged, as well she might be: this young Irishman is demonstrably neither witty nor charming, and his "intellectual attainments" scarcely pass muster as a parody of John Tanner. She will have nothing more to do with him. "Did he think"—she thinks furiously—"that men had a monopoly on brain power in the World, that Women were incapable of acquiring Knowledge? Well, she would show him his mistake" (p. 17). Armed with a stout bergstock, she enters the Ashdown Forest in search of Knowledge, leaving the Irishman talking.

Her ensuing adventures are crowded, rushed, and, by and large, illustrations of pandemonium rather than Knowledge. First to appear is the Devil, a gorgeous black gentleman, who tries to seduce her while magically divesting her of most of her clothes; next is Solomon the Wise, who also tries to seduce her while removing what is left of her clothing; then Mr Grundy, whose myopic eyes pop out on proverbial stalks when he sees her naked, and who is revealed, when Sylvia makes him take off his clothes, as the redoubtable Mrs Grundy herself.

Her next meeting, with a "noble Greek," promises a more positive approach to Knowledge, but he has time only to warn her against the "hemlock of democracy" and suggest that the Ideal State may yet be found in Reality. Next in line is an eighteenth-century Dean with a predilection for addressing his remarks to an oak tree and calling Sylvia "Stella." Like Plato, Swift is rather offhand about Knowledge, but he obligingly takes Sylvia to Babel and Bedlam (Hyde Park Corner on a more than usually noisy Sunday), where sundry crusaders and revolutionists are yelling at the top of their voices. Violence in the uniform of fascism erupts, and Sylvia flees back into the forest, where she meets "a young girl dressed in a golfing suit and carrying a niblick"—Maxwell's White Girl, as we discover:

The golfer surveyed Sylvia pityingly.

"I suppose you are a Nudist?" she said.

"No," said Sylvia, who was in no mood for conversation and resented the other's foolish smile of condescension.

"Ah," said the golfer, "You have missed the mark. I, too, once spent my life missing the mark, but now I have found Him and am starting afresh." (*Max.iv.22 and 23*)

"Him?" said Sylvia. "Whom?"

"God," said the golfer. "I found him with the aid of the Apostle Maxwell. He led me to Him. I had a conviction of sin, and I felt that the Holy Spirit was pleading with me." (*Max.iv.22*)

"Look here," said Sylvia, jumping up in alarm. "You're a Babel and Bedlamite!"

"The Holy Spirit was pleading with me," repeated the golfer softly to herself.

"Don't be tempted," said Sylvia. "Remember Mary." And she walked off. (p. 36)

Hyman explains in an Epilogue why he included this scene in the book. He had, he says, come upon a "pamphlet in boards entitled *The Adventures of the White Girl in Her Search for God,* written by one Charles Herbert Maxwell. This pamphlet appeared to me to be a rather spiteful, but ineffective, attack upon the author of *The Adventures of the Black Girl,* and an extraordinarily weak and maudlin defence of the Bible" (p. 61). He thanks Maxwell for providing the opportunity to ridicule him. He does not, however, explain the cryptic "Don't be tempted. . . . Remember Mary," although, considering Sylvia's experience of male concupiscence, it is not hard to guess.

The next highlight of her quest is a take-off of the League of Nations, which becomes a Gastronomic Conference attended by the dogs of all nations. A long-haired dachshund (an illustration shows him sporting a small black moustache) is prominant with a snarling *"Dachshundland über Alles!"* and a Japanese dog kills a Pekingese. Snarling and bickering continue until the Dean flings a huge meat bone into the center. A free-for-all ensues.

Next on Sylvia's agenda is the Theosophical Museum, in which she sees all manner of weird and wonderful, but essentially trivial, exhibits. (Since Hyman's stout Dean is in attendance when Sylvia visits the museum, Hyman may have attempted a take-off of Swift by presenting a parallel to Gulliver's visit to the Grand Academy of Lagado.) This is followed by a brief meeting with a "murderous-looking villain," a representative of civilized twentieth-century man. He, least of all, can show her the way to Knowledge.

Fortunately the fountainhead of truth is not far off. Sylvia reaches it when, in a clearing in the forest, she comes upon a glass hut mounted on a high wooden platform. In it, seated at a desk writing, is a "tall, exceedingly thin and bearded old gentleman" dressed in a nightshirt. He looks extraordinarily like God in *The Black Girl* who nailed Job in argument, but not quite, for his white hair, bushy eyebrows, remarkably high forehead, long nose, and nostrils which curve sardonically do not express self-satisfied cunning but a "distinctly mephistotelian" quality. Sylvia tells this old gentleman, "I am seeking Knowledge. Can you advise me?" He responds in a soft Irish brogue (to be sure, Job's argumentative God did not have an Irish brogue), and she is reminded of the young Irishman she had left talking at the haystack. "Get rid of your clothes, sit in the sun, and read *The Intelligent Woman's Guide to Socialism and Capitalism*," he says (pp. 55–56).

> "I've done all that," said Sylvia, and she ran up the steps and entered the hut.
> "Heavens!" said the old gentleman, spinning round in his chair. "I am not only hearing Voices but seeing Visions as well. How did you get in here?"
> "I just walked in," said Sylvia. "I am looking for a Republic where women are treated as more than mere incubators and vehicles for pleasure; where the rulers are chosen from women as well as men; where women and men share the privileges and bear the responsibilities of citizenship equally; where the women are common to all men and the children are the children of every citizen."
> "I have spent the best part of my life trying to persuade the English to build such a State," said the old gentleman, "but they are still too stupid to do so. Yet the Russians who, on the whole, are a much more ignorant people, have adopted my entire stock of ideas and are now busily engaged in putting them into operation."
> "Then we must go to Russia," said Sylvia.
> "You may," said the old gentleman, "but I won't. I've just come back."
> "But why didn't you stay?"
> "Strictly in confidence," said the old gentleman, "I feared I might change my mind and denounce my own ideas which now form the basis of the prevailing religion in Russia. Such a denunciation would rightly be treated by Mr. Stalin as counter-revolutionary, and as I have a natural antipathy to killing of any kind, I came away before they shot me. Besides Russia is still a very uncomfortable place to live in, and life is unbearable without a town and country residence and a couple of cars at least. But I am starting on a world tour very soon and hope to discover the ideal state yet."
> "Then I will accompany you," said Sylvia, "and meanwhile, if I may, I should like to stay here with you in your sensible sun hut."

> So she stayed with him and listened to his sermonising. And the sun
> shone on this odd pairing of a mephistotelian-featured old Adam in a
> nightshirt and a lovely young Eve in nothing at all. (pp. 56–57)

That elusive, sought-for "Knowledge" remains as woolly as ever, but
Sylvia seems happy; here, one might expect, her quest will end. But
Hyman, whose own "Sylvia" apparently "inspired" this book,[31] cannot
leave his heroine in the arms of Wisdom alone, not when personified in a
"sermonising" geriatric gentleman. So he spins out his tale, introducing,
by way of contrast, a procession of conspicuously unedifying Eminent
Contemporaries: "Herbert" (H. G. Wells), who passes by "Making Outlines"; then "Hotaire Billycock" (Hilaire Belloc), eating onions and scowl-
ing at "Herbert"; then "Glib T. Tunnerchest" (G. K. Chesterton), guz-
zling beer; and finally "Professor Fundamentalaski" (Harold Laski), followed by a train of adoring females.

One person remains: Sylvia's talkative school friend, George, who is
standing on his head in the clearing. He responds to her call by turning
several somersaults and executing a neck-spring before striding to the
hut. Sylvia sees the resemblance between the young fellow and the old
gentleman at once. So does the old gentleman, who wastes no time in
clearing out.

> "I'm off!" he said.
> "But what about the world tour?" said Sylvia disappointed.
> "It starts immediately," said the old gentleman. "You see," he said
> apologetically, "I happen to know that wild young man rather well, and
> I'm not particularly anxious to meet him again. Take my advice and
> chase him till you get him to marry you." (p. 58)

Sylvia follows this advice and, after some difficulty, à la Ann Whitefield,
she captures young George and marries him. She is then so busy setting
up home that she has no time to think about her search for Knowledge
and the Ideal State. George refuses to wear a nightshirt; consequently
she is never quite able to determine the precise extent to which he
resembles the old gentleman.

Hyman's White Girl suffers from overcrowding and a lack of focus and
direction, and there is confusion about the meaning of "Knowledge" in
relation to "Wisdom." The two representations of Shaw, as the young
"George" and "the old gentleman," are amusing but inaccurate. Even so,
the book is entertaining and inventive in a high-spirited, racy way; and it
does arrive at some kind of point in the end. This seems to be that
"Knowledge" ("Wisdom"?) will come to those who, like Sylvia, reject the

false prophets of the twentieth century and cleave to Shaw. Through him, in spite of the inconsistencies and contradictions of his career, one may grow to Methuselah-like "Knowledge." In this at least Hyman signals a welcome reversal of attitude to both Shaw and his Black Girl.

This was the last of the immediate replies. *The Black Girl* was to continue to prompt responses as late as the early 1970s, but those are another story.

Notes

Thanks are due to Professors Stanley Weintraub and Dan H. Laurence for their assistance in identifying and helping me track down some of the texts discussed in this article.

1. The question whether the *Black Girl* is a parable or fable or allegory is academic. Shaw himself once referred to it as a "large pamphlet"; reviewers of the book when it first appeared tended to call it a "parable"; "fable" would not be incorrect, and "allegory" is obviously acceptable.

2. An unreliable report has it that Shaw and Charlotte were house guests of the Prime Minister, General J. B. M. Hertzog, at least for a couple of days, at his holiday residence at the Wilderness. I have been unable to verify this.

3. Preface to *The Black Girl in Search of God and Some Lesser Tales* (London: Constable, 1954), p. 3.

4. Shaw had completed *Too True to be Good* in 1931; it was given its world premiere in Boston while he and Charlotte were in Knysna. *On the Rocks* was completed and produced in 1933.

5. For a more detailed report on the motor accident and the Vassall-Phillips affair, see my "Upset in a Sun-Trap: Shaw in South Africa" in *Shaw Abroad,* ed. Rodelle Weintraub, *Shaw: The Annual of Bernard Shaw Studies* 5 (University Park: Pennsylvania State University Press, 1985), 155–57.

6. *The Cape Argus* (Cape Town), 18 March 1932.

7. *The Cape Times* (Cape Town), 25 May 1935.

8. *The Black Girl in Search of God*, p. 21

9. See Shaw's description of Mabel Shaw in a letter (12 May 1930) to Lady Astor, Weintraub's comment, and Shaw's letter to Mabel Shaw (30 January 1928) in *The Portable Bernard Shaw*, comp. and ed. by Stanley Weintraub (Harmondsworth: Penguin, 1977), pp. 632–35.

10. *The Black Girl in Search of God*, p. 3.

11. An account of their long friendship, including their dispute over the *Black Girl*, is in A Nun of Stanbrook, "The Nun and the Dramatist: Dame Laurentia McLachlan and George Bernard Shaw," *Cornhill Magazine* (Summer 1956), pp. 415–58. D. Felicitas Corrigan's *The Nun, the Infidel & the Superman* (London: John Murray, 1985) covers the same ground. The author comments pertinently on the "ambiguity of the word 'inspiration' " (pp. 123–24).

12. See Dan H. Laurence, *Bernard Shaw: A Bibliography*, vol. 1 (Oxford: Clarendon Press, 1983), pp. 210–12, for the complete bibliographical history.

13. *The Times* (London), 6 December 1932.

14. *The Times Literary Supplement* (London), 8 December 1932. Coincidentally, the companion work in this critique is Archibald Henderson's *Bernard Shaw: Playboy and Prophet*, which the reviewer tore to shreds.

15. *The Times* (London), 24 December 1932.

16. *The Times* (London), 27 January 1933.

17. *The Times* (London), 3 February 1933.

18. *The Times* (London), 23 March 1933.

19. One title has not come to light: *The Adventures of the Black Man in his Search for God*, by H. M. Singh, listed in the Cumulative Book Index of 1937 as having been published in Lahore. Another elusive text, if it exists in published form, is Christopher Isherwood's stage adaptation of *The Black Girl*, produced by the Minnesota Theater Company at the Mark Taper Forum, Los Angeles, in 1969. Assistance in tracing and obtaining these texts would be appreciated.

20. Charles Herbert Maxwell, *Adventures of the White Girl in Her Search for God* (London: Lutterworth Press, 1933), 24 pp.

21. *The Times Literary Supplement* (London), 4 May 1933.

22. W. R. Matthews, *The Adventures of Gabriel in his Search for Mr Shaw: A modest companion for Mr Shaw's Black Girl;* illus. by Ruth Wood (London: Hamish Hamilton, 1933), 60 pp.

23. See Matthews's obituary in *The Times* (London), 5 December 1973.

24. The "pale green volumes" are Shaw's *Collected Works*, published in 1930–32, augmented in 1934 and 1938.

25. *The Times Literary Supplement* (London), 14 September 1933.

26. I. I. Kazi (Mr. and Mrs.), *The Adventures of the Brown Girl (Companion to the Black Girl of Mr Bernard Shaw) in Her Search for God* (London: Stockwell, 1933).

27. Ibid. (Kashmiri Bazar, Lahore: Sh. Muhammad Ashraf), 170 pp. (Page references are to this text.)

28. Mr. I. I. Kazi appears to have been Vice-Chancellor of the University of Sind in Hyderabad in the 1950s. (Uncorroborated testimony in an unknown hand on the cover of this copy in the Dan H. Laurence Collection, University of Guelph.)

29. C. Payne, *Four Men Seek God: A Reply to a Famous Author's Book* (London: Stockwell, 1934), 78 pp.

30. Marcus Hyman, *The Adventures of the White Girl in Her Search for Knowledge* (London: Cranley and Day, 1934), 62 pp.

31. "I was inspired to write this little book," Hyman says, self-importantly echoing Shaw's words, "by the original Sylvia, whom I met shortly after reading Mr George Bernard Shaw's *The Adventures of the Black Girl in Her Search for God*." Epilogue, p. 61.

Vivian Ducat

BERNARD SHAW AND THE KING'S ENGLISH

The Pronunciation Unit of the BBC is unique in broadcasting. Its function, in part, is to maintain a standard of pronunciation for English words—for example, *dispute,* which is widely used as a noun in Britain these days (thanks to an intensified clash, under the Thatcher Government, between representatives of labor and those of management) and which is increasingly heard with the accent placed on the first syllable (a pronunciation popularized by trade-union leaders hailing from the north of England). Another part of the unit's job is to provide an accurate, or at least a consistent, rendering of foreign words and proper names (*guerilla, Chernobyl, Khaddafy*) into spoken English. The Pronunciation Unit enjoys no veto or disciplinary power, even over BBC announcers, but the very fact that it exists, as a functioning organ of the chief broadcasting outlet of the people who invented English, gives it a certain stature.

It used to have—or, more precisely, its bureaucratic predecessor used to have—far more stature and far more authority. There was a time when the phrase "the King's English" had not only a substantial and particular meaning but also, for those who mastered the intricacies of the language summed up in that phrase, potentially significant social and economic consequences. In England accent was (and, to an extent, remains) a shibboleth of social class. Not surprisingly, then, when radio and television came to Britain—a few years after the one and then the other had come to the United States—the British took pains to apply a special sort of care for the language, which was as admirably foresighted as it was ineffective.

This essay is revised and augmented from the original, which appeared in *The Atlantic* (September 1986). The additional Shaw material is published with the authorization of the Shaw Trustees.

American broadcasting was already well developed when the British, in the early 1920s, got around to setting up a broadcasting system of their own. Alarmed at the "chaos of the ether" in the United States— where, by 1922, more than 500 local radio stations were in operation— the British established a very different system indeed: a nationwide broadcasting monopoly, the British Broadcasting Company (later, Corporation), whose directors could exercise total control over the quality of both signal and content. Unlike American broadcasters, the BBC's administrators and announcers were drawn from the ruling elite, from the top of a staunchly hierarchical social system. With a high-minded pride reminiscent of those who shouldered the "white man's burden," the early BBC directors saw it as their mission not only to entertain but also to educate. Accordingly they created a number of influential advisory committees, whose members included prominent experts in fields unrelated to broadcasting, to help the BBC produce programming of the very highest quality.

The task of one of these committees, the Advisory Committee on Spoken English, was to ensure proper English pronunciation on the airwaves. The committee laid down strict rules, from which BBC broadcasters departed at their peril. Announcers were expected to be men of "culture, experience, and knowledge"; their "pronunciation of the King's English must be faultless." A group photograph of the BBC's radio announcers in 1930 shows the men dressed in dinner jackets, the standard attire for reading the news. The English they spoke was supposed to be equally formal and uniform—Southern Educated Standard, or Received Pronunciation, as phoneticians call it. This was the accent of the upper-middle classes—of the officer corps, the civil service, the church, and the public schools—the accent of less than five percent of the British population. To the remaining 95 percent of the British public, Received Pronunciation came to be known simply as BBC English, and the advisory committee did its utmost, both by precept and by example, to spread BBC English among the lower classes. A didactic pamphlet called "Broadcast English," containing lists of controversial words and the pronunciation preferred by the BBC, was made available to the listening public for "price 3*d*, post free." The lists were also published in the popular weekly *The Radio Times.* The committee produced a two-record set, *Broadcast English,* for use in British schools. Once, in 1936, a member of the committee traveled around the United States in the hope of inspiring American announcers to "follow the example of their British confreres" by setting up an advisory committee of their own. (The Americans declined.)

Throughout the thirteen years of its active life, from 1926 to 1939, the

Advisory Committee on Spoken English maintained the official pretense that it was merely an in-house organ for promoting consistency in the language employed by the BBC's announcers. But the real agenda of some of its members was more ambitious. The great Lord Reith, who guided the BBC in its formative years, conceded, "So long as the announcer is talking good English, and without affectation, I think it is much to be desired that he should be copied." (Lord Reith, however, continued to speak like the Scot he was.) Going further, A. Lloyd James, the Honorary Secretary of the committee, saw its task as nothing less than "the preservation of mutual intelligibility throughout the English-speaking world."

It was a valiant effort, even if the results have been disappointing. The English spoken in Great Britain today is by no means homogeneous. Turn on the BBC and you are likely to hear accents very different from those that were prescribed by the advisory committee. A range of "nonstandard" accents—Scottish, Northern Irish, and various English accents—have joined what is now a somewhat modified version of Received Pronunciation. In England the accents on radio and TV increasingly reflect those of the British population as a group. And yet the advisory committee's recommendations of a half century ago have not been entirely cast aside. Its work, in perhaps unexpected ways, lives on.

They came by rail from Oxford or Cambridge or Rugby, or by taxi from lunch at their clubs. They came from the "talks studio" and from elsewhere inside Broadcasting House, the BBC's battleship-shaped headquarters in central London. The Advisory Committee on Spoken English convened twice a year to conduct its business. Its routine, always the same, is spelled out in a large black notebook that survives in the BBC's archives. Dutiful assistants made sure to reserve the second-floor conference room, "because it is nearest to the library." They gathered together copies of five current dictionaries, "save the *N.E.D.* [*Oxford New English Dictionary*], which is too bulky." They anticipated the needs of the flesh, as well. One injunction reads, "Send list of expected persons, with the time tea is required, to Mr. Chieman."

The list of expected persons, the number of whose entries varied over the years from ten to thirty-five, included some of the leading intellectuals of the day. There were phoneticians such as A. Lloyd James and Daniel Jones. There were lexicographers, literary scholars, writers, and other "educated users of English"—for example, the scientist Julian Huxley, the art historian Kenneth Clark, and a young British journalist named Alistair Cooke. The D.G. (Director-General), the D.P.P. (Director of Programme Planning), the D.T. (Director of Talks), the D.S.B. (Director of Schools Broadcasting), and other senior officials of the BBC also participated. Two of the committee's members were women, namely Rose Macaulay, the novelist and critic, and Lady Cynthia Asquith, an editor and writer of children's books who for twenty years was a secretary to J. M. Barrie, the author of *Peter Pan*. (Virginia Woolf was asked to join the committee but, for reasons that are not recorded, never did.) Bernard Shaw was the second, and most long-standing, chairman of the committee.

Prior to each meeting the participants were asked to submit lists of words that they felt warranted discussion. The Reverend H. Costley-White, the headmaster of Westminster College, a public school, was always extremely forthcoming. In February 1935, for example, he submitted *rationale, pogrom, concordat, format, dour,* and *intransigent.* A few months later he suggested *tripod, scone, preferable, palaver,* and *videlicet.* The following years he turned in *aqueous, truculent, savants, allies,* and *shamefaced men.* The words submitted were checked in all five dictionaries (one of which, from 1934 onward, was American—*Webster's Second New International Dictionary*) and the pronunciation options were spelled out in a simplified phonetic script and typed onto formatted sheets of paper. Each member would find one of these, together with an expense form, in front of his place at the conference table.

After coming to order, the committee would first consider some of the letters that it had received from BBC listeners. There was never any shortage. During its December 1937 meeting, the committee discussed a letter from Messrs. Unilever, Ltd., who objected to a committee dictum that the name of the oleaginous substance the company produced be pronounced with a soft *g*: marjareen. Unilever argued that the *g* in the product's name should be hard, "because of its derivation [from the Greek word *margaron,* meaning "pearl"; margaric acid, a component of margerine, has a pearly luster] and the pronunciation already in use amongst educated speakers." The committee members were not to be swayed. According to the minutes, "In view of the fact that the form MARJARINE"—that is, with a soft *g*—"was commonly used both by those who bought and those who sold the product, there was not sufficient justification for reversing their previous recommendation." The secretary was instructed to write to Messrs. Unilever, Ltd.

There were always a few business matters to discuss—the latest sales figures, say, for "Broadcast English"—but by far the most time-consuming portion of each meeting was the discussion of words, with members ultimately accepting one pronunciation in preference to the others by a show of hands. They might decide on one round that the word *ukelele* should be pronounced "uke-*lee*-ly,"and on another that the

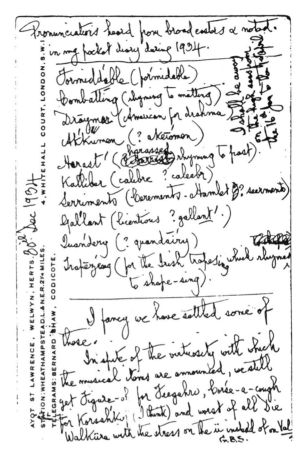

Fig. 14. A Shaw postcard
to A. Lloyd James dated
3 December 1934.
Reproduced with
permission of the Society
of Authors on behalf of
the Bernard Shaw Estate.

bas in *bas relief* should be pronounced like *bass,* the fish. The *zen* in *zenith,* they once decided, should be pronounced like the *Zen* of Buddhism, and also the word *beret* should rhyme with *ferret.* At issue on some occasions was not pronunciation but a choice of words—as between *aviator* and *airman* to designate the one who flies an airplane. (The committee chose *airman.*)

After a decision had been made by the committee, BBC announcers were expected to abide by it; a superior was likely to be listening. Lord Reith himself once upbraided an announcer for a pronuciation of *Scotland* that sounded too much like "Scutland." Bernard Shaw kept a list in his pocket diary of faulty pronunciations he had heard on the BBC, and from time to time would convey these to the Honorary Secretary or the

Director-General. In one note he complained about the music announcers who persisted in saying "*Figure*-oh" instead of "*Fee*-garoh" and "Die
Wal-*küre*" instead of "Die *Wal*-küre." Shaw's communications were always signed simply "G.B.S."

The advisory committee frequently had trouble making up its mind.
Should the place where one kept one's car be called a "*ga*-rraazh" or a
"*ga*-rredge"? The committee initially, in 1926, inclined toward the
former, but eventually, in 1930, embraced the latter. After considerable
public controversy (*controversy*, by the way, is a word that the BBC has
always pronounced with the accent on the first syllable, despite the popularity elsewhere in Britain of "con-*traw*-versy") the committee in 1934
returned to "*ga*-rraazh." The word *landscape* went from "*lan*-skip" to
"*lan*-scayp" to either (that's "*eye*-ther," not "*ee*-ther"). The word *banal*
provoked heated debate over four years, before a majority could be
mustered to promote "ba-*naal*" over "*bay*-nal."

The discussions were characterized by a mixture of seriousness, origi-
nality, common sense, and contrariness. Alistair Cooke remembers one
debate over the length of the vowel *a* in the word *canine*. Shaw insisted
that the word be pronounced "*cay*-nine" rather than "*cah*-nine," arguing
that it was his wont to pronounce words the way they were pronounced
by people who used them in a professional capacity. Shaw's dentist, it
seems, said *cay*-nine. A member of the committee objected, on the
grounds that Shaw's dentist was obviously an American. "But of course,"
Shaw replied. "Why do you think, at seventy-six, I still have my teeth?"
Shaw was, however, overruled. The BBC stuck to its short *a*.

The process by which the BBC reached decisions about language was
by no means uniform. The BBC could, for example, be maddeningly
autocratic. Thus the corporation decided by fiat that the verb *broadcast*
should be conjugated like the verb *cast*, so that the past tense would be
broadcast and not *broadcasted*. (In justifying this decision Lord Reith said,
sniffily, "After all, it is our verb.") However, the Advisory Committee on
Spoken English was at times willing to confess ignorance and seek counsel. During preparation of a booklet on English placenames, in 1928, the
committee's secretary dispatched letters to vicars and postmasters in
1,946 towns and villages around the country, asking them how *they*
would pronounce the name of their community. The committee registered its preference only in those seventy-seven cases in which the parson
and the postman were "at variance."

Shaw did not flinch from taking his case for proper pronunciation of
the King's English to the people. On 2 January 1934, having been chairman of the Advisory Committee since 1930, he published a letter in *The
Times:*

Sir,—As chairman of the committee which in the discharge of its frightful responsibility for advising the B.B.C. on the subject of spoken English has incurred your censure as it has incurred everyone else's, may I mention a few circumstances which will help towards the formation of a reasonable judgment of our proceedings?

1. All the members of the committee speak presentably: that is, they are all eligible, as far as their speech is concerned, for the judicial bench, the cathedral pulpit, or the throne.

2. No two of them pronounce the same word in the English language alike.

3. They are quite frequently obliged to decide unanimously in favour of a pronunciation which they would rather die than use themselves in their private lives.

4. As they work with all the leading dictionaries before them they are free from the illusion that these works are either unanimous or up-to-date in a world of rapidly changing usage.

5. They are sufficiently familiar with the works of Chaucer to feel sincerely sorry that the lovely quadrisyllable Christemasse, the trisyllable neighebore, and the disyllable freendes should have decayed into krissmus, naybr, and frens. We should like to vary the hackneyed set of rhymes to forever by the Shakespearian persever; and we would all, if we dared, slay any actress who, as Cleopatra, would dare degrade a noble line by calling her country's high pyramides pirramids. But if we recommended these pronunciations to the announcers they would, in the unusual event of paying any attention to our notions, gravely mislead the millions of listeners who take them as models of current speech usage.

6. We are not a cockney committee. We are quite aware that Conduit Street is known in the West End as Cundit Street. Elsewhere such a pronunciation is as unintelligible as it is incorrect. We have to dictate a pronunciation that cannot be mistaken, and abide the resultant cockney raillery as best we can.

7. Wireless and the telephone have created a necessity for a fully and clearly articulated spoken English quite different from the lazy vernacular that is called modd'ninglish. We have to get rid not only of imperfect pronunciations but of ambiguous ones. Ambiguity is largely caused by our English habit of attacking the first syllable and sacrificing the second, with the result that many words beginning with prefixes such as ex or dis sound too much alike. This usage claims to be correct; but common sense and euphony are often against it; and it is questionable whether in such cases it is general enough to be accepted as authentic usage. Superior persons stress the first syllable in dissputable, labratory, ecksmplary, desspicable, &c.; and we, being superior persons, talk like that; but as many ordinary and quite respectable people say dispūtable, laborratory, exemmplary, and despickable, we are by no means bound to come down on the side of the pretentious pronunciation if the popular alternative is

less likely to be confused with other words by the human species called
listeners-in.

We have to consider sonority also. The short i is much less effective
than the long one; and the disturbance I created in the United States last
April by broadcasting privvacy instead of pryvacy was justified. Issolate is
a highly superior pronunciation; and wind (rhyming to tinned) is considered more elegant in some quarters than wynd; so that we get the common blunders of trist (rhyming to fist) for tryst and Rozzalind for Rosa-
lynde; but we recommend the long i to the announcers for the sake of
sonority.

Some common pronunciations have to be rejected as unbearably ugly.
An announcer who pronounced decadent and sonorous as dekkadent
and sonnerus would provoke Providence to strike him dumb.

The worst obstacle to our popularity as a committee is the general
English conviction that to correct a man's pronunciation is to imply that
he is no gentleman. Let me explain therefore that we do not correct
anyone's pronunciation unless it is positively criminal. When we recommend an announcer to pronounce disputable with the stress on the second syllable we are neither inciting him to an ungentlemanly action nor
insinuating that those who put the stress on the first ought to be ashamed
of themselves. We are simply expressing our decision that for the purposes and under the circumstances of the new art of broadcasting the
second syllable is the more effective.

Yours, &c.,

G. Bernard Shaw,
Chairman

Responses to *The Times* impelled Shaw to write again in order to have
the last word on the subject. Besides, in the interim, on 22 January, Shaw
had listened to Sheila Barrett read from Byron's *Childe Harold,* and to
Stephen King-Hall discourse on "Economics in a Changing World." *The
Times* published his second letter on 25 January 1934. GBS offered the
letter gratis—not at all his usual practice. While *The Times* felt they were
seizing the best literary bargain of the year, Shaw was implicitly revealing
how much the issue meant to him.

Sir,—The correspondence on the subject of B.B.C. pronunciation has
proved very amply that the pronunciation of the English language is not
the simple matter, perfectly agreed among gentlemen, that most of your
correspondents supposed.

Last Monday two broadcasters discoursed on literature and economics.
They used the words combated and inextricable respectively. I, who am

just as good an authority on pronunciation as either of them, usually say cumbited and ineckstricably. They, being just as good authorities as I, said cmbatted (rhyming to fatted) and inixtrickably. Clearly neither they nor I can claim usage on our side. As cumbited is easily mistaken when atmospherics are raging for comforted I think I shall say cmbatted when next I broadcast, unless indeed I shirk the word I am no longer quite sure about. As to the other, go as you please. There are thousands of words which have no usage because they are not very often used. Thoughtless speakers always bounce at the first syllable and stress it: others have an instinct for the characteristic syllable. Sometimes the first syllable happens fortunately to be the characteristic one: only children say ludickrus instead of loodicrous. But what about exemplary?

My grandfather, an educated country gentleman, occasionally swore by the virtue of his oath. He said: "Be the varchew o' me oath!" He called lip salve sawve. The actors of his time called lute lewt and flute flewt; and their be and me for by and my lasted well into my own day. I can even remember when obleege was heard from old people as well as varchew; but the spelling beat that, as it always does in the long run except when the word, like would or could, is in continual use. Pronunciations are always obsolescing and changing. If the B.B.C. had existed a hundred years ago it would have been reviled for recommending vertew and oblyge instead of varchew and obleege. To-day it has to deal with America, which would have it pronounce necessarily, rhyming to merrily.

Then there is the trouble about accents. In choosing an announcer regard must be had to the psychological effect of his accent. An Oxford accent is considered by many graduates of that University to be the perfection of correct English; but unfortunately over large and densely populated districts of Great Britain it irritates some listeners to the point of switching off, and infuriates others so much that they smash their wireless sets because they cannot smash the Oxonian. The best English to-day is literally the King's English. Like his Royal grandmother before him King George is the best speaker in his realm; and his broadcasts are astonishingly effective in creating loyalty. If he delivered a single broadcast in an Oxford accent his people would rise up that very day and proclaim a republic.

How little the situation is appreciated is shown by the ridiculous extent to which this correspondence has been occupied with the trivial case of Conduit Street. The name of that street is either grossly misspelt or grossly mispronounced: I do not know which. I have no doubt that if one of the new streets made by the London University and the British Museum be appropriately named Pundit Street it will be solemnly labelled Ponduit Street. What most of those who are supersensitive on the subject seem to mean is that if the name of a street is mispronounced by the inhabitants that name shall always be so mispronounced in every possible context. Let me remind them that Conduit Street is not the only street in London. There is in the City an ancient thoroughfare labelled Ave Maria Lane. The more cultivated of its denizens call it Aivmeryer Lane, the less fastidious Hivemerawyer Line. Are we of the B.B.C. Committee expected to instruct the announcers to say: "Miss Jenny Lind will now sing a group of songs beginning with Schubert's Aivmeryer"? Are we to beg the songstress to adapt that pronunciation as best she can to Schubert's notes?

These are the questions that go over such bumptious novices as my friend Mr. Edward Marsh[1] like a steam-roller. They have long since left me as I remain at present,

In extreme humility,

G. Bernard Shaw

From time to time the advisory committee would also appeal to BBC listeners. In an article titled "How Do You Pronounce 'Wednesday'?" (answer "*Wens*-dy"), written by A. Lloyd James for the 19 April 1935 issue of *The Radio Times,* the public was asked to help the BBC come up with a word for the television equivalent of a radio listener. Lloyd James revealed that the committee had tentatively settled on *televiewer* or *viewer* but was not wedded to either term. He wrote, "It is not unlikely . . . that the man-in-the-street, with his customary genius for the *mot juste,* will hit upon the word that will finally be accepted into the language. Here is a good chance for the Reading Listener or the Listening Reader to help us to decide what name shall be given to those who look as well as listen." The man in the street came up with numerous suggestions: *auralooker, glancer, looker, looker in, optovist, optovisor, seer, sighter, teleseer, teleserver, televist, telobservist, telvor, visionaire, visionist, visor, vizier, witnesser.* The BBC was not impressed; in the words of an internal memorandum, "none of [the submissions] deserves serious consideration." In 1936 the advisory committee created a Subcommittee on Words to resolve this and similar matters of new terminology. This subcommittee ultimately accepted the original BBC suggestions, *televiewer* and *viewer.*

The Subcommittee on Words had the broad mandate to pass judgment on, or even invent, any new terms made necessary by the continuing advance of broadcast technology. It was chaired by Logan Pearsall Smith, an American who had attended Oxford and then remained in Britain, ensconced in Bloomsbury among London's literary set. (Smith is credited with the aphorism "People say that life is the thing, but I prefer reading.") Perhaps because he had been exposed to the somewhat more inventive variety of English spoken in the United States, Smith was open to popular suggestions, believing that "it may often happen that mechanics, labourers, soldiers, sailors, and their wives will best be able to supply us with the vivid terms we want." He saw the subcommittee as an opportunity to teach the Englishman "to overcome in himself the prejudice against new English compounds." He was, in other words, something of a zealot, and it was not long before his Subcommittee on Words strayed far from the realm of broadcasting terminology.

Thus Smith proposed that the new traffic circles, which were most frequently referred to as *gyratory circuses,* should be called *roundabouts* instead. This was a sensible suggestion, and it caught on. However, Smith also decided that the term *stop-and-goes* would be a welcome substitute for *traffic lights,* and that *mindfall* should be promoted as a less colloquial alternative to *brain wave.* He suggested the verb *unlike* to describe "the neutral feeling of neither liking nor disliking a person or thing." The other subcommittee members soon caught Smith's enthusiasm. Rose Macaulay proposed the word *yulery* for Christmas festivities. Edward Marsh suggested *inflex* as a superior term for an inferiority complex. It was finally moved that more than a dozen words be brought before the entire advisory committee for further discussion and a vote.

That, however, was as far as the matter went. When the Subcommittee on Words distributed its minutes, the Director of Programme Planning sounded the alarm. In the view of the D.P.P., many of the subcommittee's neologisms were "so ludicrous that irreparable harm to the main Committee's prestige might be done, should any of these suggestions be broadcast." In a talk to the full advisory committee in 1937, the Director-General himself put an end to Logan Pearsall Smith's ambitious little enterprise. He declared, "The responsibility for thus modifying the general English vocabulary is one which seems to the Corporation to be altogether outside its functions and which the Corporation, therefore, feels it cannot accept."

Although chairman since the death of the founding chairman, Poet Laureate Robert Bridges, Shaw was continually skeptical about the value and effectiveness of the committee. (Bridges, incidentally, had initially favored a northern pronunciation—with characteristics like the *a* that is heard in the American pronunciation of *grass* for words like *castle* and *bath,* and the *oo* of *took* for the *u* in *pub*—as the BBC standard.) Although Shaw frequently threatened to resign (in order to "save my own credit as a talk merchant"), he remained in the chair until 1937.

Shaw was particularly disturbed by the sometimes arbitrary way in which decisions were made. In one of his many letters to the Director-General, he complained that decision after decision at a recent committee meeting had been carried by an excessively narrow margin, and that in three cases a decision had required the vote of the chairman—a man in his eightieth year, Shaw noted—to break a tie. This was no way to enforce standards, Shaw said. Later, in a postcard to the D.G., he argued that the committee "should be reconstituted with an age limit of 30 and a few taxidrivers on it. The young people just WON'T pronounce like the old dons. . . . Are we to dictate to the mob or allow the mob to dictate to us? I give it up."

His frustration is understandable. The committee did bring a measure of linguistic order to the airwaves which is without parallel in the history of broadcasting. At the same time, it clearly suffered from the weaknesses Shaw identified, as well as from others. It grew too big. It was much too often in the limelight, whose reflections were not always flattering. In a country where people paid close attention to what was said on the radio, and were prone to communicate their views to the local newspapers, the committee's controversial decisions, occasional flip-flops, and irritating inconsistencies at times evoked anger or derision. (Why, for instance, should the first syllable of *zoology* be pronounced "zoo" but the first syllable of *zoological* be pronounced "zoe"?) The committee had few friends, moreover, in the regional press, which resisted what it saw as an attempt to stamp out Britain's great diversity of accent and vocabulary and to impose a single spoken standard. The author of one BBC memorandum observed, "Nothing that the Corporation did could prevent the idea growing up that [the committee's] recommendations were national injunctions" rather than simply rules "for the use of Announcers." Of course, some committee members had welcomed such an idea; it was not, after all, undeliberate that the committee's ever-increasing list of recommended pronunciations was published in "Broadcast English" and *The Radio Times*. In 1937, however, on the grounds that "the public persistently misunderstands its motive," the BBC decided that the edicts of the Advisory Committee on Spoken English should be circulated to announcers but no longer be made public. In 1939, after Germany's invasion of Poland, members were notified that the committee, being a relative frivolity at a time of national need, was to be disbanded pending a cessation of hostilities.

The war itself raised urgent new questions of correct pronunciation. Edward Marsh replied thus to his notification: "As a member of the now-suspended Advisory Committee on BBC Pronunciation, may I raise the question of how the frequently heard phrase 'direct hit' should be pronounced? I am glad to notice that Mr. Edward Ward and Alvar [Lidell] give it what I believe to be the right sound, viz: a short i and the accent on the second syllable; but I think all the others give it a long i, and some put a strong accent on the first syllable, so that it sounds like *dye*-wrecked. I think you will agree that there should be uniformity. I should greatly prefer that all should say dĭ rect.'" The BBC announcers themselves used the suspension of the committee as an excuse to overturn one of its recent decisions: the placement of the stress in *Allies* on the second syllable. A memo dated 3 November 1939 from the head announcer to all other announcers stated, "There seems to be general agreement that we should overlook BBC ruling and put stress on the *first* syllable. Similarly (or rather *according* to BBC ruling) let's agree all to say marjarine."

The Advisory Committee on Spoken English, *per se,* was never heard from again. In postwar Britain, where Clement Attlee headed a Labour Government, its reestablishment would have smacked of elitism. The BBC itself had changed.

There is probably no simple answer to why BBC English survives in the popular imagination as the best English—the linguistic equivalent, as it were, of the official meter, which is engraved on a platinum bar in Paris. But it is somehow reassuring that such a standard—arbitrary though it is, temporary though it is—exists. If nothing else, it serves as a gentle counterforce against the vigorous centrifugal tendencies of English, and it serves to remind English-speakers around the world that there is a form of the language that we all can understand.

Note

1. Critic, biographer, and editor of the *Georgian Poetry* volumes, Edward Marsh was a member of the Advisory Committee, which by 1935 numbered twenty-three (including the Chairman). Some of the other members were W. B. Maxwell (Royal Society of Literature), Lord David Cecil, Sir Johnston Forbes-Robertson, I. A. Richards, Harold Orton, Professor H. C. K. Wyld, Lascelles Abercrombie, W. W. Greg (British Academy), S. K. Ratcliffe (Glasgow *Herald*), F. L. Lucas (Kings College), and Kenneth R. Barnes (R.A.D.A.).

James Fisher

"THE COLOSSUS" VERSUS "MASTER TEDDY": THE BERNARD SHAW/EDWARD GORDON CRAIG FEUD

G.B.S with so much too much brain and so little else, goes about with his eyes closed—thinking . . . thinking it out—reasoning and arguing brilliantly about it all—now yes, now no—taking up a pencil and dotting down all the pros for it and all the cons against it—doing this week after week, year in and year out—looking at the thing calmly and clearly—and considering, estimating, eliminating. Getting it quite in shape, all this . . . and letting the whole thing slip. What shall that profit a man? Theoretically, how admirable is Shaw—practically, how flimsy—in action, how like a duffer—in apprehension, how like a God! Thus, the simplest clues to life escape him, as he scales impossible pinnacles of unnecessary thought, only to slip down the other side.[1]

—Edward Gordon Craig

If ever there was a spoilt child in artistic Europe, that child was Teddy Craig. The doors of the theatre were far wider open to him than to anyone else. He had only to come in as the others did, and do his job, and know his place, and accept the theatre with all its desperate vicissitudes and poverties and inadequacies and impossibilities as the rest of us did, and the way would have been clear before him for all the talent he possessed. But that was not what he wanted. He wanted a theatre to play with, as Irving played with the Lyceum; a theatre in which he could frame his pictures in the proscenium, and cut the play to pieces to suit them, and forbid the actors to do anything that could distract the attention of the audience from his pictures.[2]

—George Bernard Shaw

At the beginning of the twentieth-century, two men of Irish heritage and temperament radically influenced the development of modern theater and drama in quite different ways. Bernard Shaw, in his role as drama critic for the *Saturday Review,* promoted the revolutionary new drama, especially the plays of Henrik Ibsen. Later, in his own plays, Shaw introduced the significant, socially-conscious drama onto English stages. Edward Gordon Craig (1872–1966), son of actress Ellen Terry (1847–1928), called for a theatrical revolution in the early twentieth century that would replace the theater's dependence on photographic realism and dramatic literature with productions by a master-artist guiding highly controlled actors through a poetically abstract visual scheme, raising the play's emotions to superhuman heights. Although both Shaw and Craig aimed to elevate the quality of theater and drama in their time, a relentless exchange of personal and professional vitriol between them prevented opportunities to collaborate on a single production or, more significantly, toward their shared goal of a serious new theater.

It should be pointed out that the Shaw-Craig feud was largely one-sided. Craig was a difficult and eccentric personality, tempestuous in his personal and professional relationships, and rarely able to separate the two. Spoiled by his mother, who referred to him as "the Feather of England," the adult Craig sought to be similarly spoiled by an array of mistresses, including the legendary dancer Isadora Duncan (1878–1927). When they invariably became inconveniently pregnant, Craig abandoned them, cloaking his insensitivity in the guise of "artistic temperament." Craig was undoubtedly jealous of Shaw's dominance of the English stage, while he was able to achieve only a few "artistic successes" in the mainstream English theater.

Despite the continual assistance of his mother, and many others who recognized the extraordinary potential of his ideas, Craig was rarely able to see his concepts realized in production, due mainly to his petulance and inability to compromise. In four critically acclaimed productions for the Purcell Opera Society [*Dido and Aeneas* (1900), *The Masque of Love* (1901), *Acis and Galatea* (1902), and *Bethlehem* (1902)], Craig managed to experiment with his ideas on a very limited budget and with mostly amateur performers. Later collaborations with Eleonora Duse (1858–1924), on a 1906 production of Ibsen's *Rosmersholm,* and Constantin Stanislavsky (1863–1938), as well as a 1903 season at London's Imperial Theatre starring his mother, were realized despite Craig's difficult ways. But other possible collaborations with scores of Europe's theatrical greats, including Max Reinhardt (1873–1943), Otto Brahm (1856–1912), Herbert Beerbohm Tree (1853–1917), and Hugo von Hofmannsthal (1874–1929), fell apart as a result of Craig's outrageous demands and virulent temper.

Craig's frustration turned him away from the practical theater toward his partially self-created role as a prophet of a new theater stifled by the harsh realities of the workaday theater. Through numerous publications, including more than twenty books and his provocative periodical, *The Mask,* which he published between 1908 and 1929, Craig stood on the sidelines, continuing to promote his idealistic principles while attacking much that he saw in the contemporary theater. Shaw served him well as a target, and his reactions to Shaw were undoubtedly heightened by his resentment of Shaw's relationship with his mother as well as by his misguided belief that Shaw, as leader of the English theatrical establishment, was plotting to deprive Craig of a theater of his own and of the recognition that he felt he deserved. Although this was a grotesque distortion, it is true that the English theater was very slow to warm to Craig's theatrical concepts while many artists in the continental theater were finding his ideas a striking source of inspiration. In public and in private, Shaw often acknowledged Craig's achievements, but he and Craig remained, as a result of their personal and professional differences, locked in adversarial roles.

The Shaw-Craig feud began very early in their theatrical careers. Aside from the often amusing character of their attacks and counterattacks, their conflicts offer many insights about their highly conflicting individual understanding of the art of the theater. Shaw and Craig shared a desire to destroy the dramatic conventions and theatrical traditions of the nineteenth-century stage, as exemplified by Terry's co-star Henry Irving (1838–1905), but this did little to endear them to each other. Although both wanted to move away from superficial Victorian entertainments, Craig turned to antirealistic, aesthetically inspired stagings of poetic dreams while Shaw used the stage as a utilitarian platform, arranging life's truths in a way that exposed the need for particular social reforms. To Shaw, the theater was "my battering ram as much as the platform or the press: that is why I want to drag it to the front,"[3] but to Craig the theater was much more:

> . . . the Art of the Theatre is neither acting nor the play, it is not scene nor dance, but it consists of all the elements of which these things are composed: action, which is the very spirit of acting; words, which are the body of the play; line and colour, which are the very heart of the scene; rhythm, which is the very essence of dance. . . . One is no more important than the other, no more than one colour is more important to a painter than another, or one note more important than another to a musician. In

one respect, perhaps action is the most valuable part. Action bears the
same relation to the Art of the Theatre as drawing does to painting, and
melody does to music. The Art of the Theatre has sprung from action—
movement—dance.[4]

After giving up a promising acting career, Craig began publishing a
modest arts journal called *The Page* (1898–1901) and cut and sold numerous woodcuts and bookplates. Beginning in 1900, he began producing
and designing regularly in London, including his experimental works
for the Purcell Opera Society. It is unclear when Shaw first became
familiar with Craig's productions, but in a letter to William Archer
(1856–1924), dated 1 and 2 March 1902, Shaw advised Archer that,
when hiring staff for a production, "the wardrobe master should be a bit
of an artist, like Teddy Craig."[5] While working with the Purcell Opera
Society, Craig began to develop his notion of total theater:

> I am now going to tell you out of what material an artist of the theatre of
> the future will create his masterpieces. Out of ACTION, SCENE, and
> VOICE. Is it not very simple? And when I say *action,* I mean both gesture
> and dancing, the prose and poetry of action. When I say *scene,* I mean all
> which comes before the eye, such as the lighting, costume, as well as the
> scenery. When I say *voice,* I mean the spoken word or the word which is
> sung, in contradiction to the word which is read, for the word written to
> be spoken and the word written to be read are two entirely different
> things.[6]

Craig's theories and productions stressed a visual symphony of impressions and symbols in which the playwright's contribution would only be
one among many equally important production elements. For inspiration he looked to the Greek classics, traditional Oriental forms, *commedia
dell'arte,* and Shakespearean plays, completely rejecting the movement
toward realism and the polemical social dramas of Shaw:

> The modern Realistic Theatre, forgetful of all the Laws of Art, sets out to
> reflect the times. It reflects a small particle of the times, it drags back a
> curtain and exposes to our view an agitated caricature of Man and his
> Life, a figure gross in its attitude and hideous to look upon. This is true
> neither to life nor to art. It has never been the purpose of art to reflect
> and make uglier the ugliness of things, but to transform and make the
> already beautiful more beautiful.[7]

Despite difficulties in finding interested producers, Shaw's plays were
given occasional productions around the turn-of-the-century. At the

same time, Craig sought his own theater where he could demonstrate his theories on a larger scale than the Purcell Opera Society had allowed. In 1903, less than a year after Irving and Terry had ended their long-time stage partnership, Terry leased London's Imperial Theatre for a season of productions and designs by Craig. He persuaded Terry to open the season with Ibsen's 1857 saga of tenth-century Scandinavian warriors, *The Vikings at Helgeland.* During her years with Irving, Terry had harbored a desire to act in Ibsen's plays and other modern dramas, but Irving would have nothing to do with contemporary theater. The earliest English productions of Ibsen's works during the 1880s were generally vilified by critics, excepting Shaw and William Archer, both outspoken supporters of Ibsen's controversial plays.

Terry, who was backing the Imperial productions with her life-savings, nervously stood by her son as he proceeded to gut the theater's stage house to make room for a light bridge and his massive settings. He pushed his reluctant cast (including Oscar Asche, Hutin Britton, and Conway Tearle) toward a movement-oriented style of acting more suited to his evocative designs. The actors were uncomfortable with Craig's approach, and Terry worried about her suitability for the role of Hiordis, the towering and horrifying heroine of Ibsen's dark tragedy:

> a part like that for me would be like *3* Lady Macbeths—It's superb and I'd like to—but I'm afraid I could not get at it—could not do it—but it's wonderful—and as *I think of it* I feel like getting up and *trying* —but nobody would believe me in such a part and I'm too old now to experiment *handicapped.*[8]

Despite Terry's doubts, *The Vikings* opened on 15 April 1903 to a large and enthusiastic audience who had undoubtedly come to see her debut in a major role by a major contemporary dramatist. *The Daily Chronicle* reported the next day that the response "was enthusiastic, and after being summoned many times at the conclusion of each act, she [Terry] was compelled at a quarter of an hour before midnight to lead forward Mr. Craig and to deliver a few words of thanks for the public recognition of efforts that she admitted had occasioned some anxiety."[9] Craig's sets, costumes, and lighting brought on the expected controversy, critics finding "an obvious discord between the story told on the stage, and the atmosphere of its mise-en-scene."[10]

Although Craig was praised for moving away from customary scenic practices, he "has not yet perfected the means of doing without them."[11] Shaw saw the production and, in a letter to Terry, suggested an epitaph for Hiordis, quoting from *Great Expectations:* "For, whatsome'er the fail-

Fig. 15. Edward Gordon Craig's design for the banquet scene
in Henrik Ibsen's *The Vikings at Helgeland*, 1903. Courtesy
The Edward Gordon Craig Estate.

ings on her part, Remember, reader, she were that good in her eart."[12]
Shaw also notes that Craig is "a young man of much talent,"[13] but ultimately guilty of "matricide. In dealing with you his faculty for stage art
totally deserted him."[14] Accusing Craig of "treachery to the author,"[15]
Shaw wrote,

> Now the first act of The Vikings should be a most lovely morning scene,
> all rosy mists, fresh air, virgin light, and diamond dewdrops. The men

Fig. 16. Edward Gordon Craig's woodcut for a scene from
Henrik Ibsen's *The Vikings at Helgeland,* 1903. Courtesy The
Edward Gordon Craig Estate.

should be glowing from their baths, robust, solid, with no nonsense about
them. Into this cheerful and real scene there should come a woman like
the shadow of death— a woman in black, with white face and snakes in
her hair, so to speak, a messenger of death to every man in the play.

Instead of which, Signor Teduardo [Craig], not being able to manage full
light and local color, turns the dawn into night; makes the warriors fantastic and unreal; and finally introduces comfort and color in the shape of a
fine figure of a woman in a particularly cosy bearskin mantle which heaps
her shoulders up to her ears and gives her an air of jollity which positively
radiates goodnature in spite of the unfortunate lady's efforts to make
mischief. Result: the play drops stone dead the moment you walk on the
stage."[16]

In his 1930 biography of Henry Irving, Craig rebutted Shaw's comments by quoting Ibsen's original stage directions:

> Alas! I had done a foolish thing—I had followed the directions of a playwriter. Ibsen distinctly states in his first five lines, that "it is a stormy snow-grey day." This is what I gave: I made it rather darker than I should have done with more experience, but it was a stormy winter day right enough. In Helgoland the sky on a stormy winter day is lead-colour.[17]

However, Craig typically felt no compunction to honor the specific stage directions of the playwright. Suggesting that Terry would be blamed for Craig's liberties, and reacting defensively as a playwright, Shaw wrote,

> If Master Teddy wants to use plays as stalking horses for his clever effects, let him write them himself. To take an author of Ibsen's importance, and deliberately alter his play to suit the limelight man, is the folly of a child, not the act of a responsible man. If he did that to a play of mine, I would sacrifice him on the prompter's table before his mother's eyes.[18]

Terry's initial anxiety about *The Vikings* was well founded. Performances were poorly attended, and she was forced to close the play after a mere three weeks. Nearly thirty years later Craig, explaining the failure, wrote that "the London of 1903 which didn't want Ibsen and loathed to see E. T. [Terry] in a 'wicked woman's part,' was a grievous spectacle: and my way of producing a play or an opera attracted very few people in England at that time."[19]

Craig's staging innovations continued to concern Shaw, especially when he learned that Terry was rushing into a production of *Much Ado About Nothing*, hoping to recoup her losses on *The Vikings*. Terry had played Beatrice in the Shakespearean comedy intermittently since the 1870s. Shaw had described her Lyceum Beatrice as filled "with a charm and intuition that I have not seen surpassed."[20] Although Craig had spent relatively little on the settings and costumes for *The Vikings*, the cost of gutting the interior of the Imperial, and the poor returns at the box office, required that Craig design a modest setting. Departing from the elaborate two-dimensional painted realism of the Lyceum Theatre production of *Much Ado* two decades before, and anticipating the simplified pre-World War I renderings of Shakespeare popularized by Harley Granville-Barker (1877–1946), Craig designed an austere and evocative setting. He looked to the work of two Italians: the paintings of thirteenth-century artist Taddeo Gaddi and the architectural theories and designs of Sebastiano Serlio. From these inspirations, and from his memory of the Lyceum production, Craig created a set of pillars and arches with painted fabric inserts for various scenes.

Shaw continued to monitor the Imperial experiment and offered advice on many aspects of the play before it opened. He also managed another swipe at Irving in a letter to Terry:

> . . . do not copy the Lyceum production: it was a most unskilful one in many points. For instance, you had to play the scene "The prince's jester: a very dull fool &c" in the middle of a crowd of people, where it was entirely lost. . . .
>
> Dogberry was an utter failure at the Lyceum. This was because Dogberry's first scene was omitted—the one where he calls on Leonato with Verges. Without this to prepare the audience for the Ass scene, it falls perfectly flat. With it, Dogberry is irresistible. I implore you not to trifle with Dogberry; for the play, which is a bad one, cannot do without him. . . . This venture of yours makes me uneasy; dont, for heaven's sake, risk anything serious over it."[21]

But Terry had already risked, and lost, most of her financial resources. She also ignored Shaw's production suggestions, as he noticed when he attended a performance on 2 June 1903:

> I went to see Much Adoodle-do yesterday evening. It is a shocking bad play, and can only be saved by Dogberry picking it up at the end, when Beatrice and Benedick are worn out after the church scene. But Dogberry *cannot* pick it up unless he has his scene before the wedding, because without that the audience is unprepared for the examination scene and does not find him out until too late. Why dont you believe me when I tell you these things? You believe everyone else; but nobody else tells you the truth.[22]

Surprisingly, Shaw admired Craig's scenic achievements, and remarked cynically on the quality of the audience's taste:

> As usual Ted has the best of it. I have never seen the church scene go before—didnt think it *could* go, in fact. He should have done something better for the monument scene or else left it alone altogether; but still, when all is said, nothing quite like it has been done before; and if only the extra people were trained dancers instead of athletic amateurs, and Asche were Dogberry with his first scene left in, and the choir were complete instead of having one twopenny tenor and no basses, and the stalls were abolished and replaced with a comfortable half crown parterre right up to

Fig. 17. Edward Gordon Craig's design, with notations, for the
church scene in *Much Ado About Nothing*, 1903. Courtesy The
Edward Gordon Craig Estate.

the orchestra, why, something might be done with it all, especially if the
public were born over again and born different, and the guillotine freely
used in Trafalgar Square for a few months beforehand.[23]

But to the shock of everyone involved, *Much Ado About Nothing* failed
commercially within a few weeks. Terry abandoned the Imperial and took

to the provinces with the production and several other plays (deleting *The Vikings* from her repertory) in an effort to recover her financial losses.

Shaw was later to take note of Craig's one other attempt to stage a Shakespearean play. With the help of Isadora Duncan, who inspired many of Craig's theories on movement, Craig had secured an opportunity to co-direct and design a production of *Hamlet* with Constantin Stanislavsky at the Moscow Art Theatre. Despite many setbacks and delays, and the usual Craigian tantrums, *Hamlet* made it to the stage in early 1912. Craig made use of his patented scenic screens, and although there were some discordances between Craig's visual scheme and the realistic acting style of the Moscow Art Theatre company, the production was a success. News of Craig's *Hamlet* production drifted back to England, and Shaw was sufficiently impressed to recommend Craig and the production to Granville-Barker in a letter dated 13 February 1912: "turn your eyes now to Moscow, where Teddy Craig has staged Hamlet (or induced the papers to say so). Why not collar Craig's production with Wilkinson, Ricketts, or another, and play Hamlet yourself? If Teddy would play the ghost of a lost soul (he could), all the better."[24]

Craig longed for a theater of his own, but due to the controversial nature of his theories, as well as his extremely unrealistic demands for financial support and creative liberty, he had become something of a pariah. It is surprising, then, that Shaw subsequently attempted to interest Craig in designing some of his plays. Max Reinhardt commissioned designs from Craig for a production of *Caesar and Cleopatra* in 1905, but Craig, in what became a pattern after the Imperial Theatre failures, made outrageous demands. At least initially, the play seemed to inspire him. In a letter to his sometime patron, Count Harry Kessler (1868–1937), on 26 November 1905, Craig wrote,

> I am enjoying myself designing scene after scene for *Ceasar* [sic] *and Cleopatra*—they rush out like steam & I am obliged to put them down on paper though so many must be destroyed.[25]

Craig's enthusiasm led him to challenge Shaw's use of stage directions. In his 1913 book *Towards a New Theatre,* he included three designs for *Caesar and Cleopatra*. One design for Act One, Scene One, was accompanied by a pointed explanation:

> I hardly think that Mr. Bernard Shaw will like this design, but that is his own fault. He should have designed the scene for us. He wrote the play, he also wrote the stage directions in full, then why did he omit to design

the scene and the costumes? If you meddle with the tools of a trade, it is best to master them—and for a dramatic writer to add stage directions to his written play, and to omit to show how those directions are to be carried out, is to tinker. In the Greek and Elizabethan drama you will find no stage directions.

I was asked to produce this play in Berlin, and the only thing I could do was to forget to read the author's stage directions, so that I might make sure of getting at the meaning of the play. And as I read the words, I wanted to omit these too, for the Scenario Scene seemed so excellent. When I had got the words out of my head I looked to see what was left of the First Scene, and I found this First Scene to be a great rat-trap in which figures were hurrying and scurrying to and fro like so many squeaking animals, one real figure standing out in a comic tragic mask— Ftatateeta. So you will see in my design no other individuals whom you can recognise, and only the figure in the centre rivets the attention.[26]

But Craig's work progressed slowly, and in a letter to Terry on 15 November 1905, Shaw could not hold back his frustration: "Teddy is delaying my Caesar & Cleopatra very badly in Berlin."[27] Two days later, in a letter to his German translator, Siegfried Trebitsch, Shaw was particularly frank about Craig's involvement:

Craig usually promises to be ready in a week and devise beautiful effects which cost only twenty pounds. The effects *are* beautiful; but he keeps you waiting six months; and the cost is £50,000,000,000 or thereabouts. You must be careful that his system of lighting does not ruin the play. Remember that a comedy scene in the dark is impossible. Unless the faces of the persons on the stage are well lighted, the dialogue will fall flat. If Craig makes beautiful mysterious silhouettes of the speakers, all will be lost. "Caesar and Cleopatra" must not be two ghosts; they must be vivid personalities. For the rest, you may trust Craig, who is a real artist. Outside the art he is probably as unscrupulous as most artists; so he will probably cost the management more than they bargain for.[28]

To his great distress, Craig was continually asked to modify his designs, and finally the Craig/Reinhardt collaboration fell apart. Shaw, writing again to Trebitsch on 30 January 1906, was relieved, but also aware of the artistic loss to the production implied by Craig's departure:

I am not at all surprised about Craig. It is impossible to hold him to anything. Reinhardt is well out of his hands, for with all his artistic genius, he is ruinously expensive & uncertain. The new artist will do his best to shew that he is as good as Craig. Probably he isnt; but Craig might easily have sacrificed the play to the picture.[29]

After the aborted *Caesar and Cleopatra,* Craig rarely worked on an actual production again. He continued his published attack on the contemporary theater in numerous books and articles, but mostly through *The Mask.* He occasionally responded to Shaw's public postures on a variety of subjects in *The Mask.* It is perhaps not surprising that Craig, once a victim of Shaw's reviews during his days as a novice actor at Irving's Lyceum Theatre, took particular note of some remarks Shaw had made regarding critics. In an unsigned editorial note in 1909, Craig coyly interviewed himself:

> What is the matter with Mr. George Bernard Shaw? In an Interview, (January 25, Daily Telegraph) he flattered all the actors whom he had previously abused like pickpockets: he attacked critics for being cruel to actors, as though he had himself never written the cruellest things about actors in the Saturday Review, and he made all sorts of rash and incorrect statements which he used not to do in the time of Henry Irving. Reading the interview we came across a passage relating to Mr. Gordon Craig in which Mr. Shaw says that, as he could not annex Mr. Craig as an actor he would annex him as a scenic designer, and would "borrow his curtains." But on making enquiries we ascertained that no such curtains exist. This is Mr. Craig's reply as given to our representative, "I know nothing about any curtains . . . and I possess none. I cannot guess what Mr. Bernard Shaw can mean. Years ago when I was a boy, and Mr. Shaw in his prime, I made an experiment or two with some draped stuff instead of scenery, but that was because the theatre was not rich enough to run to wood and canvas. I was excused the offence I suppose on account of my youth, but I gather that Mr. Shaw is quite old enough to know better. I suppose it is this old threadbare curtain idea which Mr. Shaw is alluding to . . . and I hope for his own sake he will find it of a piece with his plays. If he is keen about it he is perfectly welcome to it. Why not? . . . everyone may borrow ideas, but I feel that it's alway [sic] best to borrow the latest, . . . they are so much more likely to be fresh. Still, for Shakespeare, those curtains are rather nice: they will do . . . anything does for Hamlet & Cymbeline. But when it comes to supplying scenery to the author of 'Mrs. Warren's Profession' and 'Don Juan in Hell' something sterner, grander, is necessary; something more like Trafalgar Square on a Sunday. . . . No?"[30]

A year later Craig acknowledged that Shaw was "one of the most remarkable men in England, and we fully recognise this fact although we entirely disapprove of Mr. Shaw and all that he says and does."[31] Craig clarified his objections to Shaw in an unsigned editorial in the April 1911 issue of *The Mask:*

> It is good to hear through the *Daily Mail* that the "Little Theatre" of
> London is about to become for a few weeks the home of the intellectual
> Drama; but it is a bit disheartening to learn later that the only people who
> can supply the Intellectual Drama are Mr. Bernard Shaw, Mr. John Gal-
> sworthy and Mr. Granville Barker. We always had an idea that Shake-
> speare could be put down as intellectual as well as lovely, loveable, stupen-
> dous and all the other qualities. And Chapman, Marlowe, Beaumont and
> Fletcher, Webster, ... are not these intellectual? Was not the writer of
> "Everyman" intellectual? We suppose what the *Daily Mail* wanted to say
> and didn't dare to was that the "Little Theatre" is to be made for a few
> weeks the home of that demned [*sic*] dull *discursive* Drama. Ah! that's
> quite another thing."[32]

Both the intellectual and political aspects of Shaw's plays troubled
Craig. He had a particularly strong distrust of political drama, although
Terry had noted in a letter to Shaw on 13 October 1896 that Craig
himself had "caught socialism"[33] in his youth. But to Craig, politics were
destructive to the artist:

> *Politics*—It's absurd and detrimental to an artist or an actor, to have any
> politics. It is absurd because his whole time is given to discovering how to
> write, paint, or build or compose little things which are quite difficult
> enough to learn and perfect, even if he possess talent. And it is detrimental
> to him, because politics can separate him from too many of his fellow artists
> or actors, and also prejudice large sections of the public against him, and
> these will never tolerate his work—very likely not even see it. . . .
>
> H. I. [Irving] had no politics—he had no time for them. It would be
> useless to regret that G.B.S. gave most of his time to them—and put his
> talent as a journalist and a Hyde Park orator at their service.[34]

To Craig, there was no art in the realistic and polemical drama, as he
noted in assessing the quality of Shaw's plays in *The Mask* during the
summer of 1909:

> He is unable to create a work of Beauty, . . . a work of Art. . . . Unable to
> understand Beauty, and unable to create a work of Beauty through lack
> of a certain nobility of spirit which has since time immemorial possessed
> the great artists, he vents his spleen on us all, creating thereby works of
> mischief.[35]

Two years later, as "Louis Madrid," one of the more than eighty pseud-
onyms he employed in *The Mask*, Craig pressed his disdain for propaganda in the theater:

We of the theatre dislike Mr. Shaw only when he brings his social propaganda on to the stage, for it explains too nicely how little Mr. Shaw
understands the nature of the Theatre, and it is hardly necessary to
repeat here that the Theatre is a temple or house for Art, and Art has
never flourished when in connection with Social or Political reform, it
having nothing in common with either.[36]

In late 1912, however, Craig grudgingly acknowledged the effectiveness
of Shaw's *The Shewing-Up of Blanco Posnet*, "which seems to me to be
Bernard Shaw's best play. I thought some years ago that Bernard Shaw
would come out of that strange dry thing which we can call the chrysalis,
and fly into the air, and he seems to be doing it. He is a kind of brown
moth but a good strong one."[37]

Shortly thereafter, a personal tragedy for Craig temporarily stemmed
his cynical attacks on Shaw. On 15 April 1913, Mrs. Patrick Campbell
(1865–1940) wrote a touching letter to Shaw after she had learned of the
death of Isadora Duncan's children in a freakish auto accident. One of
the two children, Deirdre, born in 1906, was Craig's:

> I open the paper to read of Isadora Duncan's heart rending sorrow—
> poor Singer [Paris Singer, father of Duncan's son Patrick. Patrick was also
> killed in the accident]—poor Ellen Terry, poor Gordon Craig—poor all
> of us that have hearts to ache. It is as though one must go to her these
> first awful days and try to keep her from going mad—She can never
> dance again—love to her will mean death—and the sight of little children
> will always break her heart—she loved them and defied the world with
> their loveliness—it's pitiable—.[38]

After this, Shaw is silent on Craig for many years, although Craig
continued to take an occasional swipe at Shaw in *The Mask,* particularly as
Shaw represented the predominance of literary, political, or realistic
drama:

> A playwright is one who masters the craft of playmaking to the greater
> lustre of the Dramatic art. Primarily (and indeed to the end) a craftsman,
> he may, as he progresses, fashion a masterpiece and so win the title of
> artist.
>   I cannot think Mr. Shaw has won that title, and for my part I believe he
> never strove for it.
>   The title is his, it has been forced on him, but I fear that is all.
>   He gives us not what an artist gives us but what a very clever man
> failing to be an artist falls back on.
>   I am grieved at what is lost. I grieve that by shouldering, elbowing

forward, he has thrust aside too many a real English artist playwright.
That is a very great pity for the English Drama. . . .

Mr. Shaw has been what the England of the day urges practical people
to be—a talker. He has not been a brilliant talker but a mighty one.
Brilliance delights and charms; it wins the hearts of men and women.
Sheridan is a brilliant talker, but I believe Shaw could bear him down.
Shaw is like a great wind; he will, I like to think, have done a power of
good when these days are gone and we gone [*sic*] and the sun shines out
again. Shaw is a noble man and his forced assumption of cap and bells is
the unkind thing the age did to him. And I, least of all, intend in anything
I say any unkindness. The trees bending underneath the blast hardly
intend unkindness to the howling storm.[39]

Referring to Shaw as "The Colossus," and coyly emphasizing this title by
signing his article in lower-case initials ("e.g.c."), Craig went on to compare Shaw's viewpoints to the incessant one-note ring of a neighboring
convent bell.

After years of ignoring Craig's attacks, Shaw responded to "The Colossus" in the next issue of *The Mask:*

You are quite right in saying that the contribution I and my followers (in
the chronological sense) have made to the drama is not an artistic contribution. Wycherley could say what he had to say as well as I, and could put
it on the stage with as much art. Congreve was as fine an artist as
Granville-Barker. . . . Wycherley and Congreve thought women over
thirty ridiculous, venereal disease funny, and the betrayal of an old husband by a young wife screamingly laughable. That covers their entire
recorded body of thought. I do not share these tastes; and if I did, I have
something more important to think about and make an audience think
about. I have nothing in common with Wycherley and Congreve except
our art, and an indefensible but irresistible love of acting for its own sake.
And I daresay Granville-Barker would say the same.[40]

Shaw cleverly turned the tables on Craig by acknowledging the achievements of artists like Craig: "In the nineteenth century they did not
know what you were talking about: today they may not know much
better; but you are the most famous theatre man in Europe."[41] Immediately following Shaw's letter, Craig replied, not very subtly, imitating
Shaw's graciousness:

I see that you allow me to print your letter in "The Mask" for you send it
almost as an article: you enclose a card *with George Bernard Shaw's compli-*
ments and the kind after thought *This—if you care for it—shall remain exclu-*
sive to The Mask.

That, if you will allow me to say so, is typical of the generous sort of thing I am told you do and most people would forget to do; it is also typical that you should take the care to give a head line to your letter "THE COLOS-SUS SPEAKS". "The Mask" might otherwise have been so daring as to put as a heading, "THE COLOSSUS REPLIES",—thereby attempting to snatch at a chance of making itself more important than it is.[42]

Craig waited until the next issue of *The Mask* to offer a more pointed counterattack:

"I being familiar with all the arts, . . . "

Bernard Shaw.
"The Sanity of Art," 1907.

I said in my first note on the Colossus that I did not read anything Mr. Shaw writes because he prevents me. . . .

To know something of an art seemed to me good: to know much of any one art seemed even better: to know a good deal of several arts might perhaps do: but to be familiar with them all seemed ridiculous. And to announce it as something to be proud of is so queer.

I have never known of any artist who said so, did so, or dreamed of pretending to "be familiar with all the arts."[43]

The Mask, succumbing to financial pressures, ceased publication in 1929, but the most public collisions between Shaw and Craig were yet to come.

In an interview with G. W. Bishop, published in *The Observer* on 26 October 1930, Shaw responded to the publication of Craig's book *Henry Irving,* in which Craig had made numerous unkind assertions about Shaw. His resentment of Shaw certainly had to do with the literary and political emphasis of Shaw's plays, but it was equally tied to a complex web of real and imagined personal conflicts. During Shaw's reign as a drama critic for the *Saturday Review,* Craig's earliest acting performances were included in Shaw's savage attacks on Irving and the Lyceum productions. This must certainly have offended Craig, who idolized Irving despite his own resistance to many of the old-fashioned plays and theatrical conventions Irving favored.

But Shaw felt that Irving, and everything he stood for, had to go. He wrote of Irving's liberties in shaping his characterizations and productions, stressing that Irving "never did and never will make use of a play otherwise than as a vehicle for some fantastic creation of his own."[44] Irving's habit of cutting and changing the texts of Shakespeare's plays, Shaw felt, "disembowels them. A man who would do that would do anything—cut the coda out of the first movement of Beethoven's Ninth

Symphony, or shorten one of Velasquez's Philips into a kitcat to make it fit over his drawing room mantelpiece."[45] Despite Shaw's relentless assault on the Lyceum, he tried to interest Irving in producing his plays, especially *The Man of Destiny*, and Craig implied in *Henry Irving* that Shaw offered his plays to managers while a drama critic, thus inviting bribes. Stating emphatically that he had done "nothing of the sort,"[46] Shaw explained that Irving had accepted *The Man of Destiny* for production at the Lyceum, dropping it later when "the expected change in my criticisms did not take place."[47]

The final public exchange between Shaw and Craig began almost simultaneously with the publication of Craig's *Henry Irving*. Not long after the death of Ellen Terry on 21 July 1928, Terry's daughter and Craig's sister Edith "Edy" Craig (1869–1947) contacted Shaw about the possibility of publishing his correspondence with Terry, which had spanned thirty years (1892–1922). According to Craig, he first learned of the letters in early 1929 and wrote to Shaw about them on 4 April 1929. "Do you want the correspondence between E.T. and G.B.S. to be published?—or is anyone pushing you to do so—or what? . . . I wish you would drop me a word to just say *you want it* or *you don't want it*."[48] In typical Craigian fashion he added, "I am reading it [the correspondence] and it seems to me that what's good in it is too good to allow the public ever to have it."[49] Craig added that Shaw had written back on 12 April 1929, saying that he did not wish to have the letters published, but that "as money was needed [it wasn't] here was a fine cheap way to make it— to publish the correspondence."[50] Again, according to Craig, Shaw wrote to him on 7 September 1929, indicating that Edy Craig and Terry's executors had sold the letters for publication. At this point Craig rose up in moral indignation, explaining that a man holding "letters from a woman, as Shaw held my mother's, does not part with them or show them to anyone. I won't discuss why—it's simply not done—it's an old and everlasting courtesy, observed by all."[51]

But the correspondence, edited by "Christopher St. John" [Christabel Marshall (1874–1960), lesbian companion of Edy Craig], was published and very well received. Craig responded by writing a biography of Terry called *Ellen Terry and Her Secret Self*, which included a pamphlet titled "A Plea for G.B.S." (dedicated to Irving's memory!) in which Craig depicted Shaw as a ruthless manipulator of Craig's mother's memory. An annoyed Shaw responded to this in an interview with G. W. Bishop in *The Observer*: "The baby is squalling again, I suppose. It always squalls when it sees me; and nobody will whack it because it is Ellen Terry's baby. Well, let it squall."[52] Shaw goes on to assert that Craig's problem was that he had not successfully gained his independence from his powerful mother,

Fig. 18. Ellen Terry as Lady Cecily Waynflete in *Captain Brassbound's Conversion.*

as his sister Edy had, and that was "why the brother and sister are at loggerheads over the publication of the letters."[53] Describing Craig as a self-conscious "thwarted genius,"[54] Shaw offered the caution that to Craig "people like myself, for instance—are the curse of the theatre because they accept its poverty and insecurity and subjection to commercial considerations instead of going on permanent strike against them, like Craig."[55]

When asked about Craig's account of the publication of the Shaw-Terry correspondence, Shaw presented Craig's signed permission, noting that Craig's "consent was extorted by circumstances, and his heart was not in his promise."[56] Shaw added his version of events leading to the publication: "At first I was almost as stupid as Craig: I remembered only the very intimate and affectionate character of the letters and declared that their immediate publication was impossible."[57] Shaw explained further that he had decided that, since the correspondence would inevitably be published after his death, he would write a document explaining it, a copy of which he sent to Craig. But Craig assumed instead that the document was being circulated by Shaw to "confound, destroy, insult, and ruin himself [Craig], his father, and his entire family."[58] Finally Shaw agreed to the publication of the letters in a limited edition to benefit a fund established to turn Terry's home into a memorial museum. Shaw claimed that at this point he read the correspondence in full for the first time and changed his mind, deciding his initial hesitation had been foolish. He suggested publication of an ordinary edition of the correspondence, and Craig was invited to contribute a preface. According to Shaw, Craig seriously considered this until "he learned that the proposal was suggested by me, whereupon he repudiated it with vehemence, declaring that it was a trap for him."[59] Finally, in responding to Craig's furious view of the situation, Shaw stated that Craig

> has allowed his psychosis to carry him to the length of suggesting that his mother's last days were darkened by his sister's excessive surveillance, and then making the crazy statement that the stroke which killed her was caused by eating something that disagreed with her when his sister was absent, implying that he was orphaned by this neglect. Here he seems to me to go beyond the bounds within which it is possible for even his greatest admirers to defend him: and at this point accordingly I throw up my brief for him and wish you good morning.[60]

Following this there were no further public exchanges between Shaw, then in his mid-seventies, and Craig, then nearly sixty. Both lived on until their mid-nineties, and Craig, in his various diaries and daybooks, continued to depict Shaw as a towering example of the proliferation of a politicized social drama that was destructive to artists and the theater in general. Craig's deeply rooted paranoia unquestionably shaped his attitudes about Shaw's real and imagined slights. But, more significantly, Craig resisted all that Shaw stood for as a playwright and man of the

theater, in much the way that Shaw resisted Irving as the representation
of Victorian stage traditions. Craig may even have been thinking of Shaw
when he wrote in his diary that "Our theatre is the worst in the world—
our dramatic literature one of the very best."[61]

Shaw gave no further public attention to Craig after the furor over the
Shaw-Terry correspondence and seems to have closed the book on it all a
few years later. When he gave Terry's letters to the British Museum, he
wrote to Mrs. Patrick Campbell that not all of them had been published:
"For instance, her [Terry's] description of Mrs. Kendal as 'my idea of
hell' could hardly be published during Dame Madge's lifetime. And
Gordon Craig had to be considered."[62]

It is not likely that their temperaments would have permitted them a
successful theatrical collaboration, but a Craigian design for a Shavian
play like *Man and Superman* would most certainly have been memorable.
It might be suggested that the Shaw-Craig feud shows these two great
men at their worst, mainly due to their mutual inability to separate their
personal animosity from their significant professional differences. Craig
obviously resented Shaw's flirtation, by mail, with his mother—even
though the flirtation was only epistolary, to woo her to the new drama—
and this resentment was certainly fueled by the publication of the Shaw/
Terry correspondence. Shaw, for his part, was privy to Ellen Terry's
many anxieties concerning her thoughtless and irresponsible son and, as
a result, developed a disdain for Craig he was never able to shake. Also,
they were divided by Craig's loyalty to Irving's memory and Shaw's need
to obliterate the remnants of a theatrical style he considered, at best,
superficial. Their feud reveals much about their individual approaches
to the art of the theater, and it remains one of the most unfortunate
omissions of the modern English stage that Shaw's extraordinary plays
were never theatrically expressed by Craig's aesthetic stage visions.

Notes

1. Edward Gordon Craig, *Ellen Terry and Her Secret Self* (New York: E. P. Dutton, 1932),
p. 13.
2. E. J. West, ed., *Shaw on Theatre* (New York: Hill & Wang, 1958), p. 203.
3. Christopher St. John, ed., *Ellen Terry and Bernard Shaw: A Correspondence* (New York:
G. P. Putnam's Sons, 1932), p. 110.
4. Edward Gordon Craig, *On the Art of the Theatre* (New York: Theatre Arts Books,
1980), pp. 138–139.

5. Dan H. Laurence, ed., *Bernard Shaw: Collected Letters, 1898–1910* (New York: Dodd, Mead, 1972), p. 265.

6. Craig, *On the Art of the Theatre*, pp. *180–81.*

7. Edward Gordon Craig, *Towards a New Theatre* (London and Toronto: J. M. Dent & Sons, 1913), p. 89.

8. Edward Gordon Craig, *Gordon Craig: The Story of His Life* (New York: Alfred A. Knopf, 1968), p. 174.

9. Unsigned Notice, *The Daily Chronicle* 16 April 1903, p. 8.

10. Unsigned Notice, *The Daily Telegraph,* 16 April 1903, p. 7.

11. Unsigned Notice, *Referee* 19 April 1903, p. 2.

12. *Bernard Shaw: Collected Letters, 1898–1910,* p. 324.

13. Ibid.

14. Ibid.

15. Ibid.

16. Ibid., pp. 324–25.

17. Edward Gordon Craig, *Henry Irving* (New York and London: B. Blom, 1969), p. 158.

18. *Bernard Shaw: Collected Letters, 1898–1910,* p. 325.

19. Craig, *Ellen Terry and Her Secret Self,* p. 138.

20. George Bernard Shaw, "Ghosts at the Jubilee," *Saturday Review* (3 July 1897), pp. 12–14.

21. *Bernard Shaw: Collected Letters, 1898–1910,* p. 326.

22. St. John, pp. 293–94.

23. Ibid.

24. C. B. Purdom, ed., *Bernard Shaw's Letters to Granville Barker* (New York: Theatre Arts Books, 1957), p. 180.

25. Edward Gordon Craig to Count Harry Kessler, 26 November 1905, Newberry Library, Wing Ke, n.p.

26. Craig, *Towards a New Theatre,* p. 51.

27. *Bernard Shaw: Collected Letters 1898–1910,* p. 582.

28. Samuel A. Weiss, ed., *Bernard Shaw's Letters to Siegfried Trebitsch.* (Stanford: Stanford University Press, 1986), p. 90.

29. Ibid., p. 94.

30. Unsigned, "Editorial Notes," *The Mask,* 1 (February 1909), 256.

31. J. S. [Craig pseudonym], "Editorial Notes," *The Mask,* 3 (July 1910), 43.

32. Unsigned, "Editorial Notes," *The Mask,* 3 (April 1911), 195.

33. St. John, p. 75.

34. Edward Gordon Craig, "Extracts from a Diary," 8 January 1933, *Radio Talks* (London: Discurio, 1962), n.p.

35. John Semar [Craig pseudonym], "Mr. Bernard Shaw and the Censor," *The Mask,* 2 (July 1909), 40.

36. Louis Madrid [Craig pseudonym], "Brieux and Bernard Shaw: A Note on Two Social Reformers," *The Mask,* 4 (July 1911), 13.

37. E.G.C. [Craig], " 'Blanco Posnet' at Letchworth," *The Mask,* 5 (October 1912), 177.

38. Alan Dent, ed., *Bernard Shaw and Mrs. Patrick Campbell: Their Correspondence* (New York: Alfred A. Knopf, 1952), p. 119.

39. e.g.c [Craig], "The Colossus. G.B.S.," *The Mask,* 12 (January 1926), 22.

40. G. Bernard Shaw, "The Colossus Speaks," *The Mask,* 12 (April 1926), 81–82.

41. Ibid.

42. Gordon Craig, "A Word From Mr. Gordon Craig," *The Mask,* 12 (April 1926), 82.

43. Gordon Craig, "The Colossus," *The Mask,* 12 (July 1926), 116–117.

44. George Bernard Shaw, *Our Theatres in the Nineties*, (London: Constable, 1948), II: 291.

45. Ibid., p. 199.

46. West, p. 202.

47. Ibid.

48. Craig, *Ellen Terry and Her Secret Self*, p. 5.

49. Ibid.

50. Ibid., p. 6

51. Ibid., p. 7.

52. West, p. 206.

53. Ibid., p. 208.

54. Ibid.

55. Ibid., p. 209.

56. Ibid.

57. Ibid., p. 210.

58. Ibid.

59. Ibid., p. 212.

60. Ibid.

61. Craig, *Radio Talks*, n.p.

62. Dent, p. 361.

JOHN R. PFEIFFER*

A CONTINUING CHECKLIST
OF SHAVIANA

I. Works by Shaw

Shaw, Bernard. *Arms and the Man,* in *Literature: Structure, Sound, and Sense.* Edited by
Laurence Perrine and Thomas R. Arp. Fifth Edition. San Diego: Harcourt Brace
Jovanovich, 1988. Not seen. Replaces *Professional Foul* by Tom Stoppard.

———. Article on Japan (Untitled), 30 April 1934. In Bernard F. Dukore's "George Bernard Shaw on Japan, Dateline 1934," *Asian Affairs,* XIX (Old Series Vol. 75), (February
1988), 45–48. Dukore's article presents an unpublished piece by GBS on Japan and
details the facts of the Shaws' travels to China and Japan which provided the occasion
for it. Shaw warns in 1934 that imperialism and capitalism will ruin Japan, or drive
Japan to a further and losing war.

———. *Collected Letters, 1926–1950, Volume 4.* Edited by Dan H. Laurence. New York:
Viking, 1988. The concluding volume of the GBS correspondence, with 740 letters,
two-thirds unpublished.

———. *Dear Mr. Shaw. Selections from Bernard Shaw's Postbag.* Compiled and edited by
Vivian Elliot. Introduction by Michael Holroyd. London: Bloomsbury, 1987. This
conflation of letters to GBS and interventions and interpolations by Blanche Patch also
includes numerous samples of Shaw's answers. There is no index.

———. *G. Bernard Shaw, Nine Answers.* As Privately Printed for Jerome Kern in 1923, with
an Introduction by Christopher Morley, including a Frontispiece after Max Beerbohm. Lewisburg, Pa.: Bucknell University Press, 1988. The "answers" are to questions that ask about the life and works of an 1896 GBS, one of the many transparent
perpetrations for comic self-advertisement concocted by Shaw. Kern issued sixty-two
copies of the 1923 version, which was not cleared by Shaw. This 1988 edition has been
authorized by the estate.

———. "The Inside Ceremony," in "A Report from *The Star,* Correspondents from *The
Star,* including Bernard Shaw." *SHAW: The Annual of Bernard Shaw Studies.* Volume
Eight. University Park: Pennsylvania State University Press, 1988. Shaw's "The Inside

* Professor Pfeiffer, *SHAW* Bibliographer, welcomes information about new or forthcoming Shaviana: books, articles, pamphlets, monographs, dissertations, reprints, etc. His address is Department of English, Central Michigan University, Mount Pleasant, Michigan
48859.

Ceremony," reprinted with articles by two other reporters, for context, from the 9 May 1893 London *Star*. The subject is Queen Victoria presiding at the opening of the Imperial Institute in South Kensington.

———. "Memoirs of An Old-Fashioned Physician." *SHAW: The Annual of Bernard Shaw Studies*. Volume Eight. University Park: Pennsylvania State University Press, 1988. One of Shaw's earliest published pieces on doctors and medicine, from the *Pall Mall Gazette*, 25 November 1885, pp. 4–5.

———. "The Process of Reading Drama," in *Literature: Reading Fiction, Poetry, Drama, and the Essay*. Edited by Robert DiYanni. New York: Random House, 1986. Not seen. Publisher's brochure indicates volume contains part or all of a GBS play.

———. "Progress an Illusion" (1903), in *Theme and Variations: The Impact of Great Ideas*. Edited by Laurence Behrens and Leonard J. Rosen. Glenville, Ill.: Scott Foresman/ Little, Brown, 1987. Not seen.

———. Quotations, in *The Wit and Wisdom of the 20th Century: A Dictionary of Quotations*. Edited by Frank S. Pepper. New York: Peter Bedrick Books, 1987. Lists 160 samples from Shaw. About half as many from Bertrand Russell. Two from Shakespeare.

———. From *The Revolutionist's Handbook*, in *The Norton Reader*. Edited by Arthur M. Eastman et al. Seventh Edition. New York: W. W. Norton, 1987. Not seen.

———. Two letters to Edith Nesbit in Julia Briggs's *A Woman of Passion: The Life of E. Nesbit, 1858–1924*. Century Hutchinson, 1987. Not seen. See Briggs, Julia, in "Books and Pamphlets," below.

II. Books and Pamphlets

Adams, Elsie B., and Donald C. Haberman, comps. and eds., *G. B. Shaw: An Annotated Bibliography of Writings about Him, Volume II: 1931–1956*. Dekalb: Northern Illinois University Press, 1987. The volume lists 2,394 items. It is the last of a three-volume set, the first and third already in print. See Weintraub, Stanley. "At Last . . . ," below.

Anderson, Sherwood. *The Sherwood Anderson Diaries, 1936–1941*. Edited by Hilbert H. Campbell. Athens and London: The University of Georgia Press, 1987. In entries between 1936 and 1938 Anderson reports seeing *Androcles, Devil's Disciple, Getting Married, Candida, Joan,* and *Misalliance,* as well as hearing read an uncut version of *Man and Superman*—"a ghastly bore."

Anonymous. "An Interpretation of Shaw," in *Critical Essays on H. L. Mencken*. Edited by Douglas C. Stenerson. Boston: G. K. Hall, 1987, pp. 40–41. A review of Mencken's *George Bernard Shaw: His Plays,* from the *Chicago Tribune,* 2 January 1906, p. 8.

Auerbach, Nina. *Ellen Terry, Player in Her Time*. New York and London: W. W. Norton, 1987. The complex relationship of GBS, Ellen Terry, and her daughter Edy Craig is treated here. Works mentioned are *Methuselah, Candida, Brassbound, Man of Destiny, Pen Portraits, Quintessence,* and *Joan.* Reviewed by Brigid Brophy. See below under "Periodicals."

Bentley, Eric. *Thinking about the Playwright: Comments from Four Decades*. Evanston, Ill.: Northwestern University Press, 1987. Five of these reprinted pieces present substantial commentaries on Shaw, including "Shaw in 1978."

———. See Bloom, Harold, below.

Berg, Alban, and Arnold Schoenberg. *The Berg-Schoenberg Correspondence: Selected Letters*. Edited by Juliane Brand, Christopher Hailey, and Donald Harris. New York and London: W. W. Norton, 1987. Both composers were concerned with Shaw's seventieth birthday. Here Berg is concerned to write his congratulations on paper of special quality. Schoenberg has dedicated a canon to GBS. The footnote says, "In the six-voice G.B. Shaw canon the first soprano begins on the tonic, the alto enters a fifth below (which Schoenberg indicates with a '5'), the second soprano enters at the unison, followed by the first tenor at the fifth below, and finally the second tenor an octave below, followed by the bass at the fifth below that. The canon was also published in *Bernard Shaw zum 70. Geburtstage* (Berlin, 1926), . . . a collection that included contributions from 105 German authors, artists, and intellectuals."

Berst, Charles A. See Bloom, Harold, below.

Bloom, Harold, ed. *George Bernard Shaw: Modern Critical Views.* New York, New Haven, and Philadelphia: Chelsea House Publishers, 1987. Includes "Introduction" by Bloom, "Introduction to Shaw" by Stanley Weintraub, "The Critic" by G. K. Chesterton, "*Pygmalion:* A Personal Play" by Eric Bentley, "The Shavian World of *John Bull's Other Island*" by Frederick P. W. McDowell, "*Caesar and Cleopatra*" by Louis Crompton, "Shaw and Revolution: The Politics of the Plays" by Martin Meisel, "The Virgin Mother" by Margery M. Morgan, "*Heartbreak House:* Shavian Expressionism" by Charles A. Berst, "*Back to Methuselah:* A Tract in Epic Form" by Maurice Valency, "The Marriage of Contraries: *Major Barbara*" by J. L. Wisenthal, "Ann and Superman: Type and Archetype" by Sally Peters Vogt, "Shavian History" by Nicholas Grene, and "*Fanny's First Play:* A Critical Potboiler?" by Barbara M. Fisher. All the pieces except Bloom's introduction are reprints.

The Book Box: G. B. Shaw & Some Associates. London: S. & M. Morgan, 1987. A book sale catalogue: "The largest section is devoted to Bernard Shaw; there is a separate section for other, contemporary Anglo-Irish writers, including Yeats; stage designers associated with Shaw and/or Granville Barker (e.g., Craig, Ricketts, Norman Wilkinson) are distributed through the catalogue in alphabetical order."

Briggs, Julia. *A Woman of Passion: The Life of E. Nesbit, 1858–1924.* Century Hutchinson, 1987. Not seen. Claire Tomalin, in *TLS* (20–26 November 1987, p. 1281), says of "An unrequited passion for Shaw" that " 'Unrequited' " is not exactly the right term, for Shaw did initially get in quite deeply. . . . The two best, wittiest, strongest letters in this book were both from Shaw; his power to upstage all his women friends posthumously would have pleased the old fox infinitely, no doubt."

Brown, Geoff. " 'Sister of the Stage': British Film and British Theatre," in *All Our Yesterdays: 90 Years of British Cinema.* Edited by Charles Barr. London: British Film Institute, 1986. A deft set of judgments on the general weakness as films of *How He Lied, Arms, Major Barbara,* and *Caesar.* Too talky. GBS, however, is recognized for having grappled decisively with the practical problems of merging theater and cinema.

Busoni, Ferruccio. *Selected Letters.* Translated and edited by Antony Beaumont. New York: Columbia University Press, 1987. In addition to his achievement as a composer, Busoni was a wonderful letter writer. He admired GBS early and came to know him well, as several of these letters document. From one to Egon Petri of 8 September 1907: "This new impression and the fact that Shaw was (and is?) part musician gave me the idea of prevailing upon him to write something for music. He would certainly create a new direction in music-theatre, even if unintentionally, and something could well come of it. I am thinking of myself as the composer; but he doesn't know me at all, so how am I to convince him of my ability? [new paragraph] You have spoken to him; perhaps it would be agreeable to you—as representative of this idea—to get to know him better."

Chesterton, G. K. See Bloom, Harold, above.

Conrad, Peter. *The History of English Literature, One Indivisible, Unending Book.* Philadelphia: University of Pennsylvania Press, 1985. Several pages are given to a discussion of evolutionism in *Superman, Disciple, Caesar, Heartbreak, Methuselah,* and *Joan.* Works by Shakespeare, Wagner, Hardy, and Yeats are drawn into the commentary for comparison.

Cooper, Wayne F. *Claude McKay: Rebel Sojourner in the Harlem Renaissance.* Baton Rouge and London: Louisiana State University Press, 1987. Provides a substantial account of McKay and GBS, whom McKay always found very fascinating. McKay on Shaw: "There was something about him that reminded me of an evergreen plant grown indoors. As an animal he suggested an antelope to my mind. And his physique gave an impression of something brittle and frail that one would want to handle with care, like chinaware. I thought that perhaps it was his vegetarian diet that gave him that remarkably deceptive appearance." The contacts of Shaw and Afro-American writers are extensive, so it is interesting to be told here that McKay felt that GBS exhibited sympathy for the problems that confronted blacks in English society, but that the great satirist had a shallow understanding of the world's racial problems.

Crawford, Fred D. "The Shaw Diaries" (review). *SHAW: The Annual of Bernard Shaw Studies.* Volume Eight. University Park: Pennsylvania State University Press, 1988.

Crompton, Louis. See Bloom, Harold, above.

Dietrich, Richard F. "Shaw and the Uncrucifying of Christ." *SHAW: The Annual of Bernard Shaw Studies.* Volume Eight. University Park: Pennsylvania State University Press, 1988.

DiGaetani, John Louis. *Puccini the Thinker: The Composer's Intellectual and Dramatic Development.* Bern, Frankfurt am Main, New York, and Paris: Peter Lang, 1987. DiGaetani reminds us of modern music critics' respect for GBS the music critic when he presents a long quotation from a Shaw music review of Puccini's *Manon Lescaut* to advance his discussion of the similarity between Puccini and Wagner.

Dinnage, Rosemary. *Annie Besant.* Penguin Books, 1986. Several pages are devoted to the Besant/Shaw relationship. "Between 1885 and 1887 Annie was certainly serious about Shaw. They played piano duets together and she wrote poems as well as letters to him. Unable as she was to marry legally, at one point in their friendship she drew up a contract for a 'free union' like that of Eleanor Marx and Aveling." Shaw's reaction: " 'Good God! This is worse than all the vows of all the Churches on earth. I had rather be legally married to you ten times over.' . . . It was little consolation to Annie [at this time] that his admiration for her was genuine and durable."

Eide, Elisabeth. "Performances of Ibsen in China After 1949," in *Drama in the People's Republic of China.* Edited by Constantine Tung and Colin Mackerras. New York: State University of New York Press, 1987. Although the focus is on Ibsen, Eide describes the 26 July 1956 banquet (in Peking?) held to commemorate the 50th anniversary of Ibsen's death and the 100th anniversary of Shaw's birth. An act from *Apple Cart* and two acts from *Mrs Warren* were "shown." Mao Dun, the president of this arrangement, said, "The works of Shaw and Ibsen inspire a love for peace and freedom."

Elliot, Vivian, ed. *Dear Mr. Shaw: Selections from Bernard Shaw's Postbag.* London: Bloomsbury, 1987. See above under "Works by Shaw."

Ellmann, Richard. *Oscar Wilde.* New York: Alfred A. Knopf, 1988. Ellmann's extraordinary biography of Wilde, already widely reviewed as this Checklist goes to press, collects much of the information on the relationship of Shaw and Wilde.

Evans, Maurice. *All This . . . and Evans Too!* Columbia: University of South Carolina Press, 1987. There is much here on Shaw because Evans was a devotee of the works of GBS. There are comments on *Androcles, Apple Cart, Arms, Disciple, Major Barbara,* and *Pygma-*

lion, with a much longer discussion of *Joan,* and a chapter subtitled "Man and Super-man" wherein Evans tells of his negotiations with Shaw to acquire the play. Part of the strategy included plying GBS with Hershey bars. Evans's impression of Shaw at the time: "The first thing that struck one about the Sage of Ayot St. Lawrence—the vigour and beauty of his voice. I hadn't seen him since he was an active youngster of seventy-nine, and I was a little apprehensive over the possible changes in him on the threshold of his ninety-first birthday. I needn't have worried. He emerged from his study, his white beard bristling like the quills of a porcupine. Leaning lightly on a cane, he advanced slowly and offered me his hand in greeting. The famous eyes, more sunken than I remembered, still had a mischievous twinkle under those bushy brows. The red pigment that used to adorn his hair and beard seemed to have concentrated itself in his nose, giving him a faint resemblance to the clown he so often declared himself to be at heart."

Everding, Robert G. "Bernard Shaw, *Misalliance,* and the Birth of British Aviation." *SHAW: The Annual of Bernard Shaw Studies.* Volume Eight. University Park: Pennsylvania State University Press, 1988.

Firchow, Peter Edgerly. *The Death of the German Cousin: Variations on a Literary Stereotype, 1890–1920.* Lewisburg, Pa.: Bucknell University Press, 1987. Includes a chapter, "Into Cleanness Leaping: Brooke, Eliot, Shaw, and Lawrence," that treats *Heartbreak:* "Although there is some justification for reading *Heartbreak House* as an anti-war play, the action paradoxically climaxes in a *Walpurgisnacht* of wartime destruction, with bombs dropping out of the sky and with Germans acting almost as the agents of God, wreaking vengeance upon Satanic capitalists in the Garden of England." Later: "*Heartbreak House* is a profoundly symbolic play. Captain Shotover's country house stands for an entire culture that, ineffectual despite great incidental charm, has reached a dead end. Put on the simplest level, it poses the old problem of the division between action and contemplation, the heart and the hand, Heartbreak House and Horseback Hall. Power is vested among the ignorant barbarians, culture among the knowledgeable decadents. Nowhere, except in a qualified sense in Captain Shotover, do the two meet."

Fisher, Barbara M. See Bloom, Harold, above.

Fowler, Alastair. *A History of English Literature.* Cambridge, Mass.: Harvard University Press, 1987. Shaw receives a page in this, and a mixed review: "There was nothing new, and certainly nothing of modernism, in an obviously didactic stance; while his subversive wit is as entertaining—as little disturbing—as Wilde's. Shaw's modernism lay in the great innovation of introducing into England that alien genre, the drama of ideas" [mentions *Arms, Superman, Barbara, Pygmalion.*]. His characters lack "credible substance" and partly fail in the attempt at "emotional engagement" [in *Heartbreak* and *Joan*].

Friedman, Lenemaja. *Enid Bagnold.* Boston: Twayne Publishers, 1986. Sometime secretary and lover of Frank Harris, Bagnold came to know Shaw. Friedman repeats the comparison of Bagnold as a playwright to Wilde and GBS a number of times, "especially in the use of aphorisms, in the wit and humor, and in the vigorous spirit of her characters."

Gibbons, Luke. See Rockett, Kevin, below.

Glendinning, Victoria. *Rebecca West, A Life.* New York: Alfred A. Knopf, 1987; London: Weidenfeld and Nicolson, 1987. West's association with the Fabians and H. G. Wells is well known. She met GBS also: "She admired his 'greyhound' appearance, his athletic bearing, his voice, and his eloquence. 'The effect he created was more stupendous since in those days every well-to-do man wore stuffy cloths, ate too much, took too little exercise, and consequently looked like a bolster.' But she did not, in her maturer years, admire his work: 'I passionately resent the fact that God gave him a beautiful style and that he used it to preach tedious and reactionary ideas.' Nor did she continue to admire him as a male specimen: on account of his sexless marriage, he became 'a eunuch perpetually inflamed by flirtation.' "

Greenfield, John. "Bernard Shaw (26 July 1856–2 November 1950)," in *Victorian Prose Writers After 1867*. Edited by William B. Thesing. Detroit: Gale Research Company, 1987, pp. 249–62. This straightforward description of Shaw's prose neglects Shaw as a writer of letters—in volume (both published and fugitive) equal at least to all the prose he published in any other category.

Grene, Nicholas. See Bloom, Harold, above.

Haberman, Donald C. See Adams, Elsie B., above.

Hay, Peter. *Theatrical Anecdotes*. New York and Oxford: Oxford University Press, 1987. Includes a number of GBS stories, mostly from easily accessible publications.

Hayter, Charles. *Gilbert and Sullivan*. New York: St. Martin's Press, 1987. Takes note of Shaw's love of Sullivan's scores and contends that GBS's disparagement of Gilbert is surprising in view of his obvious indebtedness to Gilbert.

Higham, Charles. *Brando, The Unauthorized Biography*. New York: New American Library, 1987. Brando played in *Joan* in high school. Guthrie McClintic, husband of Katherine Cornell, then at the height of her career as first lady of American theater, caught Brando's performance in *Truckline Cafe*. Mildred Natwick was with them. Natwick and McClintic decided Brando would be a great Marchbanks in *Candida*—a "stronger, more virile Marchbanks" than that played by either Orson Welles or Burgess Meredith in previous productions. There is an account of Brando's attempt to fit himself to Shaw's character.

Hill, John. See Rockett, Kevin, below.

Holroyd, Michael. *Bernard Shaw, Volume I: 1856–1898, The Search for Love*. London: Chatto & Windus; New York: Random House, 1988. A scan of the book reveals a well-written narrative that reports nothing new about GBS. Readers who want sources must wait, apparently, until Volume IV for a list. Volume I provides no notes or sources.

James, Henry. *The Complete Notebooks of Henry James*. Edited by Leon Edel and Lyall H. Powers. New York and Oxford: Oxford University Press, 1987. Provides two entries on seeing GBS plays; one in 1911 (*Fanny's First Play*); a second in 1914.

———. *Henry James Selected Letters*. Edited by Leon Edel. Cambridge, Mass., and London: Harvard University Press, 1987. Includes a long letter to GBS (20 January 1909) answering Shaw's to HJ in which Shaw had explained why HJ's play *Saloon* was being rejected by the Incorporated Stage Society.

Jones, Judy, and William Wilson. *An Incomplete Education*. New York: Ballantine Books, 1987. A pop-knowledge book. GBS has a full page with a photo—"The Second Most Famous English Playwright."

Kendrick, Walter. *The Secret Museum: Pornography in Modern Culture*. New York: Viking, 1987. Includes a sampling of Shaw's part in the evolution of the legal definition of obscenity.

Kiernan, Ryan. "Citizens of Centuries to Come: The Ruling-class Rebel in Socialist Fiction," in *The Rise of Socialist Fiction, 1880–1914*. Edited by H. Gustav Klaus. New York: St. Martin's Press, 1987, pp. 6–27. Shaw's *Unsocial Socialist* is noted as the first major work in this account. It is compared to Grant Allen's *Philistia* (1884): "Ernest [of *Philistia*] is the kind of intense and humourless ethical socialist who lacerates his conscience constantly. Like Shaw's Trefusis, he can be relied upon at every occasion, however innocuous, to remind everyone that 'others are dying of sheer want, and cold, and nakedness' . . . while they themselves indulge in meaningless frivolity. Unlike

Trefusis, however, Le Breton has no other acts up his sleeve, certainly none that would raise any laughs, and Allen does not disguise how insufferable such a remorselessly moralistic socialist can be, not least to other socialists."

Lehmann, John. *Christopher Isherwood: A Personal Memoir.* New York: Henry Holt and Company, 1987. A letter from Isherwood of 1 June 1969 reminds us that he wrote a dramatized adaptation of Shaw's *Adventures of the Black Girl,* which had a "very successful run but hasn't yet found any other offers."

Levin, Harry. *Playboys and Killjoys: An Essay on the Theory and Practice of Comedy.* New York and Oxford: Oxford University Press, 1987. Shaw is a touchstone.

McDowell, Frederick P. W. "Some Reflections on *Back to Methuselah* in Performance" (review of Ontario Shaw Festival production). *SHAW: The Annual of Bernard Shaw Studies.* Volume Eight. University Park: Pennsylvania State University Press, 1988.

———. See Bloom, Harold, above.

McGilligan, Pat. "Norman Krasna: The Woolworth's Touch," in *Backstory: Interviews with Screenwriters of Hollywood's Golden Age.* Berkeley, Los Angeles, and London: University of California Press, 1986. Krasna mentions GBS at least three times, including the comment that "I feel that *Pygmalion* is one of the great social dramatic comments, you understand? Ibsen would shout it. I think Shaw's point is stronger and more effective than Ibsen's. Unless you write on the nose for political reasons you are not labelled a writer for social betterment."

Mansfield, Katherine. *The Critical Writings of Katherine Mansfield.* Edited by Clare Hanson. New York: St. Martin's Press, 1987. Includes 13 December 1919 Mansfield letter to J. M. Murry devoted entirely to her opinion of Shaw on Butler: "GBS on Butler is very fine indeed. He has such a grip of his subject. I admire his tenacity as a reviewer and the way in which his mind follows Butler with a steady light—does not waver over him, find him, lose him, travel over him. At the same time it's queer he should be (GBS) [*sic*] so uninspired. There is not the faintest hint of inspiration in that man. This chills me. . . . What it amounts to is that Shaw is anything you like, but he's not an artist. Don't you get when you read his plays a sense of extraordinary *flatness?*"

Marsh, Jan. *Jane and May Morris: A Biographical Story, 1839–1938.* London and New York: Pandora, 1986. This account attempts to reconstruct the relationship of GBS and May. In addition, there is much other discussion of Shaw.

Massey, Daniel. "Some Thoughts on the Acting of Shaw." *SHAW: The Annual of Bernard Shaw Studies.* Volume Eight. University Park: Pennsylvania State University Press, 1988.

Meisel, Martin. See Bloom, Harold, above.

Mogen, David. *Ray Bradbury.* Boston: Twayne Publishers, 1986. Bradbury is an admirer of Shaw and Shakespeare. His extensive treatment of GBS in various forums is not adequately described here.

Morgan, Margery M. See Bloom, Harold, above.

Packard, William. *The Art of the Playwright: Creating the Magic of Theatre.* New York: Paragon House Publishers, 1987. *Superman* is "talk, talk, talk," but *Saint Joan* is a masterpiece. Packard lists thirteen GBS plays among the major dramatic works of the nineteenth and twentieth centuries: *Mrs Warren, Arms, Caesar, Superman, Barbara, Dilemma, Dark Lady, Androcles, Pygmalion, Heartbreak, Methuselah, Saint Joan,* and *Too True to Be Good.*

Perelman, S. J. *Don't Tread on Me: The Selected Letters of S. J. Perelman.* Edited by Prudence Crowther. New York: Viking, 1987. One reference in a letter of 2 September 1940 to S. D. Cohen: "Mr. Stromberg thought we might adapt *Arms and the Man* by Bernard Shaw for the screen, and we read it, but the project was abandoned after some discussion. . . . Jeannette MacDonald and Nelson Eddy" were suggested for the roles of Raina and Bluntschli.

Pharand, Michel. "Iconoclasts of Social Reform: Eugène Brieux and Bernard Shaw." *SHAW: The Annual of Bernard Shaw Studies.* Volume Eight. University Park: Pennsylvania State University Press, 1988.

Pollak, Paulina Salz. "Master to the Masters: Mozart's Influence on Bernard Shaw's *Don Juan in Hell.*" *SHAW: The Annual of Bernard Shaw Studies.* Volume Eight. University Park: Pennsylvania State University Press, 1988.

Robinson, Harlow. *Sergei Prokofiev: A Biography.* New York: Viking, 1987. Provides a brief discussion of the conflation of Cleopatra material from Shakespeare, Pushkin, and Shaw for Alexander Tairov's *Eygptian Nights.* Prokofiev said later, "Despite Shaw's charming wit, old man Shakespeare turned out to be such a titan that one wanted to give him as much space as possible and as little as possible to Shaw. Thus edited, Bernard completely lost face and turned into an unnecessary appendage at the beginning of the production."

Rockett, Kevin, Luke Gibbons, and John Hill. *Cinema and Ireland.* London and Sydney: Croom Helm, 1987. This notes that Shaw's role in proposals to build an Irish film studio was not ultimately fruitful.

Rosenbaum, S. P. *Victorian Bloomsbury: The Early History of the Group.* Volume I. New York: St. Martin's Press, 1987. The Bloomsbury Group, including the Woolfs, Roger Fry, Desmond MacCarthy, Clive Bell, Maynard Keynes, and E. M. Forster, read GBS in strong sympathy for his attack on Idealism.

Sandburg, Carl. See Steichen, Lilian, below.

Schoenberg, Arnold. See Berg, Alban, above.

Seldes, George. *Witness to a Century: Encounters with the Noted, the Notorious and Three SOBs.* New York: Ballantine Books, 1987. Seldes, a well-known journalist, especially for *The Chicago Tribune,* writes at 96 years of age. Only a few Shaw references, one of them recounting how Seldes, present at a rehearsal of the first performance anywhere of *Saint Joan,* produced by Max Reinhardt, was able to tell Reinhardt and Elizabeth Bergner, who would play Joan, about the Preface to *Joan.* They did not know it existed. Seldes helped them translate the Preface into German. They were very appreciative.

Singer, Irving. *The Nature of Love. Volume Three: The Modern World.* Chicago: University of Chicago Press, 1987. Not seen. A review indicates this includes a substantial representation of GBS on "love."

Smith, David. *H. G. Wells: Desperately Mortal, A Biography.* New Haven and London: Yale University Press, 1986. Includes a substantial treatment of the important Wells/Shaw connections.

Steele, Elizabeth. *Virginia Woolf's Rediscovered Essays: Sources and Allusions.* New York and London: Garland, 1987. References to GBS are reported in six Woolf pieces between 1916 and 1925.

Steichen, Lilian, and Carl Sandburg. *The Poet and the Dream Girl: The Love Letters of Lilian Steichen and Carl Sandburg.* Edited by Margaret Sandburg. Urbana and Chicago: University of Illinois Press, 1987. In their support of socialism, Lilian and Carl were enamored of the writings of GBS on socialism and other topics. They refer to him a number of times, starting in the letters that mark the early stages of their relationship. In February 1908 Sandburg is putting together a lecture on Shaw, as he writes to Lilian. By April, Lilian, in her letter to Sandburg, goes on about GBS at length: "I remember your saying some words of praise about Shaw's 'Education of Children.' We must discuss it. I think it unworthy of Shaw. . . . And what he says against Darwinism strikes me as pure and simple *rot.* I could almost believe he tried to write the worst rottenest rot he could—to see how the public would take it, perhaps—. . . . Maybe Shaw was on the drunk when he wrote that about Darwinism. . . . However . . . when Shaw talks sense (as he does most of the time, directly or indirectly, straight from the shoulder or by indirection of irony)—when Shaw talks sense, he's G.B.S, a man who counts in the growth of the world."

Swartzlander, Susan. "To Learn to Respect Reality": Bernard Shaw's *John Bull's Other Island*." *SHAW: The Annual of Bernard Shaw Studies*. Volume Eight. University Park: Pennsylvania State University Press, 1988.

Thomas, David, and Joyce Thomas. *Compton Mackenzie: A Bibliography*. London and New York: Mansell, 1986. Includes a Mackenzie radio broadcast in 1969 that included recollections of GBS.

Topolski, Feliks. *Fourteen Letters*. London: Faber and Faber, 1987? Not seen. This is an autobiographical work by an artist who illustrated many Shaw works and did dozens of GBS portraits.

Valency, Maurice. See Bloom, Harold, above.

Van Vechten, Carl. *Letters of Carl Van Vechten*. Edited by Bruce Kellner. New Haven and London: Yale University Press, 1987. One reference: "Bernard Shaw tells us in one of his prefaces how he threw his mother into the struggle and forced her to make a living for him until he got on his feet." This 7 February 1919 remark in a letter to Ralph Van Vechten implies considerable familiarity with Shaw's writing at this time.

Vogt, Sally Peters. See Bloom, Harold, above.

Walker, Alexander. *Vivien: The Life of Vivien Leigh*. New York: Weidenfeld and Nicolson, 1987. Leigh played the lead in *Doctor's Dilemma*. She wanted the part of Cleopatra in *Caesar*. A number of references to GBS here. Shaw is reported to have called her the "Mrs. Pat Campbell of the age."

Watson, Barbara Bellow. "The Supersaturated Dickensian" (review of *Shaw on Dickens*). *SHAW: The Annual of Bernard Shaw Studies*. Volume Eight. University Park: Pennsylvania State University Press, 1988.

Weidhorn, Manfred. "Churchill and the British Literary Intelligentsia: Skirmishes with Shaw and His Contemporaries on the Frontier of Politics and Literature." *SHAW: The Annual of Bernard Shaw Studies*. Volume Eight. University Park: Pennsylvania State University Press, 1988.

Weintraub, Rodelle. "A Parachutist Prototype for Lina." *SHAW: The Annual of Bernard Shaw Studies*. Volume Eight. University Park: Pennsylvania State University Press, 1988.

Weintraub, Stanley. "At Last! A Secondary Bibliography" (review of volumes 1 and 3 of *G.B. Shaw: An Annotated Bibliography of Writings About Him*). *SHAW: The Annual of Bernard Shaw Studies*. Volume Eight. University Park: Pennsylvania State University Press, 1988.

———. See Bloom, Harold, above.

Wellek, René. *A History of Modern Criticsm: 1750–1950. Volume 6: American Criticism, 1900–1950*. New Haven and London: Yale University Press, 1986. Two comments in a section on Edmund Wilson: "Wilson is comprehensibly impatient with [Yeats's] *A Vision*, which he contrasts with the so much more sensible *Intelligent Woman's Guide*" and "Wilson thus could not escape from the limitations of a world view fundamentally akin to his early masters, Bernard Shaw and H. G. Wells."

Wilson, Duncan. *Gilbert Murray OM, 1866–1957*. Oxford: Clarendon Press, 1987? Not seen. Murray was the original of Cusins in *Barbara*, and Lady Brit was modeled after Murray's mother-in-law.

Wilson, Edmund. *The Fifties: From Notebooks and Diaries of the Period*. Edited by Leon Edel. New York: Farrar, Straus and Giroux, 1986. Two accounts of Shaw-related conversations. One with Max Beerbohm, after GBS's death, reveals Beerbohm's abiding complex reaction to the playwright. Beerbohm acknowledged Shaw's talent and genius, but "hadn't been able to stand it that Shaw should be attaining such fame."

Wilson, William. See Jones, Judy, above.

Wisenthal, J. M. "Master and Pupil" (review of *Shaw's Letters to Trebitsch*). *SHAW: The Annual of Bernard Shaw Studies.* Volume Eight. University Park: Pennsylvania State University Press, 1988.

————. *Shaw's Sense of History.* Oxford: Clarendon Press, 1988. Examines such works as *Caesar, Joan,* and *Good King Charles,* as well as *Superman, John Bull, Major Barbara, Heartbreak,* and *Methuselah.* "This is not a study of 'Shaw the Historian', for the good reason that Shaw was not a historian. He was a dramatist, . . ." Wisenthal searches Shaw's prose as well as the drama to make "explicit the historical attitudes that underlie the plays." He wants to place the plays in "a Victorian intellectual context."

————. See Bloom, Harold, above.

Yeats, W. B. *The Collected Letters of W. B. Yeats. Volume One, 1865–1895.* Edited by John Kelly; associate editor, Eric Domville. Oxford: Clarendon Press, 1986. Includes two references to Shaw: February 1888 and April 1894. The 1888 reference is substantive: "Last night at Morrises I met Bernard Shaw who is certainly very witty. But like most people who have wit rather than humour, his mind is maybe somewhat wanting in depth—However his stories [*Love Among the Artists*?] are good they say."

III. Periodicals

Adams, Elsie B. "Shaw: A Critical View." Review of Nicholas Grene's *Bernard Shaw: A Critical View. English Literature in Transition, 1880–1920,* 30, no.1 (1987): 95–97.

Amalric, Jean-Claude. "Du Realiste Au Surhomme: Les Métamorphoses du Héros Shavien." *Cahiers Victoriens & Edouardiens,* no. 23 (1986): 59–69. From the abstract: "The Shavian hero, an iconoclast, a realist, a mentor and an intellectual ascetic, paves the way through these various metamorphoses, for the Superman."

Berst, Charles A. "G.B.S. as a Correspondent: Eruption No. 3." Review of *Bernard Shaw: Collected Letters, 1911–1925. English Literature in Transition, 1880–1920,* 30, no. 3 (1987): 336–38.

Brophy, Brigid. "An Involving Imagination." Review of Nina Auerbach's *Ellen Terry: Player in Her Time. TLS,* 6–12 November 1987, p. 1215.

Carpenter, Charles A. "Shaw," in "Modern Drama Studies: An Annual Bibliography." *Modern Drama,* 30, no. 2 (June 1987): 196–97. Thirty items, a number of them not listed in this Checklist, by a former Bibliographer of *The Shaw Review.* Indispensable to GBS research.

Cohen, Edward H. "Shaw," in "Victorian Bibliography for 1986." *Victorian Studies,* 30, no. 4 (Summer 1987): 673–74. Nineteen items on GBS. Lists only publications "bearing on the Victorian Period for Shaw."

Conlon, John J. Review of *SHAW 6. English Literature in Transition, 1880–1920,* 31, no. 1 (1988): 120–22.

Cunningham, John. "Why Shaw Spells Big Money." *Manchester Guardian Weekly,* 11 October 1987, p. 20. Some details of the large sums of money and the terms involved in Michael Holroyd's production of a biography of GBS.

Dukore, Bernard F. "George Bernard Shaw on Japan, Dateline 1934." *Asian Affairs,* 19 (Old Series Vol. 75), (February 1988): 45–48. See "Article on Japan (Untitled)" above in "Works by Shaw."

————. "*Red Noses* and *Saint Joan*." *Modern Drama*, 30, no. 3 (September 1987): 340–51. "In certain important respects, *Red Noses* constitutes Peter Barnes's response to *Saint Joan*—his own different perspective on similar subject-matter, his alternatives to Shaw's ideas. Despite the differences between the visions of these dramatists, the similarities of the two plays is strong."

————. Review of *Bernard Shaw's Letters to Siegfried Trebitsch* and Shaw's *Diaries*. *Theatre Journal*, 39, no. 4 (December 1987): 539–42.

Everding, Robert G. "Shaw in the Lone Star State: The Evolution of the Houston Shaw Festival." *The Southern Quarterly*, 25, no. 4 (Summer 1987): 111–19. "The South is not restricted to regional stagings of the latest Broadway successes or to revivals of the major work of Southern playwrights. Indeed, this region's audiences have long made the classics, especially Shakespeare, an integral part of their playgoing experiences. Beginning in 1979, this tradition was expanded with the birth of the Houston Shaw Festival, America's only producing company dedicated to the plays of Bernard Shaw. This unique summer festival has grown in achievement and reputation and is now poised to assume professional stature." Goes on to narrate Shaw productions in Texas, beginning in 1910.

Flatow, Sheryl. "Philip Bosco: Essence of Shaw." *American Theatre*, 4, no. 1 (April 1987): 36–37. As a Shavian actor Bosco has few peers among Americans. He has played in *Misalliance, Joan, Superman, Barbara, Heartbreak, You Never Can Tell, Mrs Warren, Dilemma, Caesar, Disciple,* and *Don Juan in Hell*.

"George Bernard Shaw," in "1985–1986 Annual Review." *JML*, 13, nos. 3/4 (November 1986): 537–38. Sixteen entries, one or two not before listed in this Checklist.

Gousseff, James W. Review of Eric Salmon, ed., *Granville Barker and His Correspondents*. *Michigan Academician*, 19, no. 2 (Spring 1987): 261–64.

Henry, William A., III. "Taming the Adorable 'Iggins." Review of Broadway production of *Pygmalion. Time*, 4 May 1987, p. 107.

Holroyd, Michael. "George Bernard Shaw, Cub Reviewer," *The New York Times Book Review*, 18 September 1988, pp. 3, 36, 38, 40. An adaptation from the first volume of Holroyd's biography of GBS (see Holroyd, above, under Books and Pamphlets). Shaw as a reviewer of second-rate fiction for the *Pall Mall Gazette* and other forums is sketched.

Kalikoff, Beth. Review of *Bernard Shaw: A Critical View* by Nicholas Grene. *Victorian Studies*, 30, no. 4 (Summer 1987): 519–20.

Kennedy, Dennis. Review of *Granville Barker and His Correspondents. Theatre Journal*, 39, no. 4 (December 1987): 537–39.

Korn, Eric. "Voices Off." Review of Theatre Royal, Haymarket production of *You Never Can Tell. TLS*, 8–14 January 1988, p. 38.

MacDonald, Jan. Review of *Granville Barker and His Correspondents. Theatre Research International*, 12, no.2 (Summer 1987): 180–82.

Markgraf, Carl. Review of Shaw's *Diaries* and *SHAW 6. Victorian Studies*, 31, no. 1 (Autumn 1987): 119–22.

Meisel, Martin. Review of Shaw's *Diaries. English Literature in Transition, 1880–1920*, 31, no. 2 (1988): 215–18.

Merrill, Lisa. Review of New York Circle in the Square production of *You Never Can Tell* on 13 November 1986. *Theatre Review*, 39, no. 2 (May 1987): 241–42.

Robinson, Michael. Review of Dennis Kennedy's *Granville Barker and the Dream of Theatre. Journal of European Studies*, 17 (1987): 68–69.

"Shaw, George Bernard." In "Irish Literature/1900–1999." *1986 MLA International Bibliography of Books and Articles on the Modern Languages and Literatures*. New York: The

Modern Language Association of America, 1987. Includes twenty-six items, some not
included before in this Checklist.

Taylor, Neil. "Triangular Truths." Review of the Arts Theatre production of *Candida*. *TLS*,
22–28 January 1988, p. 86.

Weintraub, Stanley. "Exasperated Admiration: Bernard Shaw on Queen Victoria." *Victo-
rian Poetry*, 25, nos. 3–4 (Autumn-Winter 1987): 115–32. Shaw's coverage of Queen
Victoria from 1882 to her death and after. This expands on the Shaw material in
Weintraub's 1987 biography of *Victoria*.

———. Review of *Shaw's Letters to Siegfried Trebitsch*. *English Literature in Transition, 1880–
1920*, 30, no. 3 (1987): 333–36.

The Independent Shavian, 25, nos. 1–2 (1987). Journal of the Bernard Shaw Society. Includes "Apocalypse and After: Recent Interpretations of *Heartbreak House*" by Frederick P. W. McDowell; "A Rhetorical Question," "Speech! Speech!", "The World According to Shaw," and "Shavian Wisdom" by Jacques Barzun; "GBS and the ABC" by
Barbara Smoker; "Mix-Up" and "Letter from London" by T. F. Evans; "Book Reviews" by Richard Nickson; and "A New Theater and Drama Journal," "A Funny
Place," "Rewriting *The Bacchae*," "An Actor Remembers," "Edgar Snow on Shaw," "An
Apology," "Society Activities," "News About Our Members," and "Our Cover."

The Independent Shavian, 25, no. 3 (1987). Journal of the Bernard Shaw Society. Includes
"The House with No Exit: The Existential Shaw" by Rhoda B. Nathan; "The Real
Corrupters of Youth," "Shaw Redivivus," "Exemplary Music Criticism," "Luce Talk *re*
Shaw," and "The Shaw Festival: Niagara-on-the-Lake" by Richard Nickson; "A Confer-
ence Announcement," "A Correction," and "Book Review" by Lillian Wachtel; "Letter
from London" by T. F. Evans; "GBS and the ABC Revisited" by Edgar Gregersen;
"Book Review" by Jacqueline Stahl Aronson; and "Society Activities," "News About
Our Members," and "Our Cover."

IV. Dissertations

Sterner, Mark Hamilton. "*Man and Superman* and the Theatre of Dialectics." University of
Texas at Austin, 1987. *DAI*, 48 (November 1987). "*Superman* is a philosophical treatise
in a dynamic theatrical form. A representative of what critics have termed 'the drama
of ideas,' this play remains an inadequately appreciated synthesis of significant intellectual content and masterful artistic form. . . . The hallmark of the Shavian dramatic
method consists in its exploitation of the process of dialectical thought. . . . Shaw's
fusion of the 'well-made' Victorian play, the modern naturalistic drama, and the de-
vices of the classical rhetorical theatre with the great philosophies of the nineteenth
century constituted a revolutionary, and not fully recognized, artistic act."

V. Recordings

Caesar and Cleopatra. The film version on videocassette. Order VV 7028, $79.95, from
Merit Audio Visual, P.O. Box 392, New York, NY 10024; (212) 267–7437.

My Fair Lady. London, 1987. Not seen. Noted in *Time* as scheduled for release in late
September 1987.

Saint Joan. The film version on videocassette. Order VH 3003, $49.95, from Merit Audio
Visual, P.O. Box 392, New York, NY 10024; (212) 267–7437.

"Shaw, Bernard," and "Shaw, George Bernard." *InfoTrac Database*. Belmont, Calif.: Information Access Company. Disc: January 1984–February 1988. Replaces *Business, Magazine,* and *Newspaper Indexes* formerly supplied by the same publisher. Includes ten 1986 items and four 1987 items not listed in this Checklist. All are reviews of plays.

Turrell, Saul J., and Jeff Lieberman. *The Art of Film, Volume I: Screenwriting.* Described in 1988 brochure. Order #3753. Coronet/MTI Film & Video, 108 Wilmot Road, Deerfield, Ill. 60015–9925. Not seen. From brochure: "The screenplay is the foundation of the motion picture. Scenes from *Oliver Twist, Metropolis, The 400 Blows, Pygmalion* and *Caesar and Cleopatra* illustrate the role of the screenwriter as the architect of both cinematic and dramatic elements of the film." Narrated by Rod Serling. Twenty-two minutes running time.

CONTRIBUTORS

Stuart E. Baker is Associate Professor of Theatre at the Florida State University and the author of *Georges Feydeau and the Aesthetics of Farce.*

Ray Bradbury is the author of a collection of verse as well as the novelist of *The Martian Chronicles* and *Fahrenheit 451.* He is also the author of the screenplay of *Moby Dick,* directed by John Huston.

Fred D. Crawford, guest editor of this volume, is Assistant Professor of English at Central Michigan University and the author of *British Poets of the Great War.*

Vivian Ducat works as a producer and director of documentary programs for public television. From 1983 to 1986, Ms. Ducat was based in London, employed by BBC Television as a director on the BBC/PBS series *The Story of English.*

Howard Ira Einsohn is a Technical Services Librarian and occasional part-time instructor in the English Department at Middlesex Community College in Middletown, Connecticut. He is currently working on another Shaw project.

James Fisher, Chairman of the Theater Department and Associate Professor of Theater at Wabash College, is the author of the award-winning play *The Bogus Bride* and has extensive experience as director and actor. He is completing work on *The Theater of Yesterday and Tomorrow: Commedia dell'arte in the Twentieth-Century* and on *Before the Theory: The Early Productions of Edward Gordon Craig.*

Michael J. Holland is a doctoral student at the Pennsylvania State University specializing in Shaw.

Leon H. Hugo is Professor of English at the University of South Africa and author of *Bernard Shaw: Playwright and Preacher.*

John R. Pfeiffer, *SHAW* bibliographer, is Professor of English at Central Michigan University.

Lee W. Saperstein, a Rhodes Scholar with a continuing interest in the British Isles, is Professor and Chairman of Mining Engineering at the University of Kentucky, Lexington, Kentucky.

Laura Tahir is Instructor of Psychology at Felician College in Lodi, New Jersey. Her doctoral dissertation is a cognitive case study of young Bernard Shaw.

Stanley Weintraub, general editor of *SHAW,* is Evan Pugh Professor and the Director of the Institute for the Arts and Humanistic Studies at the Pennsylvania State University. He has written and edited more than fifty books on Shaw and his times.